DISCARDED

SHELTON STATE COMM
COLLEGE
JUNIOR COLLEGE DIVISION
LIBRARY

D0202602

BF
432
.A1
J47

Jensen, Arthur Rob-
ert.

Straight talk a-
bout mental tests

DATE DUE

NOV 1 6 1988			
APR 4 1995			

DISCARDED

Straight Talk About Mental Tests

Other Books by Arthur R. Jensen

GENETICS AND EDUCATION

EDUCABILITY AND GROUP DIFFERENCES

EDUCATIONAL DIFFERENCES

BIAS IN MENTAL TESTING

DISCARDED

Arthur R. Jensen

Straight Talk About Mental Tests

THE FREE PRESS
A Division of Macmillan Publishing Co., Inc.
NEW YORK

Copyright © 1981 by THE FREE PRESS
A Division of Macmillan Publishing Co., Inc.

All rights reserved. No part of this book may be reproduced
or transmitted in any form or by any means, electronic or
mechanical, including photocopying, recording, or by any
information storage and retrieval system, without permission
in writing from the Publisher.

THE FREE PRESS
A Division of Macmillan Publishing Co., Inc.
866 Third Avenue, New York, N.Y.   10022

Collier Macmillan Canada, Ltd.

Library of Congress Catalog Card Number: 80-83714

Printed in the United States of America

printing number

1 2 3 4 5 6 7 8 9 10

Library of Congress Cataloging in Publication Data

Jensen, Arthur Robert.
  Straight talk about mental tests.

  Bibliography: p.
  Includes index.
  1. Intelligence levels.   2. Intelligence tests.
3. Nature and nurture.   I. Title.
BF432.A1J47   153.9′2   80-83714
ISBN 0-02-916440-0

To three American psychologists
whose contributions to mental testing
I greatly admire:

Edward L. Thorndike (1874–1949)

Lewis M. Terman (1877–1956)

Louis L. Thurstone (1887–1955)

Contents

Preface

THIS BOOK IS FOR those of the general public who want to learn more about mental testing and its controversies. It presupposes no background in the specialized terminologies or mathematical underpinnings of psychometrics, statistics, or quantitative genetics that make most of the serious literature on the "IQ controversy" so inaccessible to the educated public who are not professionals in the field of mental measurement.

Yet this book is intended to offer nonspecialists a much greater scope and depth for understanding the main issues of this topic than are provided by the popular and sensational literature of the Sunday-supplement variety.

Readers are here allowed to view this subject very much in the same perspective as it is viewed by specialists in psychometrics and differential psychology, but without all the technical paraphernalia.

The public today is witnessing a war against psychological tests. The popular media are full of it, but they fall so far short of presenting a sufficiently systematic or complete and accurate exposition of the key issues as to frustrate the educated public's desire to be well informed on a matter of great social concern. Few, if any, of the current attacks on tests have anything to do with the topics of primary interest to professionals—the reliability and validity of tests for specific predictive purposes, their usefulness in psychological diagnosis, and the attempt to gain a scientific understanding of the nature and causes of individual and group differences as measured by various kinds of tests. The attacks on tests are mostly of a political and ideological nature, at times only thinly disguised as technical criticism, and are usually leveled by persons or organizations that know almost nothing about psychometrics.

If anyone thinks that the real criticisms of tests do not come from the test experts themselves, he need only look at the eight huge volumes of the *Mental Measurements Yearbook,* in which all published psychological tests are exposed to the merciless critical scrutiny of the many specialists in psychological testing who serve as reviewers.

The current ideological attacks on mental testing appear varied and come from many quarters, but they all seem to have one common basis, which has been most aptly described by Barbara Lerner, a psychologist and lawyer, in an address delivered at the 1978 annual convention of the American Psychological Association:

> Tests are under attack today because they tell us truths about ourselves and our society; partial truths, to be sure, but truths nonetheless and, in recent years, many of these truths have been unpleasant and unflattering. Seen in this perspective, the attack on tests is, to a very considerable and very frightening degree, an attack on truth itself by those who deal with unpleasant and unflattering truths by denying them and by attacking and trying to destroy the evidence for them. . . .
>
> Unpleasant truths in the educational realm center around the fact that our public schools are doing a seriously inadequate job: children of the poor are not learning the basics; children of the rich are not learning much beyond the basics. We know that because we have current literacy test results showing how widespread illiteracy is among the poor in general and the black poor in particular, and because we have long-term SAT results showing the magnitude of the decline in academic preparedness and competence among the college bound.
>
> In the employment realm, the problem with school-like paper and pencil tests is not that they do not work; the problem is that too many of them work too well and tell us another unpleasant truth: poor students frequently make poor workers. This is so because the skills needed for competent performance in business, industry, and government are, increasingly, the same skills needed for competent performance in school. Tests tell us this unpleasant truth and they are begin-

ning to tell us some even more unwelcome ones about the relationship
between intellectual competence and national productivity, and about
the escalating price we are paying for incompetence in an increasingly
competitive world market.

I do not view my role as that of a defender of tests, least of all of the
"testing establishment." I am essentially an outsider, a critic of tests,
of their uses and abuses. I have published no tests and I have no connections with test publishers. For all I know, I may be anathema to
them, for rocking the boat. A large part of my professional career has
been devoted to the use and study of mental tests, mainly as an adjunct
of my more basic research interests in the variety, nature, and causes of
individual differences in human behavior, particularly mental abilities.
This research has not always led to popular conclusions.

How tests fare in the public arena is not of primary interest to me,
professionally. But it is of considerable concern to me as a citizen,
because I have come to believe that well-constructed tests, properly
used, provide objective standards for evaluation in education and employment, that they can contribute substantially to human welfare and
social justice.

What has come to be called the "IQ controversy" revolves around
four main issues: (1) the nature and validity of mental tests, (2) the
question of culture bias in tests when they are used for certain minority
groups, (3) the relative contributions of heredity and environment to
individual differences in general mental ability, and (4) the causes of
the observed differences in mental abilities between social classes and
racial groups.

This book deals nontechnically, but in considerable depth, with
each of these topics. In every case, I have tried to present the generally
accepted facts and interpretations of the vast majority of scholars and
scientists in the relevant fields.

The popular media, whose stock in trade is conflict and controversy, frequently try to create the impression that most of this material
is extremely controversial and hotly disputed by the experts. I assure
you, this is a false impression.

What I have to say in this book actually expresses the quite or-
thodox standard position of the majority of scientists on these issues. I
expect only minor quibbles from the experts in psychometrics and
genetics. But one always expects quibbling; it is part of our business.

On the topic of race differences in behavioral traits, which of course
is the touchiest topic of all, the reader should keep in mind that public

pronouncements by some experts often express merely their sentiments rather than the carefully considered scientific views that they would express in private discussions with other scientists.

My own position on this emotionally loaded topic is actually a quite noncontroversial one, except to the uninformed or to doctrinaire environmentalists who insist as a matter of highest principle that environmental factors *exclusively* (and particularly those associated with socioeconomic status) are the only allowable explanation for the observed racial differences in behavioral traits. My position, since 1969, has been that it is a scientifically open question whether or not genetic as well as environmental factors are involved in racial differences in IQ; that a genetic hypothesis (which does not exclude environmental factors) is scientifically the most plausible but is far from being rigorously proven; that the observed differences cannot be adequately explained in terms of test bias; and that the most commonly invoked environmental factors have proved wanting.

Probably the two least controversial facts in the "IQ controversy" are (1) that in human populations there is a well-recognized trait that can be called general mental ability or intelligence, in which differences among persons can be measured with a fair degree of accuracy by appropriate tests (often called IQ tests); and (2) that the observed differences among persons in this trait are largely attributable to genetic inheritance.

It is an undisputed fact that individual differences in the ability to perform any kind of task that involves some degree of mental complexity for successful performance are positively intercorrelated among an extremely wide variety of such tasks. That is to say, those persons who perform better on one kind of mental task tend, in general, to perform better on many other kinds of mental tasks. We see this when a great variety of mental tasks are given to any large group of persons selected at random from the general population. The correlation among mental tests of all kinds is one of the most generally acknowledged findings of psychology. It is the basis for the concept of general mental ability, or intelligence.

Scores on IQ tests reflect individual differences in this ability quite well among persons for whom the tests are appropriate in terms of age, education, and cultural background. No single standardized test is appropriate for everyone; yet there is hardly anyone of school age for whom some test cannot provide a valid estimate of intelligence.

The IQ is most highly related to children's performance in school, especially in the more academic subjects. This is not because IQ tests measure merely what is specifically taught in school, but because the kinds of complex learning and problem solving that are emphasized in school call for the same general mental ability that IQ tests are designed to measure. Many tests that measure general intelligence have no verbal or numerical content whatever, nor do they involve any specific knowledge or skills taught in school. These tests obviously measure something more fundamental than merely what the individual has acquired in school or at home. This is indicated, too, by the fact that scores on IQ tests are correlated with brain size and with the speed and amplitude of electrical potential in the brain. Also, reaction times to complex stimuli are related to IQs. The IQ obviously reflects something related to brain functions.

The personal and social importance of the IQ is most clearly recognized by its positive relationship to educational performance and to attained occupational status and income. On the other hand, IQ is *negatively* related to certain social ills, such as delinquency.

Among various behavioral traits, intelligence is perhaps the most strongly influenced by genetic factors. It is well known that many kinds of severe mental subnormalities are caused by mutant genes and chromosomal abnormalities. These are rare, fortunately. But normal variation of intelligence in the population is also attributable, in part, to hereditary factors, called polygenic inheritance, since many genes are involved. Environmental factors, both biological and psychological, prenatal and postnatal, also contribute to individual differences in IQ, although probably not so much as heredity.

The large number of studies of the inheritance of mental ability as assessed by standard IQ tests indicate that variation in genotypes (i.e., the unique combination of genes that a person inherits) accounts for between 50 and 80 percent of the variation in phenotypes (i.e., the observed characteristic, such as IQ) in the population. The relative importance of genetic factors will inevitably increase as the environmental factors that influence mental development are made more equal for everyone.

Estimates of the heritability of IQ are derived from the methods of quantitative genetics applied to measurements of resemblance between persons of differing degrees of genetic kinship, such as identical and fraternal twins, parents and children, siblings, and adopted and unrelated children who are reared together. For example, identical twins have exactly the same genotypes; and, even when they are reared apart, they are much more alike in IQ than fraternal twins reared together, since fraternals share only about half of their genes. The IQs of adopted children are more closely correlated with the intelligence levels of their true biological mothers, with whom they have had no contact since early infancy, than with their adoptive or foster parents who have reared them. Genetic influences are clearly involved.

These are the generally accepted views on these issues among the many psychologists and geneticists who have done research in this field. You will find these main facts of the matter in the vast majority of textbooks of psychology and genetics. The currently small handful of dissenters who argue that genetic factors play no part in IQ differences are not unlike the few persons living today who claim that the earth is flat.

Practically every statement in this book could be footnoted to show supporting references in the technical literature, as is the common practice in scientific journal articles and scholarly texts. But in this work for nonspecialists I have tried to minimize the scholarly trappings, while preserving scholarly fidelity to the research literature. Those who would delve into this literature will find an entrée to virtually all of it in the books listed at the end of this volume and in the extensive bibliographies found in my other books.

Finally, I should mention that I have intentionally abstained from playing the role of social philosopher. The broader educational and social implications of research in psychometrics and differential psychology certainly demand full discussion. But I am much less interested in my own rumination on these matters than in the basic facts that an informed public must know if it is to think intelligently about their broader implications. Our faith in democracy rests on the condition that the majority of the people can know the facts and can discuss them openly.

Straight Talk
About
Mental Tests

1

The What, How, and Why of Mental Tests

THE BASIC CONCEPT of testing has probably been around at least as long as *Homo sapiens* has inhabited the earth. It is familiar to everyone. Testing means trying, probing, or sampling on a small scale, as a basis for deciding further commitment. We stick our toes in the water before diving in for a swim. The host at a dinner party takes a sip of wine before serving it to his guests. These are examples of testing.

Tests are merely indicators. They are useful when we would like to have advance knowledge of some situation before we plunge into it, or when we want to predict the outcome of some endeavor before we risk it. The indicator itself need not even remotely resemble the thing it is intended to predict, so long as it indeed predicts with reasonable accuracy. The falling column of mercury in a barometer is a good predictor of rain.

Mental tests are essentially the same as all other tests. A small sample of behavior is used to predict some more extensive or important behavior or capability. Parents, teachers, and employers have always informally used limited observations of a person's behavior as clues to broader performance capabilities. When the procedure is more formalized, as in observing a person's behavior in response to strictly defined conditions, we call it a test.

People have always felt the need to predict one another's performance in untried situations. Their predictions are based on either one

1

or a combination of two things: (1) an informal test or sample of the person's behavior, as just mentioned, or (2) knowledge of the person's past performance in a similar situation. It is often true that the best predictor of future performance is past performance in similar circumstances.

There is a certain coherence and consistency in people's capabilities that no one can afford to ignore. Just as what a person has done in the past indicates what he is likely to do in the future, so does his way of dealing with ''little things'' indicate the way he is likely to deal with more important issues. That is, performance of trivial tasks can indicate performance of big ones.

These general truths about human nature and experience have always been known, more or less, by everyone. Formal tests and the whole field of applied psychometrics are simply the attempt to capitalize on these inherent regularities in human behavior. We can increase their predictive power by making our observations systematically and under highly controlled situations. The elicited behavior samples, whatever they might consist of, are valid indicators if, in fact, they improve our prediction of the quality of a person's performance in a larger, more important sphere of activity.

Tests are utterly trivial things in themselves. They gain in importance only by virtue of the things they can predict that people deem important. It is apparent that tests arouse people's emotions and become publicly controversial in direct relation to the importance people attach to whatever the test predicts. ''Intelligence testing'' thus became an emotional and controversial issue, for surveys have found that most people value intelligence second only to good health. We all know of the public clamor over tests that claim to measure intelligence or to predict the outcomes of situations—in school, college, or the world of work—in which intelligence is realized by everyone to be a prime determinant of success. No other type of test arouses quite so much emotion. In recent years, market-wise test publishers have removed such emotionally charged words as ''intelligence'' and ''IQ'' from the titles of their intelligence tests, substituting euphemisms such as ''cognitive ability'' and ''learning potential.''

Binet's Test

The first known use of formal tests was in ancient China, where civil servants were selected for and promoted to higher positions on the basis of examinations. But the first really useful test to be expressly designed as an intelligence test was not devised until 1905, by the great French psychologist Alfred Binet (1857–1911). Binet and a psychiatrist, Théophile Simon, were commissioned by the French Ministry of Education to devise a practical and objective means for identifying mentally retarded children who then could be given special attention in school or placed in more appropriate classes before the frustration of repeated failures in regular classes had taken its toll.

It is instructive to note how Binet went about constructing his test, because the same basic principles are involved in the construction of all psychological tests.

Binet first observed that the children who were pointed out by their teachers as having inordinate difficulty in their schoolwork, especially in learning the "three R's," also had difficulty doing a good many other things that were easily accomplished by their age-mates. The least successful children behaved, in many ways, more like the average child a year or two younger. (Hence the concept of "retarded" mental development.)

To objectify and quantify this subjective impression, which was shared by many teachers, Binet tried to devise an "age scale" of mental capabilities. If properly devised, such a scale would permit a more precise determination of a child's overall capability in relation to many other children of the same age than could be made by a teacher's more casual observation and subjective impression of what constitutes the average mental capability of children at any given age.

Binet and Simon went about constructing such an age scale by first observing the kinds of nonscholastic things most children knew or could do at different ages, and then making up a lot of short questions and simple tasks that would incorporate these ordinary kinds of general knowledge and skills. They did not want to assess a child's knowledge of what was specifically taught in school. Their idea was to obtain a much broader assessment of the child's abilities, which they could then compare with his performance in school.

The many questions and tasks that Binet made up were tried out on representative groups of children of different ages. Binet recorded the percentage of children within each one-year age interval from age 3 to age 15 who could "pass" each item. He noted those items that showed the most clear-cut age differences in percent passing and assigned them to the specific age levels for which they were the most discriminating.

A "maximally discriminating" item is one passed by half the children in a given age group and failed by the other half. Thus, an item that discriminates maximally among, say, 5-year-olds would be placed at that level on the age scale of test items. Binet kept trying out items in this fashion until he had five items for each one-year age interval from age 3 to age 15. Thus he obtained a series of items evenly graded in difficulty in terms of the percentage of children in each age interval who could pass the item.

The items thus form an age scale, in terms of which a child's total score on the test can be meaningfully expressed. A child who passes as many items as the average number passed by all 5-year-olds is said to have a "mental age" of 5, regardless of what the child's chronological age happens to be. A child who has a mental age of 5 and is, in fact, 5 years old is said to have average ability for his age. But a 5-year-old with a mental age of 3 is considered retarded. Such a child would fail to keep pace with his age-mates in the very first year of school.

Binet used one other criterion besides age in his final selection of items. To ensure that the ability measured by his age scale was truly relevant to children's scholastic performance, even though the items did not include scholastic subjects, Binet tried out the scale on children identified by their teachers as consistently failing in the scholastic work of their grade level. Binet eliminated any test item that did not discriminate clearly between these failing children and the pupils who were doing well in school.

In later revisions of the Binet scale, another basis for item selection is that each should clearly discriminate between children with the highest and the lowest total scores on the whole test, when all the children are the same age. This ensures that each single item measures the same trait that is measured by the test as a whole. Binet believed that the trait measured by his test could be called intelligence, the essence of which he equated with judgment. Binet and Simon defined what they intended to measure with their scale in the following terms:

> It seems to us that in intelligence there is a fundamental faculty, the alteration or lack of which is of the utmost importance for practical life. This faculty is judgment, otherwise called good sense, practical sense, initiative, the faculty of adapting one's self to circumstances. To judge well, to reason well, these are the essential activities of intelligence. A person may be a moron or an imbecile if he is lacking in judgment; but with good judgment he can never be either. Indeed the rest of the intellectual faculties seem of little importance in comparison with judgment.

Test items on the Binet scale are individually administered to a child, who is asked in a standard way to answer certain questions or perform certain tasks. For each item, the test manual spells out, with many examples, what constitutes a "passing" or "failing" response. None of the questions has a time limit for response. Below are typical items taken from the age-graded categories of Binet's scale, described in terms of what is required for passing each item.

Age 3 : Points to nose, eyes, and mouth.
Age 4 : Repeats three digits.
Age 5 : Copies a square.
Age 6 : Counts thirteen pennies.
Age 7 : Shows right hand and left ear.
Age 8 : Notes omissions from pictures of familiar objects.
Age 9 : Defines familiar words.
Age 10: Arranges five blocks in order of weight.
Age 12: Discovers the sense of a disarranged sentence.
Age 15: Interprets given facts.

The American revision and standardization of the Binet scale was carried out in 1916 by Lewis M. Terman (1877–1956), a psychologist at Stanford University. It has been known ever since as the Stanford–Binet Intelligence Test. Later revisions were made in 1937, 1960, and 1972.

The Intelligence Quotient or IQ

For Binet, a child's score on the test was always reported in terms of mental age (MA), based on the average chronological age of children in general who pass the same number of items. A mental age below the child's chronological age (CA) indicated some degree of retardation, compared with the average rate of mental development; a higher MA than CA indicated some degree of acceleration of development.

A German psychologist, Wilhelm Stern, thought it a good idea to express this rate of mental development—the child's degree of "brightness" relative to his age-mates—in terms of the ratio of MA to CA. He called it the "mental quotient," which Terman later changed to "intelligence quotient"—the now famous IQ:

$$IQ = MA/CA \times 100.$$

Multiplying by 100 simply removes the decimal point. A 5-year-old child who performs as well as the average 6-year-old on the Binet test would be said to have a mental age of 6 and an IQ of 120. A 6-year-old child with an MA of 5 would have an IQ of 83. By definition, the average child is one whose MA is the same as his CA, placing the average IQ at 100.

Present-day IQ tests, however, are not based on the mental-age concept or on the formula IQ = MA/CA. Instead, a child's raw score (i.e., the number of items he gets right) is converted directly to IQ by use of a statistically derived conversion table based on a "normative" or "standardization" group. The IQ derived in this manner more accurately represents the child's standing relative to children of the same age in the norm group. The average IQ is set at 100 at every age level. Adult IQs are scaled in the same way. The mental-age scale is no longer useful beyond about age 16, because the mental functions measured by IQ tests do not go on steadily increasing beyond that age. Knowledge, specific skills, "know-how," and experience continue to increase, but intelligence does not. Intelligence shows much the same sort of growth curve that we see for height, with a gradually slowing rate of gain as the individual reaches maturity.

Thus the IQ expresses the person's performance on the test in terms of his relative standing among persons of the same age in some specified "normative" population. The best modern intelligence tests are standardized on highly representative samples of persons drawn from each age group of the general population.

The purely quantitative meaning of any person's IQ can be most easily understood in terms of its percentile rank. This is the percentage of the normative group of the same age as the person in question that performed less well on the test. If your percentile rank is 50, for example, it means that you scored higher than 50 percent of the people of your age in the normative population. Table 1 shows IQs with their corresponding percentile ranks.

TABLE 1

IQs and Their Corresponding Percentile Ranks

IQ	PERCENTILE	IQ	PERCENTILE
145	99.9	100	50.0
140	99.6	95	36.3
135	98.9	90	24.2
130	97.7	85	15.9
125	95.0	80	8.8
120	90.3	75	4.5
115	84.1	70	2.3
110	74.2	65	0.9
105	63.7	60	0.4

The Distribution of IQ

It is a common observation that people are pretty much the same. Most people appear rather middling in height, for example; only seldom do we meet someone who is startlingly tall or conspicuously short. Similarly, most people one meets are neither unusually bright nor unusually dull; they seem to be rather middling in intelligence. Extreme deviations from the general run of people are quite scarce.

Just as there are relatively few midgets and relatively few giants, so there are relatively few idiots and relatively few geniuses. In intelligence, as in height, the majority of the population clusters around the average, with decreasing numbers the farther one moves from it in either direction. The gradations of these numbers slope smoothly downward and outward on both sides of the cluster in the middle, creating a graceful graphic curve in the shape of a bell.

The Normal Curve

The bell-shaped distribution, or "normal curve," is characteristic of sets of measurements of many of our physical properties—height, lung capacity, blood pressure, brain weight, birth weight, strength of grip, reaction time, and so on. Scores on most mental tests also closely approximate the normal distribution, provided that a representative sample of the population has been tested and that test items are more or less evenly graded in difficulty. Figure 1 shows an idealized normal

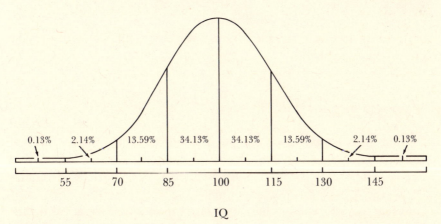

IQ

Figure 1. The IQ distribution as a normal curve, showing the percentage of scores in each segment of the curve when it is divided into standard deviations.

distribution of IQs and gives the percentage of cases falling within each interval of 15 points, the measure of what is called the "standard deviation."

Since the term "standard deviation" is so frequently used in discussions of tests, it is one of the very few technical points that must be explained here. The standard deviation of an actual distribution of scores or measurements obtained from a sample of a population is usually abbreviated as *SD* or simply *s*. The standard deviation in a whole population is indicated by the Greek letter sigma: σ. So just what is the standard deviation? It is the square root of the variance.

The variance of any set of scores is a measure of the total amount of variation that exists among all the scores. Statisticians need some way to quantify the total amount of scatter or dispersion of the scores. The index they use for this is known as the variance, symbolized as s^2 for a sample and as σ^2 for a population. To calculate the variance of a set of scores, you first determine the arithmetic mean, which is the sum of all the scores divided by the total number of scores. From each score you next subtract the mean and square the remainder. Then you sum all these squares and, finally, divide by the total number of scores. These operations are expressed more simply in mathematical notation as

$$s^2 = \Sigma(X - \overline{X})^2/N,$$

where s^2 is the variance, Σ means "the sum of," X is a test score, $\overline{X}$ is the mean of all the scores, and N is the total number of scores.

The standard deviation, then, is simply the square root of the variance, that is, $\sqrt{s^2}$, which is *s*. It, too, is a measure of dispersion. If everyone got exactly the same test score, both the variance and standard deviation would obviously be zero—there would be no dispersion or variability in scores.

Departures from the Normal Curve

The bell-shaped curve shown in Figure 1 is a perfect "normal curve," as defined mathematically. (It is also known as a Gaussian curve, after the German mathematician Karl Friedrich Gauss [1777–1855], who formulated its mathematical properties.) The word "normal" in this context has none other than a mathematical meaning. It does not connote "normal" as contrasted to "abnormal."

It so happens, in fact, that the distribution of IQs in the population corresponds very closely to the normal curve only in the central range between about IQ 70 and IQ 130. At the higher and, especially, the lower extremes, the actual distribution of IQs shows certain departures from the mathematically defined normal curve.

First of all, there is an excess of very low IQs, below about IQ 50 or so. The reason for this excess is now quite well understood. To those in the very small lower "tail" of the normal distribution, below IQ 50, must be added those unfortunate victims of various anomalies that are quite distinct from the usual genetic and environmental factors responsible for the normal distribution of intelligence. These anomalous conditions have drastic effects that often completely override all the usual determinants of a person's intelligence and cause the person to be mentally deficient, often profoundly so. These types of mental deficiency can usually be clearly distinguished from what can be called biologically normal mental retardation, most of which is found in the IQ range between 50 and 70. An IQ of 70 or 75 defines the upper limit of what is generally considered mental retardation. About 75 to 80 percent of the persons below that level are biologically normal; they simply represent the lower extreme of normal variation in the genetic and environmental factors that condition mental development. They are analogous, in the distribution of height, to persons who are very short, although they are biologically normal, in contrast to midgets and dwarfs, whose condition is the result of specific genetic anomalies.

The remaining 20 to 25 percent of the mentally retarded, mostly the severely retarded with IQs below 50, are biologically analogous to midgets and dwarfs. Their condition is due to some specific abnormality that prevents normal mental development. These abnormalities can be classified into three main categories:

1. *Major gene defects,* that is, a single rare recessive or mutant gene, the deleterious effects of which override all of the normal genetic factors involved in mental growth. Examples are phenylketonuria (PKU) and microcephaly.
2. *Chromosomal anomalies,* in which there are too many or too few chromosomes. Down's syndrome or "mongolism," for example, is the result of the the individual's having forty-seven chromosomes instead of the normal forty-six. There are a number of clinically identifiable types of chromosomal anomalies, all of which take some toll on mental ability.
3. *Brain damage* due to trauma or disease, before or after birth, such as German measles in the pregnant mother, severe anoxia during birth, and encephalitis.

It is an important fact that these three types of severe mental retardation occur with nearly equal frequency in all social classes and racial groups. A milder type of retardation, often called "familial," which is not associated with any biological abnormality, occurs with markedly different frequencies as a function of children's social class and race, as shown in Figure 2. The possible causes of these large social-class and racial differences in the prevalence of familial mental retardation are considered in Chapter 6.

The Meaning of IQ

The IQ, like any other score, derives its meaning from what we associate with it. The reason that the IQ arouses so much emotion and controversy is that people generally associate it with things they regard as very important to themselves, to their children, and to society.

No other single fact that one can determine about a child is considered more informative about his probable educational attainments, eventual occupational level, and socioeconomic status than is the child's IQ. This is especially true of his average IQ, based on several testings over three or four years after he has entered school. Neither the parents' IQs, nor their education, nor their occupational level, nor

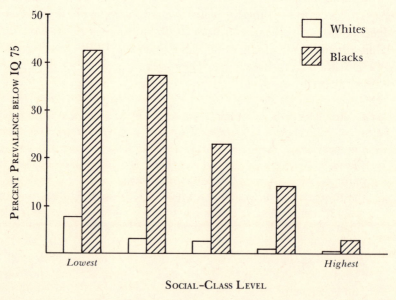

Figure 2. Prevalence of children below IQ 75 as a function of social class.

their social status, nor their income, nor all of these combined is as predictive of the child's educational and occupational future as is his own IQ. This is not to say that the IQ is a very good predictor of these things, but it is a better predictor than any others we know of.

The IQ is a fairly good, but not perfect, measure of general intelligence or of what can be called the "general factor" of mental ability, which is the main topic of the next chapter. Although the "general factor" of mental ability is a highly technical psychological concept, it does, in fact, come very close to meaning much the same thing that the layman means by "intelligence." It is people's perception of the fact that IQ tests can measure this general factor with reasonable accuracy that arouses their fascination with and anxiety about the IQ.

In contrast to the psychologist, however, the layman is often more inclined to include specialized knowledge, skills, talents, educational acquisitions, memory, and wisdom in his notion of intelligence. These things may often be valid indicators of intelligence, but they are not the essence of it, which is closer to reasoning ability, as explained in the next chapter.

Intelligence is surely not the only important ability, but without a fair share of intelligence, other abilities and talents usually cannot be fully developed and effectively used. Intelligence coordinates the person's other abilities or special talents for effective performance. It has been referred to as the "integrative capacity" of the mind.

Superior intelligence is a necessary, although not sufficient, condition for creativity in any socially valued sense. The achievements of a Shakespeare, a Michelangelo, a Beethoven, or an Edison depend on special talents and other traits and circumstances, but such achievements would not be possible without superior general intelligence as well.

Socially, it is this threshold aspect of intelligence that gives the IQ its greatest importance. It is generally perceived that when intelligence is below a certain level, there is a high probability that certain things cannot be achieved. Because of this threshold aspect with respect to education and occupation, the lower a person's IQ is, the more limited are that person's options in life. This is an awesome fact. No one knows any way to get around it. Eliminating IQ tests would certainly have no effect. The situation existed eons before mental tests were invented. Mental tests do not create individual differences in mental ability; they merely measure them.

There are four socially sensitive thresholds on the IQ scale that mark major divisions in the probabilities of educational achievement, which may have important consequences in a person's life. These thresholds are not set by arbitrary convention or by definition. They are a result of the educational and occupational structure of modern industrial societies and the demands they make on the kind of mental ability measured by IQ tests.

The four socially and personally most important thresholds on the IQ scale are those that differentiate with high probability between persons who, because of their level of general mental ability, (1) can or cannot attend a regular school (threshold at about IQ 50), (2) can or cannot master the traditional subject matter of elementary school (about IQ 75), (3) can or cannot succeed in the academic or college preparatory curriculum through high school with good enough grades for college admission (about IQ 105), and (4) can or cannot graduate from an accredited four-year college with grades that would qualify for admission to a professional or graduate school (about IQ 115).

None of these thresholds is inexorable. They merely indicate the IQ level below which the probability is very slight that the particular achievement will be realized. Similar thresholds exist in the physical realm. What are the probabilities of a pudgy girl becoming a prima ballerina? Of a 5'2" man playing on a national league basketball team? Of a skinny 120-pounder making the college football team? It *could* happen. But would we bet on it?

It is important to realize that for any given IQ there is a considerable range of behavioral capabilities. But that range is much narrower for the most intellectually demanding activities. The IQ predicts academic performance better than it predicts anything else. Except at the lowest levels, IQ is not a very good clue to performance on many of the ordinary tasks of life, or to overall social adjustment.

In our present society, however, IQ 70 or 75 seems to be the most crucial threshold. Most persons with any experience in the matter would agree that those with IQs below 70 or 75 have unusual difficulty in school and in the world of work. Few jobs in a modern industrial society can be entrusted to persons below IQ 70 without making special allowances for their mental disability, such as by greatly simplifying the requirements of the job to bring it within their capability. Also, adults with an IQ below 75 can seldom manage their own affairs; they often need assistance from their families or from social agencies. The armed services find it necessary to exclude most men and women who score below an equivalent of about IQ 75 or 80 on the Armed Forces Qualification Test. There are simply too few useful jobs that they can be successfully trained to perform in the limited time available for training.

There's no getting around it, unfortunately: a low IQ is a severe personal handicap in our competitive world. Most of this misfortune—in some 70 to 80 percent of all retarded persons—is a result of the same polygenic system of normal biological variation that is responsible for the good fortune of those with high IQs. It is no more normal, or abnormal, to have an IQ of 130 than to have an IQ of 70, in the vast majority of persons. Each is largely a consequence of biologically normal variation. The personal and social consequences of this variation are, of course, another story. But no one should be either praised or blamed for his good or bad luck in the genetic lottery.

Proper Uses of Tests

Tests that are constructed and administered can serve a legitimate and useful function in making decisions about persons. Tests themselves do not create the decisions that have to be made. Decisions were made about people long before psychological tests ever existed. Making good decisions requires relevant and dependable information. Tests can provide one source of such information.

Tests do not provide information that is of an essentially different *kind* from the information that would ordinarily be considered in making decisions without the aid of tests. But good tests can provide information that is more relevant and more accurate for decision-making purposes than any information that could be obtained by other means, with a comparable investment of time and resources. Tests also have the advantage of being sufficiently objective and explicit that the relevance and accuracy of their contribution to a particular decision-making process can be clearly established and quantified.

It should be emphasized that decisions about persons do not automatically flow from the tests themselves. Tests yield scores. Decisions are made by people. How decisions are made, how many other types of information besides test scores are taken into consideration, and how much weight is given to each kind of information in making a decision about a person are complex issues. Resolution depends on many factors: the training, expert knowledge, experience, common sense, and wisdom of the decision maker; the economic and practical considerations that dictate the time and resources that can be invested in each decision; and the purpose of the decision. Equally important to consider is the *cost* of a "wrong" decision to all the parties concerned.

There are five main practical uses of tests: assessment, guidance, diagnosis, placement, and selection.

Assessment

This means measuring the specific outcomes of a course of instruction. Achievement testing is a prime example. A well-designed test for this purpose should consist of a representative sample of the knowledge or skills that the unit or course of instruction was intended to impart. Such a test is useful as "informative feedback" to the student and the teacher. It reveals whether a standard of mastery of the course material has been met by the student, and it highlights areas of weakness, indicating the need for review and remedial study. Teachers have always used tests for these purposes; they are an integral aspect of instruction. Instructors compose their own tests to cover exactly the material they have taught.

Standardized achievement tests have two advantages and two disadvantages when compared with informal teacher-made tests.

The first advantage of published standardized tests is that they are usually carefully constructed. The ordinary teacher has neither the time nor the technical expertise that are lavished on the best standardized achievement tests, in which every item is carefully edited and selected on the basis of technical procedures known as "item analysis," based on tryouts of the items in large samples of the test's target population.

The second advantage of standardized tests is that they are "normed" on large representative samples of the group for which the test is intended—age groups, school grades, and so forth. This makes it possible to relate an individual's test score to the total distribution of scores in some reference group that is much larger and more stable than the particular small class or school of which the individual is a member. This information is usually of greater interest and importance to the teacher and school administration than to the pupils or their parents, unless they wish to know (as should be their right) how a particular school's achievement test scores compare with those of other schools or localities.

The interpretation of differences among schools in achievement levels is another matter. We know that most "achievement variation" among schools has little or nothing to do with the quality of the schools or teachers themselves. It is mostly related to characteristics of the neighborhood served by the school, to home background, and to personal characteristics that have been fairly well established before children even enter school and over which schools have little or no control. The general character of the learning atmosphere and academic standards of a school are, however, reflected by the average level of achievement in the school, and these things are of interest to parents who are concerned about their children's education.

A disadvantage of standardized tests is that they are designed to assess what curriculum experts consider the core content of a field or unit of study. But the test may not reflect the special emphases, contents, or interpretations of material that the teacher considers important aspects of the instruction. Students' acquisition of these subtler points of the course content must be assessed by the teacher's own devices.

A further disadvantage of standardized tests is that they are usually objectively scorable. That is, no decisions or judgments are required on the part of the scorer. This means that tests must be limited mainly to multiple-choice questions, consisting of a stem (the question or problem) followed by several alternative answers from among which the subject tries to pick the best answer. (The less-than-best or flatly wrong alternatives are called distractors.) Compared with essay-type exams, the multiple-choice format has the decided advantages of great efficiency, objectivity, and high reliability of scoring the tests, as well as great advantages for statistical analyses of test items. The main disadvantage of the multiple-choice test is that it does not permit the teacher to assess students' achievements in organizing knowledge and expressing it clearly in their own words; it also fails to allow for original expression, which the teacher may also wish to assess. To assess these qualities the teacher must resort to essay exams or recitation.

Guidance

Test results, when properly interpreted by an educational or vocational guidance counselor, can provide helpful information to a client trying to decide among alternative educational or employment possibilities. Specific achievement tests can inform a person of his standing in the prerequisite knowledge or skills needed for a particular choice. Vocational interest inventories and differential aptitude tests can indicate a person's relative standing among the successful and unsuccessful candidates in educational programs, job training courses, or occupations. They can indicate the person's pattern of strengths and weaknesses in different aptitudes and can match his pattern of aptitudes to the types of occupations with which such patterns are most compatible. Tests, interpreted for the client by an expert guidance counselor, can furnish much more detailed information of much greater scope as a basis for educational and vocational decisions than can be obtained from school grades alone or from previous work experience. Thus tests can be helpful to persons at educational or vocational crossroads.

Diagnosis

When a pupil repeatedly fails to maintain normal progress or to attain some minimal standard of performance, as evinced by achievement tests, and when the pupil has shown no appreciable response to his teacher's usual remedial procedures, diagnosis is needed. At some point, the teacher, after consulting the pupil's parents about the problem, refers the pupil to an accredited school psychologist. The psychologist should receive from the teacher an objective behavioral description of the pupil's specific problems. The teacher should never label the child's behavior with psychological terminology or offer a "diagnosis." All that a psychologist wants from a teacher is a clear description of the specific behavior problem that prompted the referral. Also, it is not a teacher's job to refer a pupil to a psychologist with a request for a particular test or for confirmation of a diagnostic impression of the teacher's. It is considered bad practice if a teacher requests an "IQ test" or asks for a determination whether the child is "mentally retarded" or is this or that. That is not the teacher's function.

Psychological diagnosis is an attempt to describe a problem accurately, to understand its causes insofar as possible, and, on this basis, to decide on some course of action that can benefit the pupil. It is a complex procedure calling for high-level professional skills. Individually administered psychological tests of various kinds are a useful and often necessary part of a diagnostic workup. A good psychologist could conduct his study of a pupil using no tests at all, basing his impressions on observation and structured interviews; but it would be very inefficient, and the psychologist would be seriously handicapped without the precise information that can be gained from tests. Such a study would be similar to a physician's examination of a patient without the aid of a thermometer, stethoscope, blood-pressure cuff, or tongue depressor.

An individual IQ test, such as the Stanford–Binet or the Wechsler Intelligence Scale for Children (known as the WISC), is an extremely valuable device in diagnosing children with learning problems. There are many possible causes of scholastic failure besides an insufficient level of mental maturity. These other causes can be more easily overlooked if an IQ test is not used to find out a child's general level of ability. A test such as the WISC reflects a child's capabilities over a much broader spectrum than scholastic achievement and is more generally indicative of a child's typical rates of learning and cognitive development.

In addition to this assessment of general level of mental maturity, special tests may be used to discover the presence of auditory, visual, or perceptual problems, speech problems, or highly specific cognitive disabilities that interfere with learning such school subjects as reading. To prohibit the use of any of these diagnostic instruments by school psychologists is greatly to handicap their effectiveness in arriving at the most beneficial treatment for children with unusual scholastic problems.

Placement

Some children do not benefit from ordinary classroom instruction. Their scholastic achievement falls further and further behind their classmates', and their frustration and discouragement from repeated failure can be emotionally harmful.

A teacher's usual sympathy and kindness are of little real help in such cases. Classmates are frequently less kind, and a pupil with severe problems often becomes socially isolated in a regular classroom. It can be a most unhappy and psychologically unwholesome situation.

Depending on a school psychologist's findings, a recommendation may be made for placement in some kind of special class for all or a part of the school day. "Placement," as child psychologists understand and use the term, means different treatments for different children, to meet their particular needs more effectively than would be possible in a regular classroom. Placement decisions are usually made with great reluctance, and only after it has become apparent that a pupil is more harmed than benefited by being kept in a regular class.

Then a pupil may be more appropriately placed in a special class for the "educably mentally retarded," for "educationally handicapped" or "emotionally disturbed" children, or for children with "learning disabilities."

"Placement" also encompasses special classes or programs for "academically gifted" or "high potential" pupils, often identified as those with IQs over 130 on an individually administered test.

The results of psychological testing figure prominently in all such placement decisions and, in fact, are legally required in many states. But test results alone should not dictate placement decisions. Placement is always a complex decision based on much other information in addition to that provided by diagnostic tests. The evaluation of a school's placement practices involves values and judgments in weighing real and supposed advantages against real and supposed disadvantages. Whatever else may be said for or against placement, I believe it would be far riskier, with much more room for error, if school psychologists were prevented from using the currently best standardized individual tests, including the Stanford–Binet and Wechsler scales of intelligence.

Selection

More persons today are affected by the selection function of tests than by any other use. Tests are now widely used for selection, or "screening," by colleges, industry, and the armed forces. I see no prospect of a reversal of this practice in the future.

Selection is unavoidable when the number of applicants for a college or a job far exceeds the number that can be accepted. Selection is also necessary when, as in the armed forces, a large pool of recruits, after basic training, must be assigned to a number of different specialized training courses to supply the personnel required for a variety of essential jobs. Selection is also needed when the course or job itself demands a standard of performance that not all applicants can meet, and when failures are costly.

So we are stuck with the necessity for selection. The only question, then, is *how* to select. The rational and practical course has always been to try to select the "best qualified," meaning those who are most likely to succeed, that is, to complete a course of training with an acceptable level of proficiency.

Selection has traditionally been done on the basis of educational credentials, previous experience, letters of recommendation, and personal impressions gained in interviews. Considerable subjectivity creeps into the use of such information for selection, particularly in the amount of weight given to each item of information, which leaves a good deal of room for personal biases and false impressions of the persons making the selection.

Tests can provide additional information about an applicant that is unquestionably more objective. Results of standardized tests are also unquestionably better for making direct comparisons between applicants than any other means of selection, and they can add substantially to the accuracy of prediction of the applicant's future performance.

Moreover, as a selection method, tests are much more efficient than other means of gaining valid information. This is important when a large number of applicants must be screened within a short period of time, as is most often the case.

But the practical usefulness of a test depends crucially on one thing: its cost/effectiveness ratio as compared with that of other means of selection. The cost factor is obvious; it is the average time, facilities, personnel, and monetary expense per applicant screened. The effectiveness of a test (or any other selection method) depends on its validity for predicting an applicant's level of performance or probability of success. A test's "predictive validity" is a precise quantitative index of its effectiveness for selection. It can be empirically determined for any given test used for selection for any given type of education or job. Often tests are specially devised to have validity for predicting success on a particular kind of job. Or an optimally weighted combination of scores from several different tests may substantially enhance the accuracy of prediction.

Predictive Validity

Validity is the single most important concept in psychometrics. In general, a test is said to have validity to the extent that useful inferences can be drawn from the scores. That is, a test has validity if a person's performance on the test can tell you something about his performance in some other situation.

"Predictive validity" is the accuracy with which a test score (or a combination of scores on different tests) can estimate a person's performance on some criterion, such as scholastic achievement, college grade-point average, or rated job performance.

The degree of a test's predictive validity for a *particular criterion* in a *particular population* (e.g., navy recruits, Harvard freshmen, applicants for a secretarial job) is indexed by the "validity coefficient." This is simply the coefficient of correlation between the test scores and some measurement of the criterion (e.g., grade-point average, number of words typed per minute, average number of sales per month).

What exactly does "correlation" mean? This is the only other technical statistical concept (besides variance) that the reader needs to know to understand much of this book. The concept of correlation is essential to the meaning of validity in the precise way that validity is understood by the test experts. Correlation is the degree of relationship or association between two variables. The degree of relationship is quantified by the "coefficient of correlation" on a scale that ranges from + 1 (perfect positive relationship or one-to-one correspondence) to 0 (no relationship at all) to − 1 (perfect negative relationship). The coefficient of correlation is a continuous variable that can take any value between − 1 and + 1. An example of a perfect positive correlation of + 1 (assuming no error of measurement) would be the correlation between measurements of heights in inches and in centimeters. If we rank people by height in inches, their "rank order" will be exactly the same as if we rank them by height in centimeters. An example of a perfect negative correlation of − 1 would be the correlation between people's height in inches and the reciprocal of height. An example of a zero (or very near zero) correlation would be the correlation between the first sequence of fifty numbers to come up on a roulette wheel and the second sequence of fifty numbers (assuming it is an "honest" roulette wheel!). There is a high, but far from perfect, correlation between people's height and weight—about .70. The correlation between the heights of husbands and wives is not very high—about .30. The correlation between the heights of fathers and sons (as adults) is about .50. The correlation between the number of fingerprint ridges on the index fingers of people's right and left hands is very high—about .97. The correlation between an adult's weight measured on two occasions one week apart is also about .97. The correlation between a person's IQ tested with the same test on two occasions a week apart is about .95. The correlation between a male's weight measured at age 10 and at age 18 is .70; the correlation between weights at age 2 and age 18 is only about .30. Thus, the precise degree of relationship between any two variables can be expressed by the coefficient of correlation. The details of how it is actually computed need not concern us here; they are explained in every textbook on statistical methods.

A test's predictive validity, then, is the correlation between people's test scores and some measurement of their performance on the criterion of interest. The best prediction of the criterion performance is obtained from a "prediction line," which is mathematically determined from all the test scores and the criterion measurements. It is illustrated in Figure 3. From any given test score on the baseline, one can project a vertical line up to the prediction line, and then horizontally across to the scale of criterion measurement (i.e., the vertical and horizontal dashed lines in Figure 3). This indicates the best prediction one could make of the person's criterion performance, given his test score. "Best" simply means that the errors of prediction will be at a *minimum*—any other predictions (based on some *different* prediction line) would be more in error. The test's validity coefficient determines both the slope of the prediction line (a steeper slope being more accurately predictive) and the average amount of error in the predictions. Predictions are perfect only if the test's validity coefficient is 1, which is never the case in reality. Statistically we can only try to minimize errors of prediction; we can never eliminate them.

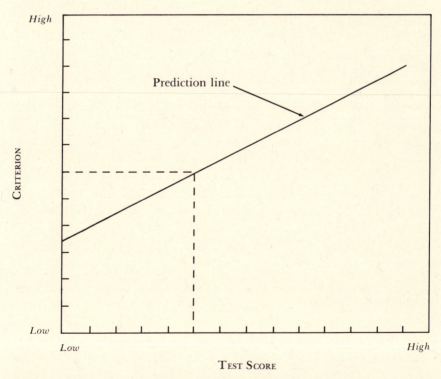

Figure 3. Graph showing how test scores predict performance on some criterion variable (e.g., grades). The location of the prediction line (which is determined mathematically from the data) is such as to minimize predictive errors; that is, it indicates the most accurate possible prediction of the criterion from a given test score that the test can provide.

Interpreting Validity Coefficients

Just what exactly does a test's validity coefficient tell us besides the correlation between the test scores and some criterion performance in a given population? How should we interpret a validity coefficient? There are three technically correct interpretations, but each one is appropriate for different purposes.

Improvement over Chance Prediction

The best *chance* prediction (i.e., best guess) you can make of a person's performance is the average performance of all persons. But if you made exactly the same chance prediction for everyone, it would be entirely uninformative for the purpose of selection. You might as well make a selection by lottery. The accuracy of such predictions is characterized as "no better than chance."

But then, you well may ask, how much better than chance will your prediction of performance be if it is based on a test score with a given validity? A measure of "better than chance" is (*a*) the amount of discrepancy between the test-predicted performance and the actual performance as compared with (*b*) the discrepancy between chance prediction (i.e., the average performance of all persons) and actual performance. If *a* is no smaller than *b*, it means the test prediction is no better than chance. If *a* is smaller than *b*, the test prediction is better than chance prediction, and the percentage of improvement can be expressed by $100 \times (b-a)/b$. The average of this value for all persons is the overall percentage improvement in the test's prediction over chance prediction. It is termed the test's "forecasting efficiency." Without showing its exact mathematical relationship to the validity coefficient, which would require too much additional explanation, the following figures give some idea of how much "better than chance" a given validity coefficient is:

Validity	Forecasting Efficiency
.40	8.35
.50	13.40
.60	20.00
.70	28.59
.80	40.00
.90	56.41
.95	68.78

It can be seen that the forecasting efficiency—that is, the percentage improvement over chance prediction—does not look very impressive in the range of validity coefficients from .40 to .70, which is the range in which most actual validity coefficients fall. Critics who wish to belittle tests and make their practical contribution to the accuracy of prediction look trivial or only slightly "better than chance" in the eyes of the public will talk about the index of forecasting efficiency. For example, under a recent newspaper headline, "Nader Calls College Entry Tests a Fraud," is the statement that "aptitude tests predict [college] grades only 8 to 15 percent better than random prediction with a pair of dice." (Prediction that is 8 to 15 percent better than chance would correspond to validities of between about .40 to .55.)

But this is an inappropriate and unfair criticism if the test is not being used to make exact "point estimates" of every individual's criterion performance (e.g., grade-point average) throughout the entire range of the criterion variable. It requires a very high test validity to make point estimates of criterion performance. But in the practical use of tests we are rarely, if ever, concerned with the accuracy of prediction of every point on the whole continuum of criterion performance. There is no need to take into account the inaccuracies of discrimination among all those applicants who have at least enough or more than enough ability to succeed on the criterion, or among all those who don't have enough ability to succeed. If the selection cutoff to get into College X is an IQ of 110, the percent improvement over chance prediction of grades for students with IQs between 115 and 140 is irrelevant. The aim is to predict who will succeed and who will fail if admitted to the college; it is not to predict the *precise* grade-point average of every admitted student. That precise prediction is, as Nader claims, only about 8 to 15 percent better than chance. His claim is technically correct but irrelevant, and therefore unfair, because college admissions officers do not use the Scholastic Aptitude Test to predict every single student's precise grade-point average.

For the usual uses of tests in selection, there are two much better indicators of the practical gain, as a function of test validity, than the percentage improvement over chance prediction.

Prediction of Odds for Success

One can properly figure the gain from using test scores in selection, as contrasted with chance or random selection, only by taking into account three things:

1. The *selection ratio*, that is, the proportion of all applicants who can be accepted.
2. The *chance success rate* on the criterion, that is, the percentage of persons who would succeed if selection were random.
3. The *validity* of the test used for selection.

Given these, and assuming that selection is from the top score on down, we can then determine the odds in favor of success of the selected persons. (Details of this calculation are explained in most textbooks on testing and personnel selection.) Say the chance of success rate is 60 percent; that is, 60 percent of the applicants would succeed (in college or on the job) if all were admitted or if they were selected at random. The average odds of anyone's succeeding, then, are .60 to .40, or 1.5 to 1. But then say we can select only 30 percent of the applicants, and we use a test with a validity of only .40 to select the 30 percent of applicants with the highest scores. Then the average odds in favor of any selectee succeeding will be .78 to .22, or 3.5 to 1. In other words, the test gives 3.5/1.5 or 2.33 times greater odds in favor of success of the selectees than if we had not used the test. Test validity gains in predictive potency as the selection ratio becomes more stringent and as the chance success rate declines. In many actual selection situations the use of a test can increase the odds for success of the selectees some three to eight times over what they would be by random selection.

Given the chance success rate and the test validity, we can also determine the probability of success for persons with test scores within any given range. For example, a college with an 80 percent chance success rate uses a selection test with a validity of .60 (for predicting grade-point averages among unselected students). Under these conditions, among students selected from the top 10 percent of all the test scores, the odds in favor of not flunking out are 99 to 1, as compared with odds of .67 to 1 for students with the lowest 10 percent of scores. In other words, the chances of the low-scoring students' flunking out, if they are admitted, are 99/.67 = 148 times greater than the top-scoring 10 percent.

Improvement in Criterion Performance

A test's validity coefficient can also be interpreted as the proportion of improvement in the overall criterion performance of a group (T) selected on the basis of test scores as compared with a randomly selected group (R) and a perfectly selected group (P). A "perfectly selected'' group is one selected *after* the fact, consisting of the top N performers on the criterion, where N is the number of persons we can accept out of all the applicants. If we obtained measures of the average performance of each of these groups (with their average performance levels designated T, R, P, respectively), then the test's validity can be expressed as $(T-R)/(P-R)$, which is the proportional improvement in performance that results from selecting by means of test scores. Obviously, if the group selected on the basis of the test performed no better on the criterion than those selected at random, the test would have zero validity in that situation.

As a simple example, say you are hiring salespeople and want to find out how valid a particular test is for the selection of future employees. There are two ways you could determine the test's validity coefficient, and each would give equivalent results. The simplest way is to give the test to everyone and calculate the coefficient of correlation between persons' test scores and their average monthly sales over one year. That correlation would be the test's validity. Say it is .33, not a very high validity but typical of many tests used in personnel selection. But you could also arrive at the same figure in the following way, which gives more insight into the practical meaning of validity. Say that in response to your advertisement 200 people apply for jobs. You want to hire them all, and you know that in each successive year you will want to hire 50 more. Here's what you should do. Give the test to all 200 applicants. Then, draw 50 applicants at random; call them group R. From the remaining 150, select the 50 with the highest test scores; call them group T. After employing all 200 applicants, determine the average monthly sales of group R and of group T, which are, say, 40 and 30 sales per month, respectively. Finally, determine the average monthly sales of the 50 salespeople who actually had the highest sales records (group P). They are the applicants you would have selected if you had wanted to hire only 50 and if you had hypothetically used a test with *perfect* validity for your purpose. Say their average sales are 60 per month. The validity of your test, then, is $(40-30)/(60-30) = .33$, which is the same as saying that selection of employees by means of this test increased the average level of performance 33 percent over what it would have been if you had selected at random. That is like 33 percent annual interest on your investment. Who would sneer at that?

A one-third increase in productivity or quality of performance would hardly be regarded as a trivial gain by most employers or college faculties. But that is the gain resulting from a test with a "mediocre" validity of only .33. Yet the Ralph Nader organization, in blasting college entrance exams, likened them to a "roulette game" on the ground that their typical predictive validity coefficients are in the range of .40 to .55. With that much predictive power at his disposal, a gambler playing the roulette wheel could easily break the bank at Monte Carlo within half an hour!

Before going on to review the actual validity of IQ and other tests, however, I must explain two other basic psychometric concepts that are based on correlation and that cannot be avoided in the discussion of mental tests: reliability and stability.

Reliability of Test Scores

People often confuse reliability and validity. Reliability means something altogether different from validity. However, test reliability is a necessary but not sufficient condition for test validity. High reliability in no way ensures high validity, whereas low reliability guarantees low validity.

"Reliability" refers to a test's consistency with itself. It can be thought of as the test's correlation with itself. A highly reliable test is one in which all parts of the test (items, subtests, and so on) measure the same trait or ability, whatever it may be. Scores based on a random selection of N number of items from a perfectly reliable test would rank-order persons exactly the same as would scores based on any other random selection of N items. That is because the test has perfect *internal consistency*. Of course, no real test ever has perfect reliability, but all good tests have quite high reliability or self-correlation.

A test's reliability is indexed by a correlation coefficient, in this case called the "reliability coefficient," which can be interpreted as the test's correlation with itself. There are a number of methods for determining a test's reliability, most of them too mathematically complicated to explicate here. The simplest, although not the most exact, method for estimating a test's reliability is the so-called split-half reliability. The whole test is given to a large number of people. Then the whole test is "split" in half—say, into the odd-numbered items and the even-numbered items. Each half of the test is scored, and the correlation is computed between the two sets of scores. This correlation between the two halves of the test is the average reliability of the two half-tests. From this, one can use a simple formula to determine the reliability of the whole test.

Most standardized tests of ability or achievement have reliabilities (self-correlations) close to .90. Individual IQ tests (e.g., the Stanford-Binet and Wechsler scales) have reliability between .90 and .95. For comparison, the correlation between the lengths of people's right and left arms is about .95. In other words, the reliability or internal consistency of most standardized tests is very high.

The reliability of a test is especially important for two reasons: it affects the test's validity and it affects the test's standard error of measurement. First, a test's validity cannot possibly be greater than the square root of its reliability. Second, no test score should be interpreted as an exact number or precise point on a scale. That would be warranted only if the test had perfect reliability. Because the reliability of any actual measurement is always less than perfect, we have to think of any measurement as having a "fringe" of error or uncertainty around it. The lower the test's reliability, the greater is the "fringe" of error. The width of this "fringe" is quantified as the test's "standard error of measurement." The term "error of measurement" does not mean mistakes in giving or scoring tests. It refers to the lack of perfect self-consistency in the test, which means that everyone would not get exactly the same scores on another test, called an "equivalent form" of the test. (The correlation between the two sets of scores would be the average reliability of the two equivalent forms of the test.) Thus a test score should really be thought of as the score *plus or minus* the standard error of measurement. The odds are 2 to 1 that the person's hypothetical "true score"—that is, the score if there were absolutely no error of measurement—falls within the interval of the standard error on each side of the score.

The standard error of measurement of the Stanford–Binet IQ, for example, is 5 IQ points. Thus a person who scores an IQ of 100 should be thought of as having an IQ of 100 ± 5 ("one hundred plus or minus five"). The person's "true" IQ would have 2 to 1 odds of falling within the range from 95 to 105. Thus we could not have much confidence that any two persons whose IQs differ by less than about 10 points *truly* differ in the intelligence measured by the IQ test. That small a difference could too easily be due to measurement error. Even much larger differences could be all error, but that probability becomes increasingly small the greater the difference between the two scores. For example, in the case of two persons whose IQs differ by 15 points, the odds are better than 50 to 1 that the person with the higher IQ would score above the one with the lower IQ on a hypothetical IQ test that had perfect reliability (and consequently zero error of measurement).

Stability of Test Scores

"Stability" refers to the consistency of test scores over a specified period of time. It is indexed by the correlation between the two sets of scores on a test given to the same group of persons on two occasions. It is often referred to as the "test-retest reliability."

"Stability" does *not* refer to the exact numerical constancy of a given score; it refers to the extent to which the scores of a group of persons maintain the same relative positions (or the same rank order) with respect to one another over some interval of time. For example, although growing children's heights steadily increase from year to year, the stability of their height measurements would be reflected by the extent to which the children's changing heights stay in the same rank order, from tallest to shortest, from one year to the next. The correlation between boys' heights at age 2 and at age 4 is .83; between age 2 and age 18 the correlation is .60. Thus height is a fairly stable, but far from perfectly stable, characteristic throughout the period from early childhood to maturity. Weight is much less stable, showing a correlation between ages 2 and 18 of only .32.

The following generalizations can be made about the stability of test scores: (1) stability differs for different traits and for different tests; (2) the stability coefficient (i.e., correlation between occasions) is lower than the test's reliability (self-correlation) on a single occasion; (3) the stability coefficient decreases as the time interval between test and retest increases; and (4) the stability of scores over any given time interval increases rapidly with age throughout the period from infancy to maturity.

For Stanford–Binet and Wechsler IQs, the stability coefficients for a one-year interval average close to .90, being slightly lower at younger ages (below 6 years) and slightly higher at older ages. The *average* change in IQ (either up *or* down) over a one-year interval is about 7 points. The IQ maintains considerable year-to-year stability for most persons and shows large changes for relatively few persons, with fewer than 1 percent showing changes as great as 20 or more points. IQ, interestingly, has just about the same degree of stability as body weight throughout the growth period from infancy to maturity. (Note: This does not imply that there is any correlation between weight and intelligence!)

Validity of IQ Tests

There would be almost no end to a tabulation of the validity coefficients of every type of standardized test in existence today. However, regardless of what they are labeled, most mental tests, except tests of perceptual-motor skills and rote memory, measure a general factor of ability common to all mental tests, as explained in Chapter 2. So-called intelligence tests, cognitive ability tests, scholastic aptitude tests, and general qualification tests all measure this general ability factor more than they measure anything else, and they all measure it to about an equally large extent. They are essentially all cut out of the same cloth and are functionally more or less equivalent. Therefore, to simplify the summation of their predictive validity or correlation with other variables, I shall refer to them all simply as "IQ tests."

The IQ (or more exactly, the general ability factor measured by all such tests) unquestionably shows significant correlations with more other variables of educational, occupational, and social importance than any other currrently measurable psychological trait.

Scholastic Performance

No other items of information that we can obtain about a child will predict his overall learning ability and academic achievement in school better than do scores on a recently administered IQ test. This is not because the IQ tests measure only what the child has learned in school, but because they meaure a general cognitive ability that plays a more important part in scholastic progress than any other trait.

At the more advanced levels of schooling, however, a student's past academic peformance, as indicated by grades or achievement test scores, can often serve to predict his future academic performance as well as—or even better than—the IQ. This is partly because past achievement is often a prerequisite, in terms of specific knowledge and skills, for success in the more advanced school subjects, and partly because past achievement also reflects other factors besides mental ability. Achievement reflects such things as motivation, study habits, and self-discipline, which are not measured by the IQ.

At any one point in time, a single IQ test will usually correlate anywhere between .50 and .80 with scholastic achievement, as assessed by standard achievement tests. If IQs and achievement scores are obtained at each grade level and averaged over three to five years, the correlation between them approaches .90, or nearly the reliability of the test.

The correlation between IQ and teachers' grades is generally .10 to .20 lower than the correlation of IQ with achievement test scores. The main reason is that grades are a less reliable measure of achievement; they vary from one teacher to another, and they are influenced by the teacher's impression of the pupil's effort, deportment, and other such factors that are not directly related to either cognitive ability or achievement. For example, teachers tend to give better grades to girls than to boys, even when the sexes do not differ in IQ or objectively measured achievement. Thus one can hardly expect other than fairly low correlations between IQ and teachers' marks.

In general, the validity of IQ for predicting academic achievement *decreases* at higher levels of schooling. The most typical validity coefficients are as follows:

Elementary school	.60–.70
High school	.50–.60
College	.40–.50
Graduate school	.30–.40

This decrease in the validity of IQ (or similar tests) for predicting achievement at higher levels of education does not imply that intelligence becomes any less important at these levels. Quite the contrary. The explanation for the decreasing validities is the narrowing "range of talent" (as it is called) as we ascend the educational ladder. The students at each higher level are a more highly select group, because the academically least successful (who also generally have lower IQs) either drop out or are screened out at each higher level. This restriction of the range of IQ and of achievement statistically limits the size of the correlation that can possibly be obtained between two variables. Imagine this situation: The basketball team of a neighborhood high school has no restrictions on height, so the players' heights range between 5'0″ and 6'8″. We would likely find a high correlation between height and the number of baskets made by each player in the course of a game, as any high school coach would attest. In contrast, on a crack professional team, where there is much less variability in height (because shorter players couldn't make it) and where players' heights range between 6' 4″ and 6' 8″, there will be only a very small correlation between height and the number of baskets made by each player. When all the players are highly selected for height, then other factors, such as speed and agility, become relatively more

TABLE 2

The Predictive Validity of IQ or Correlation of IQ
with Various Educational Criteria

CRITERION	CORRELATION
Achievement in various elementary school grades	.56–.71
IQ in grade 4 predicts achievement in grade 6	.75
Reading readiness tests	.84
Oral reading	.62
Reading comprehension	.68
Teachers' estimates of pupils' intelligence	.60–.80
Rank in high school graduating class	.62
Freshman grades in college	.44
Grade–point average in various colleges	.30–.70
Grade–point average in 48 colleges (median)	.40
Grades in law school (median)	.30
Highest level of education attained by age 40	.50–.58

important in determining the correlation. So it is, too, in the case of IQ and academic achievement at each more highly selective level of education. IQs above 115 are the bright and exceptional pupils in the top groups in elementary school. But IQs of 115 are near the bottom of the distribution of students in graduate school.

To give some idea of the range of validity of IQ (or similar scores) for predicting scholastic performance, a rather random collection of actual validity coefficients found in the literature is presented in Table 2.

IQ and Learning Ability

Teachers notice that, in general, pupils with higher IQs learn their lessons more quickly and easily, and with greater thoroughness and retention, than pupils with lower IQs. But the relationship between IQ and learning ability is not the same for all types of learning. For example, it is practically nil for the learning of certain simple motor skills in which improvement depends almost entirely on practice by sheer repetition. My survey of the entire research literature on the relationship between learning and IQ leads me to the following generalizations.

Learning is more highly correlated with IQ under these conditions:

1. When learning is *intentional* and the task calls forth conscious mental effort and is paced in such a way as to permit the subject to "think."
2. When the material to be learned is *hierarchical*, in the sense that the

learning of later elements depends on mastery of earlier elements. The dependence of learning rate on IQ can be lessened to some degree by making the hierarchical sequence of the learning very explicit for all individuals, so that the relationships between levels of the hierarchy do not have to be spontaneously discovered or inferred by the learners.

3. When the material to be learned is *meaningful*, in the sense that it is related to other knowledge or experience already possessed by the learner. IQ is much more highly related to comprehension than to memorization.

4. When the learning task permits *transfer* of knowledge or skills from somewhat different but related past learning.

5. When learning is *insightful*, that is, when it involves "catching on" or "getting the idea." Learning to name the capital cities of the fifty states, for example, does not allow this aspect of learning to come into play, as would, say, learning to prove the Pythagorean Theorem.

6. When the material to be learned is of *moderate difficulty and complexity*. If a learning task is too complex, everyone, regardless of IQ, flounders and falls back on simpler processes such as trial-and-error and rote association through sheer repetition.

7. When the *amount of time* for learning a given amount of material is fixed for all students.

8. When the learning material is *age-related*. Some things can be learned almost as easily by an 8-year-old as by an 18-year-old. Such learning shows relatively little correlation with IQ.

9. When the learners are at an *early stage* of learning something new rather than later in the course of practice, assuming that new material or concepts have not been introduced at the intermediate stages.

All these conditions influence the correlation between learning and IQ, and all are highly characteristic of much school learning. Hence the impression of teachers that IQ is an index of learning aptitude is quite justifiable. Under these conditions of learning, a child with a low IQ is a "slow learner" in comparison with children with high IQs.

Occupational Performance

People's prestige rankings of occupations or other indices of occupational status show a correlation with IQs of individuals in the various occupations of about .50 to .60 for young men (ages 18 to 26) and of about .70 for men over 40.

The correlation of IQ with grades or ratings in job training is invariably higher (averaging about .50) than with ratings of later job performance after completion of training (averaging about .20 to .25).

The predictive validity of IQ for job performance, however, depends on the type of job. Validities are low (.00 to .19) for relatively unskilled or routine jobs (sales, service occupations, machinery workers, packers and wrappers, repairmen) and are fairly high for more highly skilled jobs that require complex decisions and involve varied responsibilities (high-level technicians, engineers, managerial and professional workers).

Probably the most widely validated test used in employment selection is the General Aptitude Test Battery (or GATB) of the U.S. Employment Service. It measures nine different aptitudes, including general intelligence (called Aptitude G). The validity coefficients of Aptitude G for 446 different occupations range from − .20 to + .80, with a median of + .27. The extremely low or even negative validities are for such occupations as "tomato peeler," "onion corer," and "letter-opener machine operator." Lower-scoring persons on Aptitude G seem to work out more satisfactorily in these highly routine jobs. When scores on the other aptitude tests of the GATB are used in optimally weighted combinations for predicting performance in different occupations, the validity coefficients range from + .12 to over + .80, with a median of + .36, which is not impressively higher than for the G score alone. The predictive validities are above .40 for most jobs, which means they are of considerable practical value in personnel selection for hiring and promotion.

Aptitude test validities are higher by .10 to .20 correlation points when job performance is measured by actual on-the-job work samples than by supervisors' *ratings* of job performance. IQ is more highly correlated with job knowledge, as measured by paper-and-pencil tests, than with other measures of proficiency on the job. Workers with higher IQs spontaneously acquire more job-related knowledge per month on the job.

IQ and Creativity

So-called tests of "creativity" show as much or more correlation with IQ as with other so-called tests of "creativity." Significant creativity in the arts, science, business, and politics seems to involve superior intelligence *plus* certain personality traits. Superior intelligence is a necessary but not sufficient condition for creative achievement in a socially recognized sense. I have not heard of an authenticated case of an outstandingly creative person with a below-average IQ. When a group of 185 recognized creative contributors to socially significant fields were tested on the Wechsler Adult Intelligence Scale, their IQs ranged from 107 to 151, which encompasses the 70th to 99.9th percentiles of the population norms, with the mean at the 98th percentile (IQ 131).

Miscellaneous Correlates of IQ

The fact that IQ is significantly correlated with a large number of psychological and physical variables indicates that conventional IQ tests measure something more profound than the popular notion of IQ as reflecting merely knowledge or skills acquired in school or in a cultured home.

A number of other behavioral variables have been found to be significantly related to IQ: emotional adjustment and adaptive behavior; school deportment; delinquency and criminal behavior (which have *negative* correlations with IQ); activity level in early childhood (hyperactivity is related to lower IQs); choice reaction time; honesty; achievement in extracurricular, nonacademic activities; appreciation of humor; musical aptitude; and amount of information retained from viewing a television documentary.

Some sociologists and criminologists are now noting that below-average IQ is a major factor in delinquency, even when social class and family background variables are controlled. Delinquents from every background average about 10 points lower in IQ than their nondelinquent siblings. IQ is a better predictor of criminal behavior than socioeconomic status.

There are also a number of physical correlates of IQ: brain size (correlation about .30), brain waves (correlation of .30 to .50 with latency and amplitude of the average evoked potential), stature (correlations of .1 to .3), basic metabolic rate in childhood, obesity (negative correlation), and myopia, or nearsightedness (correlation about .25 in favor of myopes).

Types of Tests

The variety of tests and test items is far greater than most laymen ever imagine. There are many ways to divide the whole domain of psychological measuring instruments. It may be helpful to those who are new to this field to distinguish some of the main categories of tests.

Tests versus Inventories

Tests are intended to measure a person's maximum performance in attaining a standard or graded series of standards under specified conditions; the performance can be objectively scored as having attained or not attained the standard. When each item of the test measures a standard of performance, the raw score is the number of items passed.

Inventories, in contrast to tests, are questionnaires that aim to determine a person's *typical* response or behavior in some area—personality, attitudes, preferences, interests. There is no standard of performance to be passed or failed, no right or wrong answers.

Tests, on the other hand, are aimed at measuring a *capability* of some kind. "Ability" refers to a conscious, voluntary effort to attain a clearly defined standard or criterion. The criterion performance can be objectively judged as "good or poor," "pass or fail," "better or worse"; it is objective because there is agreement about what constitutes better or poorer performance.

General Ability, Aptitude, Achievement

Tests in these three categories are all essentially measures of ability. What, then, distinguishes them?

General-ability tests attempt to assess a person's overall average level of performance in a broad range of mental capabilities, so as to estimate his standing (relative to some normative population) on the general factor of mental ability that is common to a wide range of tests. (Chapter 2 is devoted to the identification and nature of this general factor.) Such tests are referred to as mental tests, because individual differences in performance are clearly not the result of differences in sensory or motor capacities. Many tests of general mental ability are called "intelligence tests" or "IQ tests." As explained in Chapter 2, they can take a great many different forms. Because such tests measure a general factor that is involved to some extent in every kind of mental performance aimed at meeting some standard, they have broader predictive validity than any other type of psychological measurement.

Aptitude tests are usually narrower or more specialized tests designed to predict performance of a particular kind, such as the likelihood of success in a specialized course of training for a particular type of job, or the level of proficiency on the job. These tests are composed of a number of parts, each of which taps some skill, knowledge, or ability found in the criterion performance it is intended to predict. Or the test component is necessary for the efficient acquisition of the criterion performance through training and experience. For example, an aptitude test battery for the selection of trainees for assembling and repairing complex electronic equipment might include measurements of visual acuity, hand-eye coordination, and finger dexterity. Many aptitude tests measure the general ability factor *plus* certain more specialized abilities that are important for success in a particular educational program or occupation. In addition to general reasoning ability, mathematical ability is important in engineering and the physical sciences; verbal ability is important in journalism and law, careers that involve a great deal of reading and writing. Nearly all scholastic aptitude tests tap a combination of general, verbal, and numerical abilities, because these are the most predictive of scholastic performance. At higher levels of education, as in college entrance or graduate selection exams, aptitude tests may, in part, resemble a scholastic achievement test, because certain prerequisite scholastic knowledge may constitute part of the aptitude predictive of success at more advanced levels of education. Reading comprehension is viewed as achievement for elementary school pupils but as aptitude for high school seniors doing college-level work. Also, among high school students who have all had much the same schooling, a standard test of reading comprehension can serve as a good measure of general ability, barring the few students with a specific reading disability, such as dyslexia. Thus there is not a clear-cut or intrinsic distinction between ability, aptitude, and achievement tests. They are distinguished in large part by the purposes they are intended to serve. The same test may serve as an ability test in one situation, as an achievement test in another situation, and as an aptitude test in still another situation.

Achievement tests are intended to assess specific attainments following a course of study aimed at imparting the specific knowledge or skills. A test that assesses achievements attained over many years in broad and varied areas of experience extending beyond the limits of formal schooling becomes, in effect, a test of general ability.

Speed versus Power

Speed tests aim to measure how quickly and efficiently a person can perform something. The items are easy enough that almost anyone could get them all right if given sufficient time. But a time limit is imposed so that few if any persons can finish the test in the allotted time. Such a test identifies those who work fastest. Tests of clerical skills (sorting, filing, alphabetizing, checking, simple arithmetic calculation, typing) are generally of this type.

Power tests consist of items so graded in difficulty or complexity, going from fairly easy to very difficult, that most persons taking the test reach their ceiling of ability well before they run out of time. From there on they can only guess at the answers to the harder items. In taking a power test there is either no time limit or a very liberal time limit. The aim of a power test is to determine the highest level of knowledge, skill, reasoning, or problem-solving ability the person can demonstrate without time pressure. The best tests of general ability are of this type, although imposing a liberal time limit is found to be more practical and yet yields about the same results as having no time limit. Some tests of general ability and achievement require that subjects be allowed enough time to attempt every item.

Group versus Individual Administration

Group tests are often referred to as paper-and-pencil tests, because they consist of printed booklets, with or without separate answer sheets, in which the person writes answers or checks multiple-choice alternatives. They can be administered to a group and can usually be scored by machine. They are therefore a very efficient method for gaining information. When subjects are normally motivated to try their best, as is typical in most assessment or selection situations in which group tests are commonly used, these tests yield quite reliable and usefully valid measurements. Their two main disadvantages, compared with individually administered tests, are that (1) they usually do not tap so wide a variety of abilities and, more important, (2) they do not allow close, detailed observation of each person being tested. Cooperation, effort, anxiety, distractability, and persistence, which are clinically revealing aspects of a person's test-taking performance, are not indicated by a test score.

Individually administered tests allow observations of all these aspects of performance, which are helpful to a well-trained psychometrist or clinical psychologist in evaluating test scores. The tester tries to put the subject at ease, usually with preliminary conversation and often with testlike practice tasks. After establishing good rapport, the tester administers the test, item by item, at a pace congenial to the subject, always trying to elicit the best performance he is capable of. If the clinician, for any reason, feels the test results were obtained under less than ideal conditions, perhaps because of the subject's emotional state or lack of confidence in the test situation, he will recommend a reexamination on the same test or an equivalent form of it.

Individual testing by a qualified professional is indicated when test results are to be used in making any placement decision that vitally affects a person's welfare. It is also called for when a person's score on a group test is markedly deviant, especially on the low side, although a retest on an equivalent form of the group test is usually the first resort.

An individual test is not just a paper-and-pencil test taken individually in the presence of a tester. It is expressly designed for individual administration. The subject is not required to read or write, but to answer a variety of questions and perform a variety of puzzlelike tasks. There is continuous interaction between tester and subject throughout the test, which usually lasts an hour or less. If a subject appears in the least fatigued or bored or becomes distracted, a good examiner will politely stop the testing and finish it on another occasion. The clinician tries at all costs to prevent the testing procedure from being an "ordeal" for the client.

The most widely used and best standardized individual tests of general ability are the Wechsler Intelligence Scales. There are three forms, for preschoolers, for school-age children, and for adults. The Wechsler scales are gradually replacing the Stanford–Binet Intelligence Scale, which was the standard for many years and is still a clinically useful test, especially with preschool children and the mentally retarded. For some diagnostic problems, clinicians prefer to use both the Wechsler and the Stanford–Binet tests.

Clinicians also use a variety of other individually administered tests for more specialized diagnostic purposes (sensory-motor and perceptual problems, brain damage, reading disability, and so on). Some vocational aptitude tests require individual administration, such as the motor coordination, finger dexterity, and manual dexterity tests of the General Aptitude Test Battery developed by the U.S. Employment Service.

Verbal, Nonverbal, Performance

Verbal tests make explicit use of language, but they may or may not require reading or writing. Typical verbal tests are general information, comprehension, verbal analogies, same-opposite, and vocabulary.

Nonverbal tests are paper-and-pencil tests that involve no explicit use of language, in some cases not even for giving instructions for taking the test, which instead can be given by example and pantomime. These tests consist of such things as figural analogies, progressive figure series, matrices, odd man out, number series completion, embedded figures, and pattern completion.

Performance tests require the subject to draw, manipulate, or construct something: form boards, bead patterns, jigsaw puzzle–type problems, figure copying, block designs, picture completion, and picture arrangement (i.e., putting a set of related pictures in some logical sequence).

How Tests Are Constructed

Test construction has become a highly technical matter, and the procedures vary for different types of tests. So I shall attempt only to outline the most basic procedures of test construction that are common to most types of tests.

1. *Purpose and specification of the test population* begin the whole process. These can usually be described in terms of (1) the specific subject area in which achievement is to be assessed; (2) the characteristics of the criterion (e.g., college grades, job performance) that the test scores are intended to predict; or (3) some theoretical conception of the psychological nature of the trait that the test aims to measure.

2. *Item writing* for achievement tests (or item invention, for nonverbal and performance tests) is done by experts in the various subject areas to be tested. Item composition is based not only on careful analysis of the abilities assumed to be involved in the criterion but on intuition, insight, experience with other tests that successfully predict similar criteria, and sheer creative imagination on the part of the item writers. Items are composed to cover a wide range of difficulty, from quite easy to very hard items, for the intended population. Many more items are created than will be used in the final test.

3. *Item editing*, the next step, is usually done by several persons, to increase the likelihood of spotting formal defects in the items. Each item is checked for clarity of wording, appropriateness of vocabulary level for the intended population, stylistic equivalence of multiple-choice distractors and the correct answer, economy of wordage, page space required in a test booklet, and what is called the "face validity" of the item. This is the property of an item that gives it the *appearance* of measuring what the test as a whole is supposed to measure. It may or may not be related to the actual validity of the item or the test, but it can affect the "reasonableness," "fairness," and acceptability of the test in the eyes of those who are taking it. The question "Who wrote *Das Kapital?*" might well show good validity for predicting the success of trainees in the police academy, but it would be judged to have poor "face validity" for police recruits taking a selection test, and the item might be discarded for that reason.

In item editing, questionable, weak, or defective items are either revamped or discarded. Unless the remaining pool of acceptable items still contains a much larger number than will be needed for the final test, more items are composed and subjected to editing until the required number is obtained.

4. *Item tryout* consists of administering the entire pool of items, presented in the format of an actual test, to large, representative samples from the population for which the test is intended. The sole purpose of this tryout is to obtain enough data for the next stage in the process of test construction: item analysis.

5. *Item analysis* is the most technical aspect of the whole process, involving a number of psychometric and statistical methods. But the purposes of these methods can be described without going into the technical details. The essential information provided by item analysis is sixfold:

1. The *difficulty level* (percentage passing) of each item.
2. The *discriminability* of each item, that is, how clearly it differentiates (in terms of percentages passing the item) the highest from the lowest scorers on the test as a whole, or how highly each item correlates with the total score on the test.
3. The *validity* of each item, determined by its correlation with the criterion measure (e.g., grade-point average), if such measures are available.
4. A *factor analysis* (see Chapter 2), which is performed for some types of tests to determine which items are correlated with one another, creating clusters of items that conform to theoretical expectations of the abilities the test aims to measure.
5. The *item characteristic curve*, which is a graphic plot for each item, showing the probability of passing the item as a function of overall ability level indicated by the total score on the test. If the plotted function deviates significantly from a normal cumulative probability curve, it is considered "suspect" and may be revised or discarded.

6. Analysis of *incorrect responses* to determine, for example, which multiple-choice alternatives are so rarely chosen as to be virtually nonfunctional.

These data permit selection of those items that will maximize the efficiency, the reliability, and the potential validity of the final test for the intended population. Practically all the characteristics of the distribution of scores on the final test can be mathematically derived from item analysis information.

6. *Standardization* of the final test is next. The distribution of raw scores (number correct) in a large representative sample of the target population is converted to some meaningful, interpretable scale such as percentile ranks, IQs, or other forms of standardized scores. Such converted scores clearly indicate any individual's relative standing in the standardization (or normative) population. Many tests are restandardized every few years, or even more often, to take account of shifts in the target population. Periodic item analyses may also lead to revamping or discarding items no longer suitable for the target population. Determination of the test's reliability and standard error of measurement in the normative population is also a part of the standardization procedure.

7. *Validation* is the final step. Test scores are correlated with the appropriate criterion performance (e.g., scholastic achievement, college grades, ratings of proficiency on the job). Often validity coefficients are determined for different subgroups or for different criteria.

All standardization and validation methods and results should be reported in the test manual for the benefit of the test users. *Standards for Educational and Psychological Tests,* published by the American Psychological Association, prescribes minimum information that test publishers should include in a test manual. Leading test publishers carefully observe these recommendations.

All currently published tests are periodically (about every five years) subjected to highly critical reviews, often by two or more experts, which are published in the volumes of the *Mental Measurements Yearbook,* the single most valuable reference for purchasers or users of psychological tests of any kind. Reviews in the *Yearbook* seldom pull any punches.

Proper execution of all procedures involved in test construction and validation is a large scale, extremely costly undertaking. It is thus hardly feasible for any but large, well-financed test bureaus and government agencies. Making and marketing a new test that would be competitive with the present, most widely used tests is beyond the resources of any individual psychometrician or small organization. Test production is therefore dominated by only a handful of large multimillion-dollar firms. The leading firms, such as the Educational Testing Service and the Psychological Corporation, can afford to employ on their research staffs some of the world's leading test experts—persons who, if they were not employed in these organizations, would most likely hold full professorships in our top universities.

College Entrance Examinations

College selection tests have recently come under such strong public attack, mostly by political, civil rights, and consumer protection groups (particularly Ralph Nader's organization) that they warrant more detailed examination.

Most of the fulmination is directed at a single test, which clearly dominates the field—the College Entrance Examination Board's Scholastic Aptitude Test, better known as the "College Boards" or the SAT. The SAT is produced, distributed, and scored, and the results disseminated, by ETS—the Educational Testing Service, of Princeton, New Jersey. ETS is the largest testing organization in the world.

The SAT is given several times each year, throughout the nation's high schools, to juniors or seniors. The tests are scored by ETS in Princeton, and results are sent to the students and to any college they designate. Most American colleges require SAT scores as part of a student's application for admission. Every year the SAT is taken by nearly one and a half million high school students. Handling all this is obviously a massive operation (as well as big business), which ETS manages with remarkable efficiency and professionalism.

The SAT is a timed, paper-and-pencil, group-administered, objective test composed of 150 alternative multiple-choice items. It has two parts, Verbal and Mathematical, designated SAT-V and SAT-M. The SAT-V consists of reading comprehension, antonyms, verbal analogies, and sentence completion. The SAT-M taps numerical ability and quantitative reasoning but not formal mathematical knowledge as such. SAT-V is generally more predictive of overall college grades than SAT-M.

The SAT-V and SAT-M raw scores are converted to a standard score scale going from 200 to 800. The average score was set at 500 in the original standardization, but today relatively few high school seniors, nationwide, obtain SAT-V scores above 500—only about 20 percent of white students and 1 or 2 percent of black students. Many highly selective colleges regard scores below 600 as "academic risks"; the average score of students admitted to such colleges is usually closer to 700.

The SAT has a standard error of measurement of 32—that is, any individual SAT score should be thought of as the score plus or minus 32 points—and the standard error of the difference between any two scores is about 45 points, which means that smaller differences than that between individuals are statistically meaningless.

Although most colleges now use the SAT in selecting students, fewer than 1 percent claim that the SAT is the single most important factor in admissions. High school grades and rank in graduating class are usually given more weight. For whites, the high school grade-point average (GPA) is a better predictor of college grades than is the SAT, but the opposite is true for blacks, probably because high school grading standards are less uniform for blacks. The SAT gives academically talented blacks a better chance of showing their strength than does high school GPA.

A poor score on the SAT does not necessarily close the door to selective colleges. A student may take the SAT again and again, and colleges generally take into account only the student's highest score, in addition to their other selection criteria.

Validity of SAT

A great many validity studies have been published, showing validity coefficients of about .30 to .70, with an average of about .50, for predicting overall college GPA. When SAT-V and SAT-M are combined with high school GPA in a multiple-prediction equation, the validities are raised to around .60. The SAT has lower validity in highly selective colleges because of the restriction of range of scores. Also, the imperfect reliability of the GPA itself puts a ceiling on the degree to which an unreliable criterion can be predicted by the SAT. When achievement in students' major fields is assessed by objective achievement tests at the time of college graduation, it is found that the achievement scores are predicted with a validity of over .70 by the SAT scores on which the student's admission to college was based. There is no question that SAT scores are highly related to academic performance when the various statistical artifacts that tend to lower the obtained validity coefficient are taken properly into account.

As I explained earlier, the meaning of the typical validity coefficients found for the SAT has been misrepresented to the public by the test's critics, by defining the validity coefficient as the percentage of the total variance in college GPA predicted by SAT scores. (The percentage of predicted variance is the square of the validity coefficient × 100.) This is an overly stringent and generally inappropriate interpretation of the validity of the SAT in terms of its typical use, which is not to make point estimates of every student's GPA throughout the entire range of SAT scores but to predict the odds of success for a student with a given SAT score.

Advantages of the SAT

Many colleges and universities, especially selective colleges with the most prestigious academic reputation, cannot possibly admit all those who apply. There simply has to be some kind of selection. The aim of most college directors of admissions is to strike a good balance of three objectives:

1. To select those applicants who, in terms of past performance (high school grades in academic subjects, rank in class) and scholastic aptitude (scores on the SAT or similar tests), are statistically the most likely to meet the college's academic standards and earn a degree.
2. To select applicants whose records evince desirable qualities other than scholastic ability, for example, leadership (class president, editor of school paper), participation in extracurricular activities (various youth organizations, summer camp counselor, 4-H member), and special talents (athletic, dramatic, musical, artistic, literary).
3. To select applicants from a wide diversity of backgrounds—ethnic, cultural, social class, and geographic.

How much weight is given to each of these factors varies among colleges. Usually, the second and third criteria come into play after initial screening on the first criterion to obtain a pool of applicants with promising academic qualifications, who can then be screened further, giving consideration to nonacademic criteria.

The use of nationwide SATs, and the availability of scores to any college an applicant designates, has made it possible for colleges to screen many more applicants and for applicants to be considered by many more colleges than would otherwise be possible. As a consequence of this enlarged freedom of choice by both colleges and applicants, specific college populations have become more homogeneous in ability but more diverse in students' personal qualities and in their social, ethnic, and geographic backgrounds.

Without nationally standardized tests that are uniformly administered and scored, and without a central office to disseminate the results, the cost to colleges of screening the current numbers of applicants would be much greater than at present. And that cost would be passed on to the applicants.

Although high school grades are often as good a predictor of college performance as the SAT, or better, predictive accuracy can be significantly improved by using the SAT scores together with high school grades. The main reasons the SAT enhances prediction are (1) the various high school courses in which students earn their grades are not the same for all students and are not of equivalent difficulty, (2) high schools in different localities differ in grading standards (a C + grade average in one school may be equivalent to an A − average in another school in terms of actual academic achievement), and (3) for some students high school grades are an exceedingly poor indicator of actual ability for college-level work. A bright student who, for whatever reason, made poor grades in high school would have virtually no chance of getting into many selective colleges if it were not for his SAT score. The SAT helps many students prove their abilities. A high-scoring applicant with poor high school grades, however, is considered an underachiever up to that point in his educational career, and is statistically a greater selection risk than a student with a less impressive test score but with excellent grades. Such students are considered overachievers, but they are generally good risks. Their past performance predicts their future performance as well as or better than their SAT scores, because the SAT does not predict a student's motivation, persistence, study habits, stability, or other traits that contribute to success and are reflected to some extent by the applicant's past achievement. For this reason college admissions officers much prefer to base selection on a combination of high school grades and SAT scores, rather than on either one alone.

If neither of these criteria is used for selection, a college has what amounts to an ''open admissions'' policy which can be wasteful in time and money both to colleges and to underqualified applicants. If the degrees granted by an ''open admissions'' college are to have worth, there must be a rigorous, costly, and painful culling of the academically untalented within the first year after admission. Many of those who fall by the wayside could have spent that year to their greater advantage in other pursuits better matched to their abilities.

The "Truth-in-Testing" Law

In July 1979, a bill before the New York state legislature was passed into law ruling that the whole college testing business, the tests, and their psychometric and statistical bases, should be completely open to public scrutiny. A similar federal bill is now before the U.S. Congress. The bill would give all college applicants who have taken the SAT (or any other admissions test for college, graduate school, or professional school) the right to examine their answer sheets accompanied by the questions and the keyed correct answers. The bill also requires the test publishers (ETS is the main target) to make public their methods of test construction, standardization, and scoring. The groups promoting these bills are opposed to current college selection procedures and would clearly like to reduce the influence of the SAT on college admissions as much as possible. Support for the bill has considerable ideological and political steam behind it, generated particularly by certain ethnic organizations, such as the NAACP, as well as by national associations with powerful lobbies in Washington, such as the National Education Association and the Parent-Teacher Association.

The practical consequences of such a law, of course, would be many. Because no set of test questions could be used more than once, new tests would have to be produced every time the SAT or other test was to be administered nationwide. Costs would be exorbitant, and applicants might be asked to share them. In all probability, tests could not be administered so frequently as now; more high school students would have to take them on exactly the same few dates each year, to prevent questions and answers from becoming widely available before each test had received maximum use. Tests would also probably include fewer items measuring specific scholastic knowledge or achievement (because that item pool is limited by school subject matter) and would have to put more emphasis on item types intended to measure general intelligence, for which there is a theoretically unlimited pool of possible items. In other words, the tests would be forced to measure general intelligence more and actual scholastic achievement less than at present. This could lower the validity of such tests for their purpose.

The SAT Coaching Controversy

Although ETS has claimed that, according to its own studies, the SAT scores cannot be appreciably raised by crash coaching, many critics of the SAT claim the contrary. There has been a boom in test coaching courses in recent years, with fees running from a few dollars up to as much as $275 per enrollee.

The issue is relevant to the question of unfair discrimination, if the coaching courses can actually make an important difference and if the cost of such courses results in the disproportionate exclusion of applicants from less affluent homes. In quality and quantity, the evidence on this issue that I have been able to find tends to support the claims of ETS. Much of the opposition's "evidence" consists of hearsay and testimonials of greatly improved scores on a retest, after coaching. Because of imperfect test reliability, there are nearly always changes in scores on repeated testing, occasionally quite radical ones. But they are largely unpredictable and inconsistent, and they occur with or without coaching. Testimonial "evidence" capitalizes on the few largest score changes that occur in a favorable direction. The overall systematic effects of coaching are always much less impressive than the testimonial "evidence" would suggest.

An independent study by the Federal Trade Commission of two commercial SAT coaching courses found that these crash courses can produce small but statistically significant gains in scores, especially for students whose SAT scores are lower than would be expected from their high school grades. These are probably the students whose basic academic qualifications are sound but who, for a variety of reasons—test jitters, lack of experience with objective tests, inefficient use of the available time for taking the test—fail to post high scores. Coaching may help to minimize these factors for such students. In any case, the average gain from coaching was not impressive—about 25 points (on a score scale from 200 to 800) in one school and zero gain in another. One course that involved several hours of individual tutoring produced an average gain of 28 points. One especially intensive coaching program conducted at the U.S. Military Academy is claimed to have produced gains of 57 points on the SAT-V and 79 points on the SAT-M, which are large enough to be of practical significance to individuals seeking college admission. Students who took crash courses are about evenly divided in their opinions as to whether they benefited. In 1979, 21 percent of Berkeley freshmen claimed to have taken special courses to prepare for taking the SAT.

It is probably wise, in any case, for students planning to take the SAT to make use of the practice booklets of sample items put out by ETS or to work through the hundreds of practice items provided in inexpensive, commercially published practice booklets for the SAT, available in most college bookstores. The SAT-M is considerably more susceptible to a practice effect than the SAT-V. Students who have not taken a high school mathematics course within the past year should brush up on their math, especially algebra; this could boost their SAT-M scores significantly.

If future research should demonstrate conclusively that some form of coaching can raise SAT scores by enough points to make a real difference (which would not be too surprising, as the SAT is partly a scholastic achievement test), and if such coaching were unavailable to many applicants, claims of unfairness would seem justified. As yet, however, there is no compelling evidence that supports this claim. If there were, the best remedy, of course, would be for all high schools to offer an elective test-coaching course for all who wish to take it. Studies have found that when coaching is given equally to everyone, a test's reliability and predictive validity are enhanced. But the evidence indicates that the advantages gained from coaching tend to fade quite rapidly, so that the sooner one can take the test after coaching, the better.

Those who feel uneasy about taking tests may gain greater confidence and composure in the test situation from coaching or practice. However, a number of studies on tests similar to the SAT show that taking an equivalent form of the test under actual test conditions is more helpful than coaching *per se*. This suggests that most students, without any coaching at all, would improve their SAT scores the second time they take the test. Much of the score gain claimed by test-coaching schools is probably attributable to the practice effect of having previously taken the SAT ''for real.''

Decline in SAT Scores

Much concern has been expressed over the gradual drop in the SAT scores of college applicants over the past fifteen or twenty years. The total decline amounts to about one-half of a standard deviation. On the SAT that is about 50 points (on a scale from 200 to 800). This much decline amounts to about six or seven fewer correct answers on the verbal and on the math parts of the SAT.

Evaluating the causes of this decline becomes a highly technical matter. A panel of test experts who have studied it find that it cannot be explained in terms of a change in the actual difficulty level of the SAT. There is a real decline in the average ability level of the students taking the SAT.

Most of the decline, probably all but about one-eighth of it, is a result of the great increase in the percentage of high school graduates who seek college admission. A much more inclusive population, including more minorities, is taking the SAT, dipping lower into the distribution of scholastic aptitude.

The drop in the frequency of exceptionally high scores, around 800, however, is more of a puzzle. It has been attributed to laxness of academic standards in school, absenteeism, grade inflation, automatic promotion, too little homework, too few written assignments, a decline in intellectual discipline, lowered motivation for academic excellence, too much time spent watching television, and too little serious reading by the majority of high school students. The SAT, after all, is designed to measure not students' innate potentials, but their *developed* scholastic knowledge and skills, which are acquired throughout their entire school careers. Just how much these hypothesized causes actually contribute to the decline of SAT scores is not clearly established, but it could only be a minor share in any case. The slight decline in frequency of top-scoring students could also be due to a declining birth rate among those ethnic groups and social strata in the population that have always contributed a disproportionate number of the highest scorers. The movement to limit family size in the past thirty years or so has made its greatest impact on the best-educated youths, who as potential parents might have had a higher percentage of academically able children than any other group in the population. If the offspring of this generation have been fewer than those of past generations, one predictable result would be a decline in the frequency of very high scores on the SAT.

Graduate and Professional School Examinations

The Educational Testing Service also produces and administers nationally standardized examinations for the selection of graduate students pursuing advanced degrees in academic fields and students in professional schools of business, law, dentistry, and medicine. These tests, like the SAT, have also come under attack because of the considerable disparity in average scores between majority and minority students (except Asians), and the resulting low success rates of minority applicants in competing for admission to graduate and professional schools where college grades and test scores are the chief selection criteria. Minority student scores on the Graduate Record Exam

(GRE), Medical College Aptitude Test (MCAT), and Law School Admission Test (LSAT) average between about 100 and 150 points below the average scores of majority students.

These advanced-level tests are generally found extremely helpful in screening applicants for graduate programs. Overall grade-point averages of college graduates fall within a quite limited range, extending from an A to a C average; further, each is an average of grades earned in a different mix of courses taken by each student. Grade-point average is thus not a highly discriminating index of academic potential for graduate work. College grades are also much more variable in meaning than high school grades; academic standards of different colleges vary enormously. Scores on the GRE, MCAT, and LSAT can serve as a "sheet anchor" for the evaluation of college grades and other selection criteria.

Numerous studies have found that personal interviews are a notoriously unreliable basis for prediction of success in graduate school and, besides, they are practically prohibitive for applicants in distant places. Nor are letters of recommendation dependable as criteria for selection, except in those very few instances in which the letter contains a strongly negative statement, prompting an especially careful scrutiny of the applicant's qualifications.

Examination scores provide the one fully objective and uniformly interpretable item of evidence to the graduate selection committee. Furthermore, many applicants whose test scores are nowhere near the ballpark of acceptability can be quickly rejected without further deliberation. Although high scores on these tests are surely no guarantee of distinguished or even successful performance in graduate or professional school, it is rare that low scores are not highly predictive of unusual difficulty in intellectually demanding curricula, even for the most highly motivated students.

Tests and Social Justice

Those who would have us do away with college and graduate school admission tests never present a compelling argument for alternative methods of selection. And selection there must be. The only question is whether there are any criteria besides test scores that are as objective, comparable, assessable in terms of effectiveness, and as fair to applicants graduating from high schools with different grading standards. No one has yet convincingly proposed a more fair basis for college selection than a combination of high school grades and SAT scores, the current practice of the vast majority of selective colleges in the United States.

Unlike teachers' marks, letters of recommendation, and interviews, test scores have been found to be essentially colorblind (see Chapter 4) as predictors of academic performance in college. They "read through" the veneer of social class background, as well. College entrance tests have made it possible for able but financially poor students to gain entrance and obtain scholarships to the nation's most selective colleges. Sociologists at Harvard have shown that test scores are considerably more advantageous to the upward mobility of low-status boys than are school grades. (Christopher Jencks et al., *Inequality: A Reassessment of the Effect of Family and Schooling in America,* 1972.) In England it was found that more working-class pupils, relative to middle-class pupils, were selected for college preparatory schools when selection was based on tests than when selection was based on teachers' grades and recommendations. The use of IQ tests instead of school grades actually *doubled* the percentage of scholarship winners coming from working-class homes. When the use of selection tests was abandoned in one county, the percentage of children of professional and managerial parents who obtained scholarships rose from 39.6 percent to 63.6 percent, while the percentage of children of manual workers fell from 14.9 percent to 11.5 percent. Interestingly, the use of selection tests was most strongly opposed by upper-class parents whose children traditionally enjoyed the advantages of a secondary education regardless of their ability.

2

The Structure of
Mental Abilities

W<small>E HAVE ALREADY SEEN</small> that there are a great many different kinds
of mental tests and an almost unlimited variety of items that make up
tests. One might therefore suspect that a great many different kinds of
abilities are measured by so many different kinds of tests.

In fact, however, that is far from true. A tremendous number and
variety of tests measure only a very small number of mental abilities.
This is because the same ability can be measured by many superficially
different tests or test items, which, in effect, are functionally
equivalent. Increasing the variety of tests does not necessarily increase
the number of abilities measured by the tests. Each test taps one or a
combination of primary mental abilities, of which there are only a
relatively small number. In addition, each test measures something
peculiar to itself, called a specific factor. Unless it is found that specific
factors are correlated with something else and are not just specific to a
particular test, they are of little interest or importance.

g, The General Factor

One of the most remarkable findings in all of psychology is that
scores on all mental ability tests of every variety are positively intercorrelated in any representative sample of the general population.

Positive intercorrelation among tests means that subjects who perform very well on any given test will, on the average, also perform well on other tests. So far it has proved practically impossible to invent a mental test of any kind that contradicts this general rule. The correlations between tests themselves, however, are seldom perfect. If we rank people's scores on one test from highest to lowest, and then do the same thing with the same people's scores on another test, the rank order of the scores will be similar though not exactly the same for both tests. But they will be much more alike than if the two sets of scores had been drawn from a random lottery, in which case the correlation would be close to zero. Also, some tests consistently show much higher intercorrelations than others.

The English psychologist Charles Spearman (1863–1945), who first discovered these facts, tried to figure out what they mean. First, it seemed reasonable to assume that any two tests that are correlated with one another measure something similar. Going a step further, the fact that all mental tests are correlated with one another to varying degrees could mean that they all measure one general factor.

Spearman gave the label g to this general factor and argued that all tests of mental ability measure it to some degree. However, since all tests are not *equally* correlated with one another, not all tests measure g to the same extent; some tests must be more "g-loaded" than others. Highly g-loaded tests show a greater number of relatively high correlations with many other tests, while the least g-loaded tests show only small correlations with other tests.

Spearman, who was trained as an engineer, thought about psychological problems more mathematically than do most psychologists. To deal with the observations just described, he developed a mathematical method known as factor analysis, which proved to be his major contribution to the behavioral sciences.

Factor analysis is mathematically much too involved to explain here. The important point is that it enabled Spearman to "extract" the g from all the intercorrelations among a collection of diverse tests, and to show precisely the correlation between each test and this hypothetical general ability factor. The correlation of a given test with the g factor common to all tests in the analysis is termed the test's g loading. The square of a test's g loading tells us the proportion of the total variance (i.e., individual differences) in the scores on a particular test that is due to individual differences in this general ability. Some tests have very large g loadings of .70 to .90 or above; many have moderate g loadings of .40 to .70; and some have quite small g loadings of less than

.40. But hardly any test can be found that does not have a *g* loading substantially greater than zero, provided the factor analysis is performed on data obtained from a representative sample of the general population.

The *g* factor may not show up on some tests given to highly selected groups, such as university students, although these same tests have modest *g* loadings when given to the general population. The reason is that these groups have already been highly selected on *g*-loaded tests, such as college entrance exams, and so the scores show less individual variation on the *g* factor. This limits the intercorrelations among the various tests and thereby prevents the *g* factor from showing up strongly in a factor analysis of the matrix of intercorrelations.

Group Factors

At first, Spearman proposed what he later acknowledged to be an oversimplified picture of mental ability. He originally hypothesized that each test measures only *g* plus some specific ability, *s*, which is tapped only by the particular test. This theory that any given test score is composed only of *g* + *s*, as well as measurement error, was soon refuted by the finding that there are other common factors besides *g*. However, they are not *general* factors, because they do not enter into all tests, as does *g*, but enter only into certain groups of tests. They are therefore called group factors. All verbal tests, for example, have *g* in common, and this accounts for their correlation with all nonverbal tests, which also measure the same *g*. But the verbal tests also share a common factor of verbal ability that they do not share with nonverbal tests. Hence we speak of verbal ability as a group factor. Other prominent group factors besides verbal ability are numerical ability, spatial visualization ability, and memory. The method of factor analysis can be extended to determine to what degree any given test measures each of these group factors, just as we can determine how well the test measures the *g* factor. Some tests are simple, in that they measure only one or two factors besides their specific factor; and some tests are very complex, measuring several factors. Factor analysis can tell us how many factors a given test measures, and to what extent it measures each factor, in terms of the test's loading on each factor.

Although psychologists can devise tests that measure only one group factor, they cannot devise a test that excludes *g*. So-called factor-pure tests, designed to measure only a single group factor, such as verbal or numerical or spatial ability, always measure *g* as well. Usually these tests are more heavily loaded on *g* than on the particular group factor they are intended to measure. Tests of primary mental abilities, for example, are measures of *g* plus verbal, or *g* plus numerical. The ubiquitous factor common to all tests is *g*, which has been aptly referred to as the primary mental ability. It accounts for about half of the total variance in any large battery of diverse mental tests, and with rare exceptions accounts for more of the variance in a particular test than any other factor. IQ tests and scholastic aptitude tests are especially highly *g*-loaded. And the same *g* permeates scholastic achievement and many types of job performance, especially so-called higher-level jobs. Therefore, *g* is most worthy of our scientific curiosity.

Just What Is *g*?

This is the question that dominated Spearman's research for many years. He never found a definitive answer, but he did show how we can identify *g* "by site if not by nature." That is, we can identify the kinds of tests that measure *g* the most, even if we don't know just what *g* is. We can subject a number of diverse tests to a factor analysis and determine their *g* loadings. Then, by comparing tests that show large *g* loadings with tests that show small *g* loadings, we can get some idea about the properties of tests that are most related to the manifestation of *g*. Spearman did just that, with over one hundred tests of various types. The tests were all homogeneous in item content. He avoided using tests made up of different kinds of items, because he could not then easily characterize the features of the test that might be responsible for its high or low *g* loading.

Even then, Spearman's task was not an easy one, because there seemed to be very little, if any, connection between the superficial characteristics of different kinds of test items and their *g* loadings. Such obvious classifications of items as verbal, nonverbal, performance, numerical, figural, general factual information, or scholastic knowledge and skills, were not related systematically to *g* loadings.

It was soon obvious that *g* could not be described in terms of the readily observed superficial characteristics of various types of test items. For example, a vocabulary test and a block design test, involving the reproduction of a mosaic-like design with colored blocks, both had the same *g* loading, even though the tests seem quite different in their content and the skills called for. Yet a spelling test, which superficially seems more similar to a vocabulary test, had a much lower *g* loading than either the vocabulary test or the block design test. And a test of speed in color-matching pairs of colored blocks had a lower *g* loading than either the block design test or the vocabulary test, and was more like the spelling test in *g* loading. It all looked quite puzzling.

The situation that Spearman faced is somewhat analogous to the situation we can imagine if a group of scientific-minded Martians invaded a large, well-stocked liquor store and tried to discover the nature of the multitudinous variety of liquids they found in all the different bottles. They might find that if they drank a certain amount from some of the bottles they could not walk a straight line. They might then use this very criterion—walking a straight line—and measure precisely how much of each liquid they could imbibe before failing the sobriety test. Each kind of liquor in the store would receive a ''score'' indicating the amount that one had to drink to fail the sobriety test. These ''scores'' could all be intercorrelated and factor-analyzed. Each liquor would show some ''*g*'' loading, large or small, depending on how much of the liquor had to be drunk to fail the test. The Martians, who would not be able to read any of the labels on the bottles, would then set about classifying the various liquors in terms of their ''*g*'' loadings, which in this case should be directly related to their potency for causing failure on the line-walking test. Their aim would be to discover what it is about the liquids that was responsible for their difference in potency, as indicated by their ''*g*'' loadings.

They would soon discover that color was not a clue. Some beer is the same color as whiskey, yet the two drinks differ markedly in potency. Vodka is colorless, yet it has about the same potency as amber-colored whiskey, and red and white wines have equal potency. Odor is also a rather inconsistent clue, although, in general, the beers, weak in potency, the wines, moderate in potency, and the whiskeys, strong in potency, have somewhat distinctively different odors. But then gin and vodka and many liqueurs do not conform to this odor rule. Taste works slightly better. The more highly ''*g*''-loaded liquids (whiskeys, gin, and vodka) somehow have a ''stronger'' taste than the less ''*g*''-loaded wines and beers. But there are many exceptions. For example, stout tastes stronger than Moselle wine, yet Moselle has a higher ''*g*'' loading. Thus some of the superficial aspects of all these liquids, like odor and taste, afford only a rough and often fallible indication of their potency.

The best our Martians could do at this level of analysis would be to generally characterize the odor and taste of the more potent liquids in

contrast to the least potent and acknowledge the exceptions and am-
biguities. By just smelling and tasting, different Martians would
seldom be in perfect agreement about the relative potencies of various
liquors, especially when these are not at the extremes of "strongness"
and "mildness" in taste or odor.

Moreover, the Martians would find it virtually impossible to relate
the potency of the liquids perfectly and consistently to any one or a
combination of their readily observed superficial characteristics. The
cause of their differences in potency is too much obscured by their
superficial characteristics. The only way they could index potency accurately without using the actual sobriety test would be to discover the
common factor in all of these liquids that makes them differ in potency.

If the Martians were able to do a chemical analysis, it would reveal
the common factor to be C_2H_5OH, or ethyl alcohol, which, interestingly, shows virtually none of the superficial characteristics of most of
the liquids in the liquor store. The Martians would then be faced by the
problem in brain biochemistry and neurophysiology of why ethyl
alcohol has its potent effect, as reflected by the sobriety test.

With respect to the common factor, g, in mental tests, Spearman
was in much the same position as the Martians in the liquor store, up
to the point where they could only describe and contrast the surface
characteristics of the most and least potent liquids. Spearman had no
means of taking the further steps analogous to the chemical and brain
analyses in our Martian fantasy. Although in the seventy-five years
since Spearman's discovery of g, psychologists have refined and extended his descriptions of the kinds of tests that are most and least
loaded with g, they are substantially no further ahead than he was in
understanding the nature of g, in terms of what brain activity causes
some types of test items to be more g-loaded than others. Until we can
understand that, we cannot really understand why people differ in g.
This continues to be one of the great questions in the history of
psychology. There has been plenty of theoretical speculation about the
nature of g, but no really satisfactory theory and no scientific consensus
on the matter. This does not mean that g does not exist, whatever it is.
Its existence is patently demonstrable in the consistently positive intercorrelations among all mental tests.

The g factor appears to be the essence of what most people think of
as "intelligence." There is excellent justification for technically defining intelligence as g. For example, mental retardation is recognized by
most people without the aid of any tests. If a number of tests of various
kinds are given to a group of persons who are easily recognized by their

parents, teachers, and acquaintances as retarded, and if the same tests are also given to groups of nonretarded persons of the same age, it is found that the tests that show the largest differences in scores between the two groups are the tests with the highest g loadings. If we rank-order the tests according to how much they discriminate between the retarded and nonretarded groups, and then rank-order the tests by the magnitudes of their g loadings, we find that there is practically perfect correspondence between the two rank orderings. The same thing happens if we compare persons who are regarded as unusually bright with the average run of people. In other words, the extent to which various tests discriminate between persons in accord with our subjective impressions of their "dullness" or "brightness" is directly related to the test's g loadings. Thus, whatever g is, it is not something technically esoteric and unrecognizable by the "man in the street." It corresponds quite closely to what he ordinarily thinks of as "intelligence."

No other factors that factor analysis is able to extract from tests make as consistent or as clear-cut discriminations between groups of persons who are generally considered especially dull or bright as does the g factor. And no superficial features of tests, such as their specific item contents and whether they are verbal or nonverbal, give any consistent clue to the g loadings or to how much the tests will discriminate between groups of particularly bright or dull persons.

How can we characterize the test items that are most g-loaded? And how do they differ from the least g-loaded items? Spearman and many others, including myself, have spent a lot of time inspecting different types of tests in relation to their g loadings to try to gain some insight into the nature of g. The results of such studies suggest two important generalizations.

First and most important is the fact that g is not related to the specific contents of items or to their surface characteristics. An almost infinite variety of test items is capable of measuring g. This observation led Spearman to a principle that he referred to as the "indifference of the indicator," meaning that the manifestation of g is not limited to any particular types of information or item types. Tests as diverse as vocabulary, number series completion, and block designs can all be equally g-loaded. This extreme variety of item types that can be highly g-loaded completely destroys the notion that g is an artifact of a narrow class of tests reflecting only scholastic and cultural attainments. Although scholastic tests can have high g loadings, the measurement of g is not at all dependent on any specific cultural or scholastic knowledge.

Second, if we arrange various tests, each composed of homogeneous item types, in the order of their *g* loadings, from highest to lowest, we notice that the *g* is related to the *complexity* of the cognitive activity demanded by the items. Test items are *g*-loaded to the degree that the mental activity they call forth involves seeing relationships between elements, grasping abstract concepts, reasoning, analysis, finding common features among superficially dissimilar things, inferring conclusions from given items of information. In the most general terms, the *g* factor shows up whenever a test item requires one to fill a gap, turn something over in one's mind, make comparisons, transform the input to arrive at the output. Spearman believed *g* was most clearly manifested in items calling for inductive and deductive reasoning and abstraction. He characterized *g* as inventive rather than reproductive.

Even more generally, *g* seems to be involved in items that require mental manipulation of images, symbols, words, numbers, or concepts. Tests that merely call for the recall or reproduction of previous learning or highly practical skills are poor measures of *g*. Tests depending on rote memory, for example, have relatively low *g* loadings.

Examples of tests with high *g* loadings:

Raven's Progressive Matrices, which call for perceiving key features and relationships among simple geometric figures and designs, and discovering the rules that govern the differences among the elements in the matrix.

Verbal similarities and differences. For example, in what ways are pairs of abstract words, such as *triumph* and *victory,* or *defeat* and *vanquish,* the same or different?

Verbal analogies. For example, "*Cut* is to *sharp* as *burn* is to (a) *fire* (b) *flame* (c) *hot* (d) *hurt.*"

Series completion. For example, "1, 4, 2, 5, 3, __, __" and "81, 49, 64, 36, 49, 25, 36, __, __."

Paragraph comprehension. Drawing conclusions based on inferences that are logically implied but not explicit in the contents of the paragraph.

Figure analogies and figure classification. Seeing common elements, patterns, or systematic progressions in varieties of simple nonrepresentational figures consisting of lines, angles, circles, dots, etc.

Arithmetic reasoning. For example, "Bob is twice as old as his sister, who is now 7. How old will Bob be when his sister is 40?"

Arithmetic *problem solving,* in which the arithmetic operations required for solutions are not explicit but must be selected by the subject in accord with the logic of the problem, is much more highly *g*-loaded than tests of arithmetic *computation,* in which all the operations called for are entirely explicit. This illustrates Spearman's characterization of *g* as inventive rather than reproductive, and as involving the discovery or inference of rules rather than merely their application. For example, about one-fourth of adults fail the foregoing arithmetic problem about Bob and his sister, but nearly all who fail give "80" as the answer, which shows they have learned to multiply 40×2. But they select the wrong operation and don't see the logical absurdity of their answer. That is a matter of *g*.

Examples of tests with only moderate *g* loadings:

Performance. Physical manipulation of form boards and puzzles, involving an element of trial-and-error in solving the problem.

Sentence completion. For example, "A body of _____ entirely surrounded by _____ is called an _____."

Handwriting speed. Counting speed.

Paired-associate learning, which consists of being given several pairs of unrelated words (e.g., *box/chair, pig/hat,* etc.) and then being asked to say the second word in each pair when given the first.

Examples of tests with low *g* loadings:

Speed of simple addition.

Speed of counting dots.

Crossing out designated letters or numbers (scored for speed and accuracy).

Recognition memory for words and numbers.

Rote memory tasks.

Tapping speed. Dotting speed.

Simple reaction time, such as pressing a telegraph key the instant a light goes on.

When large numbers of psychological tests have been categorized into four groups strictly according to their *g* loadings, the groups of tests, from highest to lowest *g* loadings, can be characterized as involving primarily (1) relational, (2) associative, (3) perceptual, and (4) sensory-motor processes.

We can gain further insight into the nature of *g* by examining certain simple tasks that have very low *g* loadings and then finding out what kinds of changes can be made in these tasks that will increase their *g* loading.

Forward and backward digit span tests are a good example of this. These tests are part of the Wechsler Intelligence Scales for children and adults. The subject is asked to listen to and then repeat a string of digits (e.g., 6, 4, 9, 1, 5) either in the order in which they were presented (termed "forward digit span") or in reverse order (termed "backward digit span"). The examiner begins with a string of only two or three

digits and works up to a number of digits so long that the subject cannot repeat all of them in the correct order after a single presentation.
The longest string of digits that a subject can repeat correctly is his digit
span, and this can be determined for repeating digits forward or
backward. Neither test is a very good measure of *g*. But the interesting
point is that backward digit span has about double the *g* loading of forward digit span. Why? Notice that the contents of the two tests are the
same—highly familiar digits. The main difference is that backward
digit span requires more mental work and manipulation than forward
digit span, which requires only reproductive memory. In the backward
digit span task, the subject must transform the input, turn the string of
digits around in his ''mind's eye,'' before ''reading'' them out. This
extra mental manipulation or active transformation of the input is the
source of backward digit span's greater *g* loading. Sheer effort or task
difficulty *per se* does not bring out more *g*. Longer strings of digits forward are not more *g*-loaded than shorter strings. Also, if we interpose a
ten-second delay before the subject is permitted to recall the series, it
increases the difficulty of recall, as shown by the fact that people generally can't recall as long a string under the delayed-recall condition,
but it does not significantly alter the task's *g* loading. Task complexity
in the sense of requiring greater mental manipulation of the input
seems to be the essential ingredient in *g*. Any relationship of *g* to task
difficulty is merely an incidental result of the fact that more complex
tasks are usually more difficult—that is, fewer people can do them.

But tasks can also be made too complex to be highly *g*-loaded.
When complexity is so great as to interfere with the perception of
relationships, logical patterns, and the like, everyone is forced to fall
back on purely trial-and-error attempts at solution. Laboratory trial-
and-error learning tasks, which can be made very difficult, are devised
so as to rule out any possibility of insight, grasping relationships, or
reasoning of any kind. Interestingly, scores on such tasks show very
low *g* loadings. By the same token, they show low correlations with IQ
tests and scholastic achievement, and they do not differentiate markedly between retarded and normal persons, or between species of
animals that differ markedly in capabilities on problem-solving tasks
that involve ''seeing'' relationships.

Another set of laboratory tasks that affords an even more basic insight into *g* involves simple and choice reaction time (RT). In simple
RT the subject merely has to lift his index finger off a telegraph key the
instant a light bulb goes on. The brief interval of time between the
light's going on and the releasing of the key is the RT, measured in

milliseconds. Many trials are averaged for a given person to obtain a stable reading. In choice RT the subject is faced with two light bulbs, side by side, and is uncertain of which light will go on next. Again, the subject waits with his index finger on a telegraph key and releases it the instant either light goes on. The greater uncertainty about which bulb will go on increases the RT considerably. In the nearly one thousand persons we have now tested, we have not found one whose RT for the two-light task was not slower than for the one-light task. But the important point is that the RT scores derived from the choice RT test are more *g*-loaded than are the simple RT scores. If we go on increasing the number of light bulbs (we've used up to eight), thereby increasing the amount of uncertainty in the task, the greater is the *g* loading of the RT measurements. In other words, having to make a decision in the face of uncertainty brings out more *g*.

Such evidence clearly contradicts the idea that what our best, most *g*-loaded IQ tests measure is merely some narrow ability that is only important in school. There is ample evidence that *g* is involved even in seemingly simple and commonplace activities that are remote from school and academia. For example, work sample tests given to U.S. Army cooks, who were equated for number of months of experience in the kitchen, showed that different routine tasks performed by cooks have different *g* loadings. Making jellyrolls is much more *g*-loaded than making scrambled eggs. On the Armed Forces Qualification Test a greater percentage of high-scoring army cooks could make jellyrolls without prompting than could low-scoring cooks. But both high- and low-scoring cooks can prepare scrambled eggs equally well. Whenever the task at hand, whatever it may be, involves complexity, novelty, uncertainty calling for choice, mental manipulation of the elements of the problem, or the recall of specific relevant items of information from memory needed to get on with solving the problem, then *g* comes into the picture. It is the same *g* that is measured with useful accuracy by our present-day IQ tests.

Fluid and Crystallized *g*

If *g* involves complexity, mental manipulation, reasoning, and inference, why do many ordinary IQ and scholastic aptitude tests include items such as vocabulary (e.g., "Define *apothecary*") and general information questions (e.g., "Who was the founder of Islam?"), which seem to involve just memory of things one has chanced to learn at some time before taking the test? After all, we have seen that tests of memory *per se* are not very good measures of g. Yet even though simply recalling, say, the meaning of a word doesn't involve much g, the original acquisition of the word's meaning is a highly g-loaded mental activity. People don't acquire vocabulary by rote learning. They don't memorize word lists and definitions by drill and repetition. Virtually all of one's vocabulary is acquired by hearing or reading words in a context from which one can infer their meaning. One might have to encounter a word used in several different contexts to be able to infer its complete meaning and its subtle difference from some similar word (e.g., *charitable* and *generous*). Brighter persons infer more of a word's meaning from any given context and don't need as many encounters with it in different contexts to grasp its distinctive meaning. Given similar amounts of exposure to the language, therefore, a more intelligent person acquires a larger, qualitatively richer, and more subtle vocabulary than a less intelligent person.

Hence tests of vocabulary and general information and other tests that require the recall of previously acquired information or skills are said to measure crystallized intelligence, or crystallized g, symbolized g_c. The inferential processes involved in the original acquisition depend upon fluid intelligence, or g_f. For persons from similar educational and cultural backgrounds, tests involving g_c and g_f are highly correlated; that is, persons who score high on g_c tests, like vocabulary, also score high on g_f tests, like matrices or figure analogies and other novel reasoning problems.

Another point: the concepts represented by some words are too complex, abstract, or subtle for some people to infer from any context or to fully understand even when the word is fully defined. A person may look up the definition in the dictionary and might even memorize it verbatim; but unless the meaning of the word is grasped at a deeper, nonverbal conceptual level, it does not become a part of his functional vocabulary. It is remarkable how hard it is to retain such words—the memorized definition soon fades beyond retrieval. And even if the memorized definition is provided again, the person's lack of a conceptual grasp of the word's meaning is shown by his inability to express the meaning adequately in words other than those of the memorized definition. There is a very high correlation between the subtlety with which people understand the meaning of words, and the sheer number of different words whose meaning they can recognize in any sense. Thus, vocabulary or word knowledge is a good indicator of g, provided, of course, that the test words are not too narrowly selected from specialized areas of learning. One could easily make up specialized vocabulary tests, for example, in which musicians, or chefs, or mechanics, or carpenters would excel over everyone else. Such specialized tests would probably be quite good measures of *g* for the persons within each specialty, when their amounts of experience in their respective fields are equated, but they would be rather poor measures of *g* for people in general.

Much the same can be said about tests of general information, although people's performance on information items has the disadvantage of being more strongly affected by differences in educational background than most other types of intelligence test items. For persons of similar education, however, well-constructed tests of "general information" are quite highly *g*-loaded.

Breadth and Altitude of Intellect

The American psychologist Edward L. Thorndike (1874–1949) described two aspects of intellect: breadth and altitude.

Breadth is measured by how many different things a person knows that are relatively easy to know; that is, they are not highly complex, abstruse, esoteric, or profound. There are many words, for example, that are known by about 50 percent of the general population. Therefore they are fairly common and simple words. The number of such words that a person knows is one indication of his mental breadth. The same goes for items of general information. There are great individual differences in the "breadth of intellect" as so measured.

Altitude is measured by the most difficult and complex problems a person can solve, or the most difficult words in a vocabulary test or the most difficult general information questions he can get right. A test item's difficulty is indexed by the percentage of the standardization population that fails the item. So items can be ranked in difficulty, from very difficult items that are failed by more than 99 percent of the population to very easy items that are failed by fewer than 1 percent. The average of the most difficult items in several types of tests that a person can pass is an indication of that person's altitude. There are great individual differences in "altitude of intellect" just as in "breadth of intellect."

But the really interesting fact discovered by Thorndike is that measures of individual differences in breadth and altitude are almost perfectly correlated. That is, these two seemingly different aspects of mental ability are both indices of one and the same general ability, or *g*. People who know rare or difficult things or can solve very complex problems also generally know a lot more than do most people of the rather ordinary kinds of words and facts that many people know. Persons with poor reasoning and problem-solving ability also possess much less common knowledge about the world around them. Brighter persons automatically pick up more information from any experience afforded by their environment.

I recall once inteviewing a young man who tested out as borderline retarded, in the range of IQ 75, to get some idea of his fund of general information. I decided to begin by trying to find out how much he knew about whatever topic he claimed to have the greatest interest in and to know the most about. It was baseball. He frequently went to baseball games with his father or watched them on television, and found them very exciting. Yet when I questioned him about baseball, I discovered that he didn't know for sure how many players are on a team, couldn't name all the positions on the team, and had only vague and at times incorrect notions of the rules of the game. He knew the names of three or four players on the local team but didn't know any of the world's most famous players or even the names of any of the Big League teams. When I probed other topics in which he claimed an interest—automobiles and gardening—I found that he possessed even less information about these than about baseball. It was evident that his quite low score on the General Information subtest of the Wechsler Adult Intelligence Scale, on which I had tested him, gave an accurate assessment of his level of general knowledge of the world around him. On the other hand, just out of curiosity, I later put the same baseball questions to a learned professor who, I happened to know, had no interest in any sport whatever. He even had a positive disdain for spectator sports and claimed never to have seen a baseball game in his life. Yet he had no trouble answering the several baseball questions I asked him, and could name three Big League teams and several famous baseball players. Interestingly, he was quite surprised to discover that he knew anything at all about baseball and seemed puzzled as to where he could have learned facts about something he cared nothing about. But conversations with him revealed that he knew a great deal about a great many things, in science, literature, the arts, economics, politics, and world affairs. In his own field he is an acknowledged world authority.

These striking differences that are so obvious between the extremes of the IQ scale exist in smaller degrees between less extreme IQ differences. But when the differences are fairly small—less than 10 points or so—they cannot be dependably recognized by casual observation. Without very carefully designed tests we cannot reliably discriminate between the g levels of persons whose IQs are within ten or so points of each other. Within that range, the more obvious differences between persons involve their special talents, developed skills, interests, personal experiences, and educational backgrounds. The ordinarily observed differences between persons, then, are a poor basis for subjective judgments about differences in intelligence or g. In general, however, someone who knows a lot about *something* is most likely more intelligent than one who doesn't know much about anything.

Fluctuations in Tests' g Loadings

A test's g loading is not a constant like the specific gravity of a metal. It can vary as a function of several conditions.

1. A test's g loading depends on all the other tests that are included with it in the correlation matrix that is subjected to factor analysis. However, if the collection of tests is fairly large (ten or more) and they consist of a number of different types of tests, a given test's g loading usually stays in the same general region of either high, medium, or low g loadings. Thus, a test's g loading is not entirely capricious, given an adequate sampling of tests in the particular factor analysis in which the g loading is determined.

More constant than the g loading of any particular test is the entire g factor extracted from any large collection of diverse tests. It is possible to give people factor scores based on the g factor (or any other factor) extracted from the whole battery of tests they took. Individuals' g factor scores remain in very much the same rank order when they are based on different batteries of tests, even when the batteries of tests seem quite dissimilar (such as the verbal and performance tests of the Wechsler scale), provided there are about ten or more somewhat diverse tests in each battery.

2. The size of a test's g loading also depends on the group of people whose test scores are factor-analyzed. If the group's range of mental ability is restricted, every test's g loading will be somewhat smaller than it would be in the general population, with its full range of mental ability. Hence tests' g loadings will not be so large when they are factor-analyzed in a group of the mentally retarded or in a group of students in a selective college. This is because factor analysis is essentially an analysis of individual differences, and it shows how much of the individual differences in the group from which all the test scores were obtained are attributable to the *g* factor or to other factors. If the range of individual differences has already been diminished on any given factor, as when college students are selected on the basis of their academic performance and intelligence, then the restricted factor is prevented from showing up fully in the factor analysis. If we factor-analyze a host of body measurements in a sample from the general population, the largest factor (the *g* of all the body measurements) is a general size factor. But if we perform this analysis on several teams of professional basketball players, who are all highly similar in height and build, it would fail to reveal a prominent general size factor.

3. A test's *g* loading may change according to the age of the subjects taking the test. The *g* factor shows up most on tests that involve some novelty, reasoning, judgment, and mental effort. Tests that have these properties for children of elementary school age may not have these properties for many high school youths, and so their *g* loadings would decrease. Mechanical arithmetic or computation is an intellectual challenge to young children who are just beginning to learn arithmetic, and so tests of mechanical arithmetic at that age show moderately high *g* loadings. But for older children and adults for whom computation is already a highly practiced routine, such tests have a comparatively low *g* loading.

For elderly subjects, tests such as vocabulary and general information tend to lose some of their *g* loading. In some old persons who have undergone some mental deterioration, scores on vocabulary and information can be likened to empty shells, only indicating the *g* that the subject once possessed but which is no longer fully functioning. Such persons get high scores on tests of vocabulary, general information, and other tests of crystallized ability, but perform relatively poorly on tests of fluid ability, such as matrices, figure analogies, number series, block designs, and backward digit span. In normal young persons there is a high correlation between scores on tests of crystallized and fluid ability. The correlation decreases somewhat in old age, and in some cases an old person's vocabulary and knowledge are better indications of former mental ability than of present fluid ability for new learning and novel problem solving. The aged brain retains the knowledge and skills acquired in the past, but no longer functions at a level that could result in the same rate of new acquisition in the present.

4. Instruction, learning, and practice on a task first increases, and then decreases, its *g* loading. Whether the *g* loading first increases depends on the initial complexity of the task. The more complex tasks at first show an increase in g loading with instruction and practice. If the nature of the task itself does not change, then instruction, learning, and practice decrease its g loading. By analogy, learning to drive an automobile takes a good deal of mental effort in the early stages. One has to concentrate fully on the requirements of the task—shifting gears smoothly, giving proper hand signals, and so on—to the exclusion of all other mental activity, such as listening to the radio, conversing, or thinking about something to be done later in the day. After sufficient practice, these tasks become routinized and automatic, freeing mental energy for other things. One could say that practice and overlearning of complex skills result in the conservation of g.

People can be taught strategies for solving certain types of highly g-loaded intelligence test items, and through prolonged practice at solving many such problems they can improve their performance on them. But this does not increase their overall standing on g. The highly practiced types of items lose their g loading, and the person's performance on them becomes a poor index of how he will perform on other types of g-loaded items.

Animal Analogs of g

The essential characteristics of g—reasoning, seeing connections, and grasping relationships—are exemplified in many of the behavioral tests that have been devised by zoologists and comparative psychologists for the study of differences in behavioral capacity among various species of animals. There is universal assent that some animals are more intelligent than others. The dog is considered more intelligent than the chicken, the monkey more intelligent than the dog, and the chimpanzee more intelligent than the monkey.

The sheer speed of learning very simple things does not discriminate among species nearly as much as the degree of complexity of a problem that an animal can solve spontaneously without special training. Problems that require the animal to size up a situation, to integrate sensory information to reach a goal, to see connections, to "get the idea" or "catch on," are the most discriminating. These aspects of animal behavior are seen in the flexibility of behavior in the face of obstacles, the amount of insightful behavior as contrasted with trial-and-error, problem-solving behavior, transfer of learning from one problem situation to somewhat different situations, and the understanding of abstract or relational concepts. These are the features of the kinds of tests that are the most g-loaded for humans.

Interestingly, the degree of behavioral complexity shown by different species of animals when placed in specially devised problem situations is related to their brain size (in relation to body size) and to the proportion of brain tissue not involved in vegetative-autonomic and sensory-motor functions. Development of the cerebral cortex, the association areas, and the frontal lobes parallels the behavioral complexity of various species.

The detour problem clearly distinguishes the intelligence of fowls and mammals. When, say, a hungry chicken is placed behind a three-sided screen-wire barrier, open at one end, and a pile of grain is placed on the other side of the wire, the chicken runs from side to side trying to get at the grain. But it never turns its back on the grain and so it is stymied. It can't solve the detour problem. It eventually gives up and walks out of the three-sided pen; it may then find the grain only inadvertently rather than by intention. How different is the dog's behavior in the same situation! A dish of meat is placed outside the barrier. The dog quickly sizes up the situation and immediately runs around the barrier to get the meat. The dog's behavior is obviously controlled by a much more subtle and complex brain than the chicken's.

But a string-pulling test will readily show that the relatively smart dog is not nearly so bright as a monkey. A hungry dog is placed in a completely enclosed four-sided pen with bars all around. Three feet outside the bars is a large juicy bone with a heavy white string tied around it. The string goes straight into the pen and has a wooden knob on the end of it to permit the dog to grasp it easily with its teeth and pull the bone into the cage. Typically, the dog tries to get the bone by putting its paws between the bars; it scratches at the bars and bites them, and does just about everything it can do in the situation—except pull on the string. Although the string is plainly visible, the dog does not "see" the connection between the string and the bone. Put a monkey in the same situation, with a banana attached to the string, and in almost no time the monkey "sees" the connection and pulls in the banana with the string.

In a number of training sessions, using gradual approximations, we can specially train the dog to drag in the bone with the string. The dog will then perform this task as readily and efficiently as the monkey. But no one believes, therefore, that the dog is as smart as the monkey. The difference, of course, is that the dog has merely learned to perform a trick and has not solved a problem. This is essentially the difference between rote learning and *g*.

The pole-and-banana problem shows the difference between the monkey and the chimpanzee, which is the most intelligent of the anthropoid apes. A banana is placed beyond arm's length outside the bars of the cage, and a four-foot pole is placed inside the cage. Monkeys rarely get the idea of using the pole to drag in the banana, but most chimps will do so. If two short poles that can be connected like a fishing rod are placed separated in the cage, the brightest chimps will attach them together to drag in a banana that is out of reach of either of the shorter poles. They will also use a short pole to drag in a longer pole with which they can then reach the banana. It all involves seeing connections. The various animal intelligence tests can be rank-ordered in difficulty along this dimension, just as we can rank-order different items in tests devised for humans. There are many other types of animal intelligence tests of varying complexity, extending from simple stimulus-response conditioning, to trial-and-error learning, to habit reversal, to learning-set acquisition (also called "learning to learn"), to simple and double oddity problems (i.e., pick the one odd object out of a set of three objects where two are identical), and so on.

Many of these tests devised to assess differences in animal intelligence have also been given to humans. Because most of them are so easy by human standards, they have to be used with young children and the mentally retarded. The various tests show the same rank order of difficulty for children and the retarded as they show for monkeys and chimpanzees. The complexity factor in these animal problems that reveals differences between various species of primates also rank-orders children the same as do standard IQ tests. The *g* factor of IQ tests reflects much the same kind of ability to see connections and size up complex situations that is measured by the animal tests which most clearly reveal species differences in adaptive capacity. Thus it seems the *g* factor of our IQ tests is not just peculiar to individual differences among persons within a particular culture, but is continuous with broader biological aspects of neural organization reflected in individual differences within other primates and even in the hierarchy of behavioral capacities between different species. The *g* of intelligence is evidently as much a biological reality, fashioned by evolution, as are the morphological features of organisms.

The Neurophysiology of *g*

Although psychologists can now measure *g* quite accurately and can identify the kinds of test items that best measure *g* in a given population, they do not yet have any satisfactory theory of the brain mechanisms underlying measurements of g. There is at present no scientific consensus about basic processes involved in g or even how they should be investigated, although there is plenty of theoretical speculation.

Some critics of mental testing use the lack of a scientific consensus about the ultimate nature of g to argue that since psychologists don't know what g is, they can't possibly measure intelligence or say anything scientifically valid about it.

Such arguments are nonsense. One can measure intelligence without knowing what goes on in the brain, just as one can measure the horsepower of a car without knowing what's under the hood. It was possible to recognize electricity and measure it precisely long before there was any generally accepted theory of what electricity consists of. Accurate thermometers existed long before the science of thermodynamics had come up with an adequate explanation of the nature of heat. Psychometrics is in much the same position today. Trying to discover the basic nature of g is one of the major frontiers of psychological research.

We already know that g is correlated with certain anatomical and electrophysiological brain measurements. There is a correlation of about $+ .30$ between IQ and brain size, taking proper account of sex, physical stature, birth weight, and other correlated variables. Such a correlation is considered quite important from a biological and evolutionary standpoint, considering that much of the brain is devoted to noncognitive functions that are not at all related to IQ. It can be argued that there has been a direct causal effect, through natural selection in the course of human evolution, between intelligence and brain size. Cerebral development, as reflected in cranial capacity, is known to have increased markedly over the five million years of human evolution, almost tripling in size from *Australopithecus* to *Homo sapiens*. The evolutionary selective advantage of greater brain size was the greater capacity it conferred for more complex intellectual functioning.

In recent years, it has been demonstrated that IQ and other highly g-loaded tests are correlated with the speed and amplitude of electrical potentials evoked in the brain by visual and auditory stimuli and recorded by the electroencephalograph through electrodes attached to the scalp.

Spearman conjectured that different parts of the cerebral cortex (the outer gray matter of the brain) could be likened to different engines performing specific functions, while the general neural energy of the whole cerebrum, which he speculated is the basis of g, could be likened to the fuel that drives the different engines. Its potential energy, therefore, enters into every activity of the brain. Another theorist and a contemporary of Spearman's, Sir Cyril Burt (1883–1971), suggested that g reflects the general character of the individual's brain tissue, such as the degree of systematic complexity in the neural architecture. Burt noted that the cerebral cortex in the mentally deficient often shows less density and less branching of neurons than in normal persons. One of the currently more popular speculations was put forth by Sir Godfrey Thomson (1881–1955) in his famous work *The Factorial Analysis of Human Abilities* (1939). The action of the brain involves a large number of elements of various kinds: the number and extent of branching of brain cells, synaptic conductivity between cells, thresholds of activation of neural elements, the production of neurochemical transmitters, the richness of the capillary network supplying blood to the brain, neural connections acquired through learning, and so on. If various kinds of mental tasks involve different samples of these many elements, the degree to which excellence of performance is correlated across different tasks will depend on the number of common elements they involve. Because more complex tasks will involve more elements, there is greater likelihood that different complex tasks will share more elements and therefore will be more highly intercorrelated.

Thus our present knowledge about the nature of g is limited to descriptions of the characteristics of tests or problems that are most g-loaded and to contrasting them with the least g-loaded tests. Practically nothing is known about the physiological and biochemical substrate of g. What we do know about g with considerable assurance, however, is, as noted earlier, that the measurement of it does not depend on any particular test or on any particular item contents. These are all merely vehicles, and g can be measured by an incredible variety of vehicles. The elicitation of g does not depend on any specific set of acquired knowledge or skills. As a psychological construct, g cannot be adequately defined in terms of any specific types of information, knowledge, skills, or problem-solving strategies. David Wechsler, the author of the Wechsler Intelligence Scales, has aptly remarked, "Unlike all other factors [g] cannot be associated with any unique or single ability; g is involved in many different types of ability; it is in essence not an ability at all, but a property of the mind."

The Practical Significance of g

The one thing you can be virtually certain of when taking any kind of mental test (other than personality, attitude, preference, and interest inventories) is that the test measures g, whatever other abilities it may measure, and it probably measures more of g than of any other identifiable ability.

The General Aptitude Test Battery (GATB) used by the U.S. Employment Service is a good example of a highly diverse battery of tests devised to measure nine aptitudes, which, in different combinations, can validly predict successful or unsuccessful performance in some five hundred different occupations. Each of the aptitudes is correlated with g, with the highest correlation of .60 to .80 for the verbal, numerical, and spatial reasoning aptitudes, and the lowest g correlations of .20 to .50 for tests measuring motor coordination, finger dexterity, and manual dexterity. The g loadings of the nine GATB aptitudes closely parallel their correlations with a number of standard IQ tests, which is not surprising, because IQ tests measure mostly g.

Also, g has greater predictive validity for job performance of all kinds than any particular aptitude, although the prediction of performance in any particular occupation can be significantly improved by taking certain special aptitudes into account, in addition to g. Certain aptitudes are completely irrelevant to success in certain jobs, but there is practically no job for which g is wholly irrelevant. Jobs differ in their g demands just as tests do, and highly g-loaded tests, such as standard intelligence tests and scholastic aptitude tests, are the best predictors of performance in g-demanding jobs. These are the jobs that cannot be routinized and that require thinking, judgment, planning, assimilating new information, and making decisions on the basis of complex and changing conditions. Such demands are most typically found in highly skilled technical and professional occupations and in high-level managerial and executive positions. Persons who are low in g, therefore, are virtually excluded from such jobs. The educational requirements for many such highly g-demanding jobs usually screen out persons of below-average intelligence, because secondary and higher education are themselves quite g-demanding.

In sum, standard intelligence tests, both group and individually administered, are all very highly g-loaded, although many of them also include some small admixture of other factors, most often a verbal ability factor. This is especially true of scholastic aptitude tests, which, besides g, contain verbal and numerical factors. The addition of verbal and numerical factors improves a test's validity for predicting scholastic performance, although the g factor usually contributes most of the predictive power.

3

The Inheritance of Mental Ability

Since ancient times, people have noticed that blood relations show some resemblance in appearance. The resemblance is far from perfect, even between next of kin, or brothers or sisters, and is even less marked between more distant relatives—grandparents and grandchildren, half-siblings, aunts or uncles and their nephews and nieces, first and second cousins.

The ancient rule "Like begets like" was recognized by the earliest known breeders of livestock, ages before there was a science of genetics. But it was apparent that "Like begets like" was only half the truth. The other half: "Like also begets unlike." This was even more puzzling to the ancients. Although they noticed unmistakable resemblance among the offspring of a pair of parents, it was also obvious that the offspring are by no means entirely alike, but often show striking differences. Variation among the offspring of the same parents is as much a fact of life as their family resemblance.

Galton's Discovery

We don't know just when people first began to wonder if these rules applied to mental ability as well as to physical characteristics. But the illustrious British scientist Sir Francis Galton (1822–1911), a half-cousin of Charles Darwin, is generally credited as the first to try to find out whether ability is inherited along lines similar to physical traits. Galton's most famous work, *Hereditary Genius* (1869), is the fascinating report of this pioneer study of the inheritance of mental ability.

When Galton did this work, mental tests had not yet been invented. The only tests were school examinations in classics, mathematics, and the like. Marks on such tests were of very limited usefulness for Galton's purposes, as it was hard to find many relatives, especially across different generations, who had the same education or had taken the same exams.

So Galton decided that the most useful and objective criterion of mental ability, for his purpose, was intellectual eminence, as indicated by the number and length of biographical accounts, entries in encyclopedias, extent of obituaries in the leading world newspapers, and the like. These are fairly good, though rough, criteria of intellectual distinction. They would clearly distinguish Darwin and Einstein from the general run of scientists, Beethoven and Wagner from the general run of musicians, Shakespeare and Goethe from the general run of writers, Lincoln and Lenin from the general run of politicians, and popes and cardinals from the general clergy.

Galton argued that, although eminence results from a variety of personal qualities, opportunities, and circumstances, the one common factor in all cases of achieved eminence is a level of ability well above the general average. Eminence, Galton claimed, is a product of outstanding ability combined with high energy and exceptional persistence of endeavor, whatever other factors might contribute. Biographies of eminent persons clearly substantiate Galton's generalization. Galton's investigation was unavoidably limited to men, because in the Victorian period, when he did his study, there were not enough eminent women to justify statistical analysis.

What Galton's study of eminent men revealed, essentially, was this: If he began with a large group (977, to be exact) of eminent men, he found that far fewer of their sons ever became distinguished. Yet a much greater percentage (48) of the sons met Galton's criteria of eminence than the percentage of prominent men found in the general population. The percentage of eminent men among the brothers of eminent men was 27. It was significant that grandsons and nephews of eminent men showed an even smaller percentage (6) who were able to attain distinction. Among the first cousins, great-grandsons, and great-nephews of eminent men, only about 1 percent achieved eminence. The percentage of these men's more distant relatives who were eminent was scarcely greater than the small percentage of distinguished men in the general population, which by Galton's criterion was estimated to be one in four thousand.

Galton termed this regular phenomenon "the law of filial regression to mediocrity." In general, the offspring of an exceptional parent tend to "regress" toward the average of the population, with respect to those characteristics in which the parent is exceptional. The more distant the relative is from the selected person, the greater is his "regression" toward the average of the general population.

Galton was the first to demonstrate this "law of regression" for physical stature. Because height can be measured precisely, Galton was able to demonstrate exactly how much regression there is for an indisputably hereditary physical trait. His physical measurements of thousands of Englishmen showed that tall men had sons who, as adults, were not so tall as their fathers but were above the average height of men in general. Short men had sons who, as adults, were not so short as their fathers but were below the average height. There are many exceptions, of course, because these are *statistical* generalizations. If we select men for tallness or shortness, their sons' heights, as adults, will, *on the average*, fall just a little less than halfway between the fathers' heights and the mean height of men in the population. The "law of regression to the mean," of course, also applies to mothers and daughters, fathers and daughters, and mothers and sons, if proper allowance is made for the average sex difference in height.

The "law of regression," Galton found, also works "backwards" across generations. The fathers of eminent men much less often achieved distinction. Interestingly, the percentage of eminence among eminent men's fathers was less (31) than among their sons. Grandfathers showed a much lower percentage (8) of eminence than did fathers of eminent men, and about the same percentage as the grandsons (7) of eminent men. The same ancestor-descendant symmetry in the percentage of eminence is also found in the collateral relatives, such as uncles and nephews. Brothers of eminent men show about the same chances of achieving eminence as their fathers. In general, among the first-degree relatives (father, brother, son) of eminent men, 32 percent were themselves eminent. Among second-degree relatives (grandfather, uncle, nephew, grandson), 6 percent were eminent. And among third-degree relatives (great-grandfather, great-uncle, first cousin, great-nephew, great-grandson), only 1 percent were eminent.

This all looked much like what Galton had found in the case of height. Second-degree relatives of tall (or short) persons show about half again as much regression toward the average height in the general population as do the first-degree relatives (parent, child, sibling).

Galton's discovery that the law of regression applied not only to height but also to intellectual eminence convinced him that mental ability is inherited in much the same way and to almost the same degree as stature and other hereditary physical traits. This is one of the important discoveries in the history of science, although it has not been regarded as wholly compelling because of the problem of assessing the extent of privilege and opportunity for attaining eminence that a man of eminence confers on his next of kin.

More than a century after Galton's pioneer investigation, we now have the results of many scores of technically more sophisticated studies carried out by innumerable scientists in Europe and America. Modern investigators have had two great advantages over Galton: the development of mental tests, permitting objective, reliable measurement of abilities; and the development of the science of genetics, which affords a theoretical basis for understanding the complex findings. The extensive research since Galton's time has not essentially contradicted his conclusions. They were basically at least as correct as other pioneer efforts in science, such as Sir Isaac Newton's picture of the physical universe or Charles Darwin's theory of biological evolution. The present scientific picture of the genetics of mental ability differs from Galton's mainly in the precision and comprehensiveness of the evidence and the theoretical sophistication of its interpretation.

Chromosomes, Genes, and Alleles

To understand how individual differences in mental abilities are influenced by heredity, it is necessary to understand some basic principles of genetics.

Every normal human being is born with twenty-three pairs of chromosomes, duplicates of which exist in the nucleus of every cell in the body. Each chromosome contains thousands of genes, each gene occupying a specific location on the chromosome, like beads on a string. The genes, which are composed of DNA molecules, are the basic units of heredity. They govern every aspect of the organism's physical development and physiological functions, from the moment of conception.

At conception, when one of the father's sperm cells fertilizes the mother's ovum, the fertilized egg (technically termed a zygote) contains the genetic "blueprint" for the new individual's whole course of development, from zygote to mature person. However, if there are too many mutant or defective genes that fail to perform the crucial functions of normal genes at certain stages of development, the effect is lethal and the embryo is spontaneously aborted. This occurs in more than one-fourth of all pregnancies. Genetic and chromosomal anomalies that are not lethal, and hence are not aborted, often result in birth defects or cause abnormalities that appear later in life.

If the two chromosomes of a particular pair are laid side by side, they are seen to be homologous. That is, on both chromosomes the same genes appear in the same locations, or "loci." The pairing of chromosomes takes place during the formation of the sex cells—the ova and sperm. The pairs of chromosomes then separate, so that only one member of each pair of homologous chromosomes goes into each sex cell (called a gamete). When the father's sperm cell fertilizes the mother's ovum, the twenty-three single chromosomes from the father unite with the twenty-three single chromosomes from the mother, giving the new individual twenty-three *pairs* of chromosomes. Thus a person receives one-half of his chromosomes, and consequently one-half of his genes, from each parent. Which half of each parent's twenty-three pairs of chromosomes goes into any one offspring is pure chance. The parents' genetic contribution to their offspring can be likened to a random lottery, like throwing dice or dealing a hand from a shuffled deck of cards.

Because the offspring receives a purely random half of each parent's genes, he will resemble each parent to some extent. Each offspring of the same pair of parents will receive different random sets or combinations of the parental genes, so no two offspring will be completely alike genetically. But there will be considerable resemblance among offspring of the same parents, of course, because all of them inherit different random combinations drawn from the same lottery of parental genes. The well-known exception is identical twins (or triplets, etc.) that result from the splitting in two, shortly after conception, of a single fertilized ovum. (Hence identical twins are termed monozygotic, or MZ, twins.) Each of the two halves of the split zygote that develops into an MZ twin contains perfectly identical alleles at every locus in their twenty-three pairs of chromosomes.

The genes at each locus on the chromosome can have two or more forms, called alleles. Different alleles have different effects on the particular functions performed by the gene at a given locus on the chromosome.

It is convenient to think of the various gene loci on a chromosome as letters of the alphabet, and to think of their different forms (i.e., alleles) as being either capital or small letters. Thus we can imagine a chromosome as a long string of letters, consisting of both capital and small letters. Homologous chromosomes have the same letters, (i.e., genes) but they need not have the same print style (i.e., alleles). For example, here is a pair of homologous chromosomes:

$$A\ b\ c\ d\ E\ F\ G\ h\ I\ j\ K\ L$$
$$a\ b\ C\ D\ e\ F\ g\ H\ I\ J\ k\ l$$

Although the genes at each locus, like A (or a), control the same function, the different alleles, A and a, have different effects on the function. These differences in alleles are responsible for the physical variations we see among members of the same family and among members of the same species—variations in eye color, skin color, hair color and texture, blood types, facial features, height, fingerprints, and so on. The differences that we see among persons in all these characteristics are the result of differences in their alleles. In our alphabet analogy, these are represented as the differences between A and a, B and b, and so on.

Mendelian Genetics

Consider the inheritance of a characteristic governed by the locus on the chromosome at which the gene can have either of the allelic forms A or a. Say A makes for red petals of a flower and a makes for white petals. Because chromosomes exist in pairs, there are three possible combinations of alleles at a given locus: AA, Aa, and aa. In sexually reproducing plants, one allele in each pair comes from the "mother" and one comes from the "father." A plant that receives the A allele from each "parent" is designated as AA, and its flowers will be red. A plant that receives A from one parent and a from the other is designated as Aa, and all its flowers will be pink, that is, a half-and-half blend of red and white. If a alleles are received from both parents, the combination aa results in purely white flowers.

Thus there are three gradations of color resulting from the three possible combinations of two alleles, A and a. Since pink (Aa) is exactly intermediate between red (AA) and white (aa), the effects of A and a are said to be additive. Their combined result, Aa, is like adding equal parts of red pigment and white pigment, which produces pink.

Now we can figure out the possible combinations of alleles that different pairs of parents can pass on to their offspring.

Genotype and Phenotype

In Examples 1–4 notice that each offspring can have any combination of the parents' alleles. Each combination of alleles is called a genotype. Every possible combination of the parental alleles is produced at random, and therefore, on the average, the relative frequencies of each combination (genotype) will be the same.

The phenotype is the observable manifestation of the genotype; it is the characteristic that we can actually see or measure. Individuals whose genotypes consist of identical alleles (*AA* or *aa*) are "homozygous" for the characteristic; those whose genotypes consist of different alleles (*Aa*) are "heterozygous."

Notice that in going from the parent generation to the offspring generation, the parental alleles undergo segregation and recombination. Because of segregation and recombination, it is possible for parents to have offspring with genotypes and phenotypes that are different from either of the parents, as shown in Examples 1 and 3. Also notice that it is only if the parents both have the same genotype and only if they both are homozygous that there will be no genetic variation among their offspring in the particular characteristic.

Finally, it is most important to notice that parents do not pass on their own genotypes to their offspring, but only their segregated alleles, which, in recombination, form *new* genotypes. Because there are so many genes with different alleles that go to make up any individual, and because the alleles at the different loci that control different characteristics all segregate independently each time a new individual is conceived, the likelihood that a parent and an offspring, or any two offspring (other than MZ twins), will have the same genotypes for a large number of traits is almost infinitesimally small. The chance that two children (other than MZ twins) born to the same parents would have the same genotypes at every loci on every chromosome has been estimated to be about one in seventy trillion, which is far more than the total number of persons who have ever lived. Thus, with the exception of MZ births, the mechanism of genetic inheritance ensures the biological uniqueness of every person.

These basic genetic principles of independent segregation and recombination were discovered by an Austrian monk, Gregor Mendel (1822–1884), who is generally recognized as the father of genetics. The

Example 1

Parents	*Mother*	*Father*

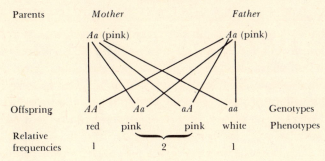

Parents   *Mother*   *Father*

Aa (pink)   *Aa* (pink)

Offspring   *AA*   *Aa*   *aA*   *aa*   Genotypes

red   pink   pink   white   Phenotypes

Relative frequencies   1   2   1

Example 2

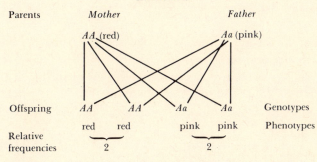

Parents   *Mother*   *Father*

AA (red)   *Aa* (pink)

Offspring   *AA*   *AA*   *Aa*   *Aa*   Genotypes

red   red   pink   pink   Phenotypes

Relative frequencies   2   2

Example 3

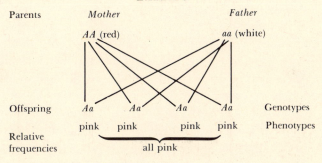

Parents   *Mother*   *Father*

AA (red)   *aa* (white)

Offspring   *Aa*   *Aa*   *Aa*   *Aa*   Genotypes

pink   pink   pink   pink   Phenotypes

Relative frequencies   all pink

Example 4

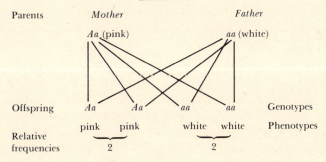

Parents   *Mother*   *Father*

Aa (pink)   *aa* (white)

Offspring   *Aa*   *Aa*   *aa*   *aa*   Genotypes

pink   pink   white   white   Phenotypes

Relative frequencies   2   2

laws that explain the inheritance of characteristics that are governed by a single genetic locus, as in the preceding examples, are referred to as Mendelian genetics, and such unitary characteristics are referred to as Mendelian characters, because their mode of inheritance conforms to the simple principles discovered by Mendel. The relative frequencies of the different phenotypes of a Mendelian character among the offspring of any given pair of parents are referred to as a Mendelian ratio.

Dominant and Recessive Alleles

Another important principle discovered by Mendel involves genetic dominance and recessiveness. This discovery is crucial for understanding differences between parents and their offspring. It partly accounts for the "law of regression" discovered by Galton. (It is interesting to note that Galton was born in the same year as Mendel—1822.)

Dominance is said to occur when the phenotypic characteristic of the heterozygote (for example, *Aa*) is not exactly intermediate between the phenotypes of the two homozygotes, *AA* and *aa*. If *A* is dominant and *a* is recessive, and if there is complete dominance, then the genotype *Aa* will manifest the same phenotypic effect as *AA*. In the case of partial dominance, the phenotypic appearance of *Aa* comes closer to the phenotype produced by *AA* than by *aa*. But when dominance is complete, the different genotypes *AA* and *Aa* will have indistinguishable phenotypes. So, even if the parents are phenotypically just alike in some trait, they may have a deviant offspring because of genetic dominance, as in the Mendelian example of complete dominance shown in Example 5. The Mendelian ratio of 3:1 is a sure sign of genetic dominance; in this case the allele for red is dominant and white is the recessive character. A mating between two red *AA* individuals will "breed true" and produce only red *AA* offspring. Similarly, two white *aa* individuals will produce only white *aa* offspring. But if two red *Aa* individuals mate, then, on the average, three-fourths of their offspring will be red (*AA, Aa,* and *aA*) and one-fourth will be white (*aa*).

Here one can see the mechanism of regression. The two red parents produce offspring who, on the average, are only three-fourths as red as the parents. If we can think of color as a measurable quantitative trait, like height, we could show that the arithmetic average of the offspring is different from the average of the two parents. For example,

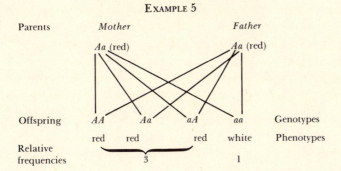

EXAMPLE 5

if $A = 1$ and $a = 0$, and if there is complete dominance, the two parents, with $Aa = 2$ and $Aa = 2$, will average 2, but the four offspring, being $AA = 2 + 2Aa = 4 + aa = 0$ will average only 6/4 or 1.5. This is the essential mechanism of the phenomenon of genetic regression.

Polygenic Inheritance

Many phenotypic characteristics that are influenced by genetic factors show continuous or quantitative variation, like height and intelligence. Such traits do not fall into discrete categories, like blood types or eye colors, but are graded on a continuum ranging from low to high values on some scale of measurement. Such continuous variation can come about genetically through the same Mendelian principles that were explained in the previous section. The only essential difference is that not just one gene but genes at a number of different loci control a trait that varies continuously. Hence such continuous traits are said to be polygenic. Instead of there being only one gene with two alleles, there are many genes, each with two (or more) alleles. Each allele has a small enhancing or nonenhancing effect on the phenotypic expression of the trait.

Just how do polygenes create continuous variation? Consider the simplest possible polygenic system—the case of just two loci, each with two alleles, A and a. The relative frequencies of the various genotypes produced by two parents who are each Aa at both loci can be determined from the binomial expansion of $(A + a)^{2n}$, where n is the number of loci (in this example, 2). Assuming that there are equal proportions of A and a alleles, the relative frequencies of all possible genotypes that can be produced by these parents are:

Genotypes		Relative Frequency	Metric Value
$AAAA$	$= A^4$	1	4
$AAAa$	$= A^3a$	4	3
$AAaa$	$= A^2a^2$	6	2
$Aaaa$	$= Aa^3$	4	1
$aaaa$	$= a^4$	1	0

Notice that with only two loci, there are five different genotypes. In general, if a genotype for a given trait involves n loci, each with two alleles, there will be $2n + 1$ different possible genotypes. Notice, too, that the most extreme genotypes (A^4 and a^4) have the smallest frequencies. As the number of loci increases, the number of possible genotypes increases, and their relative frequencies tend toward the so-called normal distribution, as illustrated in Figure 4.

We can give metric values to the various genotypes by arbitrarily assigning $A = 1$ and $a = 0$, which result in the values shown in the preceding tabulation. These are called genotypic values. The assigned allelic values 1 and 0 are entirely arbitrary, for convenience of illustration. The essential point, however, is that in theorizing about the polygenic inheritance of a continuous characteristic, such as height or intelligence, we think of the two forms of alleles, A and a, at each of many loci, as either enhancing the trait or not enhancing it. A enhances; a does not. Thus, individuals who measure high on the trait theoretically possess a greater-than-average number of the trait-enhancing alleles, and those who measure low on the trait possess fewer than the average number of enhancing alleles. This is the simplest possible model of polygenic inheritance.

Any proportion of the genes in a polygenic system may show complete dominance or any degree of partial dominance. Another complication in a polygenic system is termed epistasis. This is the interactive effect of genes at different loci. Just as dominance involves the influence of one allele on another allele at the same locus, so, too, can an allele at one locus have an influence on the action of an allele at another locus. This means that not only can the separate effects of alleles at each locus add up to create genetic variation, but particular combinations of alleles at the same loci (dominance) and at different loci (epistasis) also contribute to the variation. Thus some part of the variation among phenotypes is the result of particular combinations of alleles—some favorable, some unfavorable for the trait in question. The farther that a parent deviates from the population average, the greater is the probability that part of the deviation is due to a rare combination of alleles. Because a parent cannot pass on his own genotype

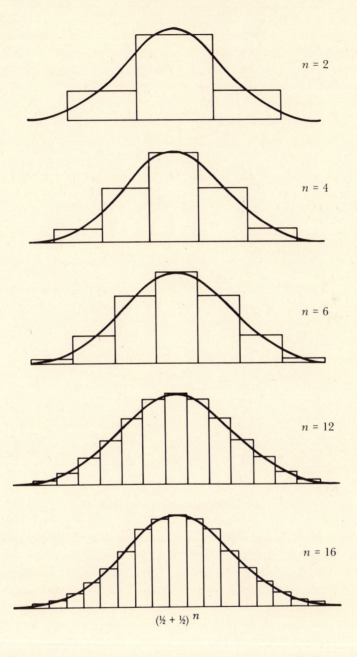

$$(\tfrac{1}{2} + \tfrac{1}{2})^{n}$$

Figure 4. Frequency distribution of genotypic values as the number of gene loci (n) increases (from 2 to 16). In each case, the normal curve has been superimposed on the actual distribution, which increasingly approaches the form of the normal curve as n increases.

to his offspring, but passes on only a random half of his alleles, it is much less likely that the offspring will receive the same rare combinations possessed by the parent. Therefore, the offspring, on the average, will be less deviant than the parent in the characteristic for which the parent is exceptional. That is essentially the explanation for Galton's "law of filial regression."

Quantitative Genetics

Individual variation in mental ability is attributable, in part, to polygenic inheritance, that is, the cumulative action of a number of genes. Polygenic inheritance is the subject of the branch of genetics known as quantitative genetics. Because each gene in a polygenic system has only a small effect, a separate gene's passage from generation to generation cannot be individually traced, as it can be in Mendelian genetics. Geneticists can trace the passage of a single gene across generations—in what is termed a pedigree study—only when the single gene, by itself, produces a large or distinctive phenotypic effect, as in the case of single-gene Mendelian inheritance.

The evidence for Mendelian or single-gene inheritance comes from pedigree studies, in which the appearance of a distinctive characteristic is traced in the direct line and collateral descendants from generation to generation. The evidence for polygenic inheritance, on the other hand, is based on a quantitative index of the degree of resemblance between relatives on the trait in question.

The Correlation Coefficient

The basic index of resemblance was first invented by Galton and further developed by his student Karl Pearson (1857–1936), who has been called the father of statistics. It is known as the "Pearson product-moment coefficient of correlation," or just "correlation," for short. In his genetic research, Galton needed some way to represent precisely the degree of resemblance between relatives, and it was originally for this purpose that he invented the correlation coefficient. It is an exact quantitative index of similarity or resemblance. In more general terms, the correlation coefficient is an index of the degree of relationship between two sets of measurements. For example, we might ask to what degree is variation in men's weights related to variation in their heights? We notice that taller men are larger and, in general, tend to weigh more than shorter men. How can we express this relationship more precisely? The relationship between height and weight can be stated precisely in terms of the correlation coefficient, which happens to be + .63 in young adult males. This coefficient of correlation was determined by measuring both the height and the weight of each of several thousand army recruits. All the measurements are subjected to certain routine calculations that can be expressed in a single mathematical formula invented by Pearson, which yields the correlation coefficient.

A correlation coefficient can take any value between zero and + 1 or − 1. A correlation of zero indicates a complete absence of any relationship between the two variables. A correlation of + 1 indicates a perfect positive relationship between the two variables, that is, as one variable increases, the other variable increases by a perfectly corresponding amount. A correlation of − 1 indicates a perfect negative correlation; that is, as one variable increases, the other variable decreases by a perfectly corresponding amount. If the correlation between two variables is either + 1 or − 1, that is, a perfect correlation, we can predict exactly any individual's measurement on one variable by knowing his measurement on the other.

The correlation coefficient can also be used to express precisely the degree of resemblance between relatives of any degree of kinship in any measurable characteristic, such as height, weight, or IQ. We simply pair up a large number of relatives, say, brothers, and measure the particular trait in each person, and then, using all of the measurements and the appropriate formulas, calculate the correlation coefficient.

The degree of relationship or resemblance as indicated by correlation can be expressed verbally as follows:

	Correlation Coefficient
Perfect correlation	1.00
Very high	.80 to .99
Moderately high	.60 to .79
Moderate	.40 to .59
Moderately low	.20 to .39
Very low	.01 to .19
No correlation	.00

Genetic Correlation

In 1918, the British geneticist and statistician Sir Ronald A. Fisher (1890–1962) wrote a highly technical paper (''The Correlation between Relatives on the Supposition of Mendelian Inheritance'') that is one of the cornerstones of quantitative genetics. It showed how one could determine the genetic correlation between relatives of any degree of kinship. The reasoning could be applied to any polygenic characteristic, in which each of the many genes affecting the characteristic is assumed to act according to the Mendelian principles previously described.

A genetic correlation is the theoretical correlation between relatives of a given degree of kinship (parent-child, brothers, cousins, and the like) if genetic factors alone were responsible for the resemblance between relatives. The genetic correlation, in other words, is the correlation between persons' genotypes for a given trait. It cannot be determined empirically, like a corrrelation between phenotypic measurements. The genetic correlation is based on purely theoretical considerations derived from the basic principles of Mendelian genetics, which apply to all sexually reproducing plants and animals. Most simply, it can be thought of as the proportion of those genes contributing to genetic variation that, on the average, are the same in relatives of a given degree of kinship. In short, the genetic correlation is an index of genetic resemblance in a particular trait.

In the simplest genetic model the effects of all alleles are additive, that is, if there are no dominant or recessive alleles, and there is zero genetic correlation between parents. Under these simple assumptions, the genetic correlations between various kinships are shown in Table 3.

A quantitative genetic analysis of a measurable trait consists essen-

TABLE 3

Genetic Correlation between Various Kinships under
the Assumptions of the Simplest Genetic Model

KINSHIP	GENETIC CORRELATION
Monozygotic twins	1.00
Dizygotic twins	.50
Full siblings	.50
Parent-child	.50
Grandparent–grandchild	.25
Half-siblings	.25
Uncle (aunt)–nephew (niece)	.25
First cousins	.125
Second cousins	.0625
Unrelated persons	.00

tially in comparing these theoretically derived genetic correlations with the actual phenotypic correlations based on direct measurements of the trait obtained on large numbers of persons in each kinship. If there is a very high degree of correspondence between the phenotypic correlations and the genetic correlations for the various kinships, it could mean either one of two things.

1. Phenotypic variation in the trait is largely due to genetic factors, because the pattern of kinship correlations closely parallels the genetic correlations, as it would if all of the variation were completely attributable to variation in genotypes.

2. Phenotypic variation in the trait is due to nongenetic or environmental influences which act in such a way as to almost perfectly mimic the kinship correlations expected in terms of genetic theory. This, however, would seem like a remarkable coincidence. But it could be argued that close relatives live in closer proximity to one another than more distant relatives, and therefore have more similar environments. In other words, the correlations between relatives could be *environmental* correlations rather than *genetic* correlations. Environmental correlation means that persons reared in very similar environments are more alike in those traits affected by the environment than persons reared in different environments.

Because of the conflict between these two interpretations, geneticists look for types of kinship data that would reasonably rule out one or the other interpretation. This means, for example, comparing the correlation between close relatives who have *not* been reared in highly similar environments with the correlation between more distant relatives, or between entirely unrelated persons, who have been reared in highly similar environments. In this way we can determine whether similarity of environments or closeness of genetic kinship makes for a greater correlation between persons' IQs.

One other point needs to be understood about genetic correlations. The correlations shown in Table 3 are based on the simplest possible genetic model. In humans, however, most polygenic traits that are of any evolutionary, cultural, or interpersonal importance do not act entirely in accord with such a simple model. Two main factors in human genetics complicate the picture: genetic dominance and assortative mating. But these complications can be taken into account in theoretically deriving the genetic kinship correlations.

Dominance, which was explained previously, can occur in some or all of the genes of a polygenic trait. Dominance reduces the genetic correlation in some kinships but not in others. Dominance affects the genetic correlations between parent and child, between dizygotic twins, and between siblings, but not between monozygotic twins or between half-siblings. It is because of these theoretically expected distinctive effects of dominance on certain kinship correlations that geneticists can determine whether dominant genes are involved in a particular trait.

Assortative mating is the tendency for like to marry like. The complete absence of assortative mating is known as random mating, in which there is no more resemblance between mates than would be expected by pure chance. Random mating is seen only in socially unimportant characteristics, such as fingerprint ridges and blood types.

The degree of assortative mating is measured by the correlation between parents on the phenotypic trait. Numerous studies show that the parental correlation for IQ is higher than for any other physical or psychological trait. In our society, the average correlation between parents' IQs is about + .45. This means that husbands and wives resemble each other in IQ almost as much as do brothers and sisters who are reared together.

If genetic factors are involved to some extent in IQ, it is extremely unlikely that the phenotypic correlation between parents' IQs does not carry with it some genetic correlation as well. Parents who resemble each other in mental ability will also be somewhat similar in the genetic factors as well as in the environmental factors that affect mental development.

Genetic correlation between parents has two especially important effects on the offspring generation.

1. It increases the variability of the trait in the population. That is, assortative mating of parents results in a larger percentage of families showing more extreme deviations from the population average. Assortative mating thus results in there being slightly fewer families in the middle of the distribution of measurements on the trait and more families nearer the high and low extremes than would occur under random mating. In other words, assortative mating spreads out the genetic variation of the trait in the population, by making different families genetically more unlike one another.

Because assortative mating for IQ spreads out the distribution of IQs, it has been estimated that the present level of assortative mating for IQ in the United States accounts for more than half the number of persons with IQs above 130, and for four out of five of those with IQs above 145. About twenty times more persons have IQs above 160 than we would find if there was no assortative mating for intelligence. Assortative mating thus greatly affects the intellectual resources of a population.

2. Assortative mating increases the correlation coefficient among siblings. Under assortative mating, the variability among all the children born to the same parents is less, relative to the total variation in the population, than would be the case under random mating. Assortative mating does not make siblings more alike in absolute terms, but as it increases the differences between unrelated persons, it has the effect of increasing the correlation coefficient between siblings. The correlation coefficient reflects the average variation among siblings relative to the average variation among all persons in the general population.

The fact that assortative mating increases the correlation between siblings (and also, to a lesser degree, between more distant relatives) means that it tends to counteract the effect of dominance, which decreases the correlation between siblings. The effects of dominance and assortative mating on the sibling correlation thus tend to cancel each other. This makes it more complicated for quantitative genetic analysis to determine the amount of genetic dominance.

The theoretic genetic correlations shown in Table 3 can be modified to show what they would be under different degrees of dominance and assortative mating. These effects on kinship correlations can be calculated theoretically for each kinship. If the actual kinship correlations then come closer to matching the theoretical genetic correlations when the effects of dominance and assortative mating are taken into account, it is reasonable to conclude that the genetic model that generated the correlations successfully explains the variation in the trait. That is how any scientific theory is validated. The theory predicts certain outcomes that cannot be predicted from other theories, and if the predictions are borne out in fact, the theory is substantiated. No scientific theory is proved absolutely, like a purely mathematical proposition, because there is always the possibility that some as yet undiscovered fact might turn up that contradicts the theory.

Kinship Correlations

The simplest way to summarize the main evidence on the degree of resemblance in IQ between various degrees of kinship is by means of a bar graph (Figure 5) showing the median or average correlation for IQ found in studies of each kinship. The correlation indicates the average degree of resemblance between pairs of persons, going from a correlation of 0 (no resemblance) to a correlation of 1 (perfect resemblance). These median correlations in Figure 5 are based on fifty-one independent studies involving over 30,000 kinship pairs from eight countries in four continents obtained over a period of more than two generations using a variety of intelligence tests.

Notice that the correlations are arranged, from top to bottom, in order of closeness of the relationship both with respect to degree of genetic kinship and environment or condition of rearing (together or apart). As the degree of closeness (both genetic and environmental) decreases, the correlation correspondingly decreases.

How close do these actual kinship correlations come to the genetic correlations derived strictly from genetic theory, as explained in the foregoing section? Figure 6 shows a plot of the actual kinship correlations in relation to the genetic correlations that would be expected under the simplest theoretical assumptions of no genetic dominance, no assortative mating, and, of course, no environmental influences or errors of measurement. It can be seen that many of the actual kinship

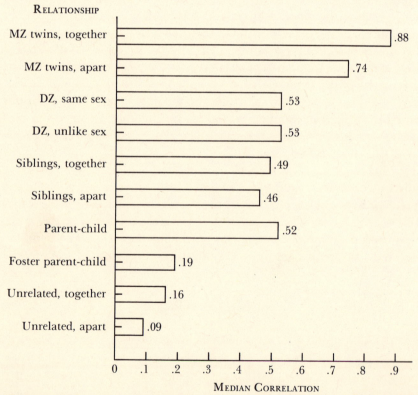

Figure 5. IQ correlations for various degrees of kinship. (From *The Psychology of Individual and Group Differences* by Lee Willerman. W. H. Freeman and Company. Copyright © 1979. Reprinted by permission.)

correlations are not markedly discrepant even from this oversimplified genetic model. Figure 6 also shows the best-fitting straight line through the data points for persons of various degrees of kinship who were reared together and for persons of varying kinship who were reared apart. The slopes of these lines provide an approximate estimate of the

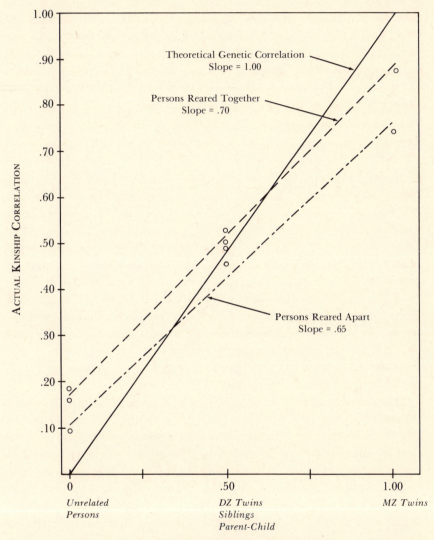

Figure 6. Actual kinship correlations (from various studies), of kins reared together and reared apart, plotted as a function of the theoretical genetic correlation for each kinship.

proportion of genetic variance in the trait. The one best-fitting line (not shown in Figure 6) through all of the data points has a slope of .69, which indicates that about 69 percent of the total IQ variance is attributable to genetic factors and the remaining 31 percent to environment and errors of measurement.

By analyzing the pattern of differences among the correlations for the various relationships, it is possible to get an idea of how we can estimate the relative contributions of genetic and environmental factors. This has been done by numerous investigators using many different sets of kinship data.

We can gain some idea of how these estimates of the relative effects of heredity and environment are obtained by looking more closely at the correlations for specific relationships.

MZ Twins Reared Together

Let us begin with the closest degree of relationship: MZ twins reared together. Because MZ twins have exactly the same genetic makeup, the genetic correlation between them must be perfect, that is, a correlation of 1. The fact that their IQs correlate only .88 means that some nongenetic factors have caused them to show less than perfect resemblance in IQ. What would these nongenetic factors be that account for $1 - .88 = .12$, or 12 percent of the total variance?

First off, there is measurement error, that is, unreliability of the IQ scores. As explained in Chapter 1, test scores, like all other measurements, do not have perfect reliability. The best IQ tests generally have about 5 percent error variance. So we can right away eliminate that from the 12 percent nongenetic variance, leaving 7 percent of the IQ variance that needs to be accounted for.

How do we account for this 7 percent? It can't be due to genetic differences, since MZ twins are genetically identical. Also, it can't be due to those aspects of the environment that the twins share in common by virtue of being reared together. Since they are reared together, many aspects of their total environments will be the same for both twins. These environmental influences that are the same for both twins when they are reared together are referred to as the common environment, or CE. Those environmental influences that are different for each member of a twin pair are referred to as the specific environment, or SE. In other words, even MZ twins reared together do not experience identical environments. The genetic factors in the mental development of a pair of MZ twins are of course exactly the same for both twins.

The CE of children reared together consists largely of such things as the fact that the children are brought up by the same parents, who treat them much alike in many ways, speak the same language to them with the same vocabulary, read the same bedtime stories to them, provide the same meals, and so on. Moreover, children reared together share many experiences. They watch many of the same television programs together, go to the same shows, visit other relatives together and have Sunday outings and holidays together, take trips together, play with the same toys, look at the same books and magazines, and attend the same classes at school. They often come down with common childhood illnesses at the same time and stay home from school on the same days. Twins are frequently dressed alike.

What does the specific environment of each twin consist of? The SE results from the fact that twins (or any other children reared together) do not share all of their experiences in common. Accidents and illnesses often befall one but not the other. They may take up different interests or hobbies which afford different experiences. Their parents may try to treat their twins somewhat differently in order to bring out and emphasize whatever little individuality they may show. It is also likely that some part of the specific environment is prenatal. MZ twins are not always situated equally advantageously in the womb. One is sometimes more "crowded" than the other, or gets less than an equal share of oxygen and nutrients from the placenta. Twins are also slightly more liable to birth injuries and brain damage than are single fetuses, and in some cases one twin is stillborn while the other survives. These prenatal environmental inequalities often show up as rather marked differences in the size, appearance, and birth weights of MZ twins—differences that are largely overcome in the subsequent course of development, which is strongly influenced by the MZ twins' common genes.

All of these specific environmental influences cause MZ twins to be slightly different in IQ to the extent of about 7 percent of the total IQ variance. Thus, a simple analysis of these findings would look like this:

Source of IQ Variance	% of Variance
Common genes } Common environment }	88
Specific environment	7
Measurement error	5
Total variance	100

Notice that the sources of variance that are *common* to both twins (that is, common genes and common environment) are what add up to the

88 percent of the total IQ variance the twins have in common. This percentage is the same (when expressed as a proportion) as the correlation between the twins. In other words, the correlation expresses the proportion of the total IQ variance the twins have in common.

Another way of expressing this is in terms of the average of the IQ differences found between the two members of many sets of MZ twins who were reared together. The average IQ difference between MZ twins reared together amounts to about 6 IQ points. But some of this difference is due to measurement error. When error is properly taken into account, the average IQ difference between MZ twins is only about 4½ IQ points—a quite small difference. All of that difference of 4½ IQ points is attributed to SE effects, those specific environmental influences that are not shared by both twins. This figure can be compared with the average difference in IQs between pairs of unrelated persons who were not reared together, that is, persons picked at random from the general population, for whom the average difference in IQs is about 16 IQ points (not including measurement error). Obviously, having exactly the same genes and being reared together results in a much greater similarity in IQs than being unrelated and reared apart.

But how much of the IQ resemblance, as indicated by the average correlation of .88, between MZ twins reared together, is attributable to their common genes and how much to their common environment? Is there any way we can tease apart these two causes of the correlation? One way is to look at MZ twins reared apart.

MZ Twins Reared Apart

MZ twins who have been separated shortly after birth and reared in different families have always been of great interest to geneticists. Such MZ twins, of course, have identical genes, but do not share a common environment, except prenatally. Since they are reared apart in different families, they presumably do not share a common environment. For the moment we will assume this is true, just to keep the argument from getting too complicated too quickly, even though we know that the environments of separated twins are not quite so different as the environments of persons picked entirely at random from the general population. When twins are separated in infancy, they usually are not placed in extremely differing environments, although there are notable exceptions. Usually twins are separated because their mother died during or shortly after giving birth, or became too ill to care for them. The separated twins are often placed in different foster homes by an adoption agency, which sees to it that both homes can provide a wholesome environment with caring foster parents, even though there is no attempt to match the two foster homes in specific characteristics. Some separated twins are reared by different branches of the same family, such as different aunts and uncles or grandparents, who would provide environmental conditions that are not as different from one another as the differences between homes picked entirely at random. Despite this limitation, the study of MZ twins reared apart is valuable, since no one would argue that they share anywhere near as much common environment as MZ twins or other children who are reared together by the same parents in the same home.

We see from Figure 5 that MZ twins reared apart show an average IQ correlation of .74. This correlation is based on a total of 69 pairs of separated MZ twins in three independent studies.

A simple analysis of these data would look like this:

Source of IQ Variance	% of Variance
Common genes	74
Common environment	0
Specific environment	21
Measurement error	5
Total variance	100

Now we can compare this analysis with the previous analysis for MZ twins reared together. The difference between 88 and 74 indicates how much of the correlation of .88 between MZ twins reared together is due to common environments. It is 14 percent. Thus, by knowing the correlations for MZ twins reared together and for MZ twins reared apart, we have been able to analyze the total IQ variance into four components:

Source of IQ Variance	% of Variance
Common genes	74
Common environment	14
Specific environment	7
Measurement error	5
Total variance	100

The average difference in IQs between separated MZ twins (not including measurement error) is about 8 IQ points, as compared with the difference of about 4½ IQ points between MZ twins reared together. MZ twins reared apart, who are assumed to have nothing in common but their genes, differ on the average by only 8 IQ points, as

compared with the average difference of about 16 points between unrelated persons who have neither genes nor environment in common.

Clearly, in terms of this particular analysis, genetic factors markedly outweigh environmental sources of IQ variance. Notice that the
correlation between MZ twins reared apart is a direct indicator of the
proportion of genetic variance, that is, .74 or 74 percent. However,
this can be regarded as an accurate estimate of the amount of genetic
variance only to the extent that there is zero correlation between the
environments of the separated twins. A zero correlation would mean
that the difference between the environments of the separated twins of
each pair is no less, on the average, than the differences between the
environments of pairs of persons picked entirely at random. As studies
of the environments of separated twins show that there is some correlation between the environments of separated twins, the value of .74 is
apt to be inflated by some unknown amount. Some part of the separated twins' correlation could be due to some similarity in their environments, as might be expected, for example, if they were reared by
different relatives, say, one by an aunt and one by a grandmother.

Therefore we need to look at still other ways of estimating the
relative effects of genes and environment on IQ, to see if the results are
very discrepant from the analyses of MZ twins reared together and
apart.

Comparison of MZ and DZ Twins

Dizygotic or two-egg twins, also known as fraternal twins, have
also played an important role in genetical analyses, mainly through
comparison with MZ twins. DZ twins have only about one-half of
their segregating genes in common. (Segregating genes are those genes
which contribute to genetic differences among persons. There are
many more nonsegregating genes which are the same in all humans
and therefore do not contribute to genetic variation within the human
species.) Thus DZ twins are genetically just like ordinary siblings. As
in the case or ordinary siblings, approximately one-half of all DZ twin
pairs are of the same sex and half are not.

Nearly all of the DZ twins studied so far have been pairs reared
together. It is instructive to compare the IQ correlation of DZ twins
reared together with the IQ correlation of MZ twins reared together.
Both types of twins share a common environment to about the same
degree, but DZ twins have only half of their genes in common,

whereas MZ twins have all of their genes in common. The genes that DZ twins have in common are called, not surprisingly, common genes (CG) and the genes that are different in each DZ twin are called specific genes (SG). Let us do a comparative analysis of MZ and DZ twins side by side, as follows:

	% of Variance	
Source of Variance	MZ Twins	DZ Twins
Common genes }	88	53
Common environment		
Specific genes }	0	42
Specific environment	7	
Measurement error	5	5
Total variance	100	100

The correlation of .53 between DZ twins is due to common genes plus common environment. Specific genes and specific environment together contribute 42 percent of the DZ variance. Now, if we assume that DZ twins reared together share as much common environment as MZ twins reared together, then by subtracting the DZ correlation of .53 from the MZ correlation of .88, we can get rid of the proportion of IQ variance due to common environment. The remainder, of course, must be one-half of the proportion of IQ variance due to common genes, which is $.88 - .53 = .35$. Recall that the correlation between twins is due to their common genes and their common environment, and that MZ twins have all of their genes in common, whereas DZ twins have only half of their genes in common. Thus the logic of this subtraction can be understood as follows:

Twin Type	Common Genes	Common Environment
MZ twins together	G	CE
DZ twins together	½ G	CE
Difference	½ G	0

The difference between the MZ and DZ correlations, then, is equal to ½ G, that is, one-half of the genetic variance. An estimate of the proportion of genetic variance in IQ, therefore, is obtained by *twice* the difference between the MZ and DZ correlations, which is $2(.88 - .53) = .70$. This value is in fairly close agreement with the value of .74 obtained for MZ twins reared apart.

How reasonable is the assumption that the environment is as similar for DZ twins who are reared together as for MZ twins reared together? We know that MZ twins are more often dressed alike than

DZ twins, and MZ twins may be treated more alike because they look and act more alike in many ways. This could conceivably make them more alike in IQ. Studies have clearly shown, however, that DZ twins who were mistakenly thought by their parents to be MZ twins are no more alike in IQ than DZ twins who were not mistaken for MZ twins. On the other hand, parents tend to treat their male and female children differently. Yet we notice that unlike-sex DZ twins show the same IQ correlation (.53) as same-sex DZ twins. The different experiences of boy and girl twins do not produce a greater IQ difference.

In any case, it would be difficult to argue that MZ twins reared apart experience more similar environments than DZ twins reared together, and yet the average correlation between MZ twins apart is .74 as compared with .53 for DZ together. The average IQ difference between MZ twins reared apart is only about 8 IQ points, as compared with the average difference of about 11 IQ points between DZ twins reared together (excluding measurement error). This fact leaves little doubt of the predominance of genetic over environmental factors in the determination of IQ.

Siblings

Ordinary siblings, who differ in age, are less likely to have as much common environment as DZ twins who are born together and reared together. Yet siblings, remember, have the same degree of genetic resemblance as DZ twins. The average correlation between sibling IQs is .49—not much lower than that of .53 for DZ twins.

We can obtain still another estimate of genetic variance by comparing ordinary siblings with genetically unrelated children (foster or adopted children) who have been reared as siblings. The IQs of unrelated children reared together show an average correlation of .16. Here's the analysis of siblings and unrelated children:

	% of Variance	
Source of Variance	Siblings	Unrelated
Common genes	49	0
Common environment		16
Specific genes	46	79
Specific environment		
Measurement error	5	5
Total variance	100	100

The logic of subtracting the unrelated children's correlation (.16) from the sibling correlation (.49) can be understood as follows:

Relationship	Common Genes	Common Environment
Siblings together	½ G	CE
Unrelated together	0 G	CE
Difference	½ G	0

Thus, the difference between the IQ correlations for natural siblings reared together and unrelated children reared together estimates half the genetic variance, so twice the difference estimates the total proportion of genetic variance, which in this case is $2(.49 - .16) = .66$. This value is lower than our previous estimates of .74 and .70. The most likely reason for the lower value is that unrelated children who are reared together are usually adopted children, and adoption agencies tend to favor "selective placement," matching the characteristics of the adopted child with those of the adoptive parents and of the other children in the family. For example, a baby born to a college girl and given up for adoption is more apt to be placed with adoptive parents who are college-educated. Such selective placement slightly increases the correlation between unrelated children reared together, and between adopted children and adoptive parents, over what could be attributed to common environment alone. So the value of .66 in this case probably underestimates the true proportion of genetic variance in IQ.

Parent-Child and Foster Parent–Foster Child

The average correlation between the IQs of parent and child is .52. Foster children or adopted children correlate only .19 with their adoptive parents, or even less when they are older. The proportion of genetic variance can be estimated by twice the difference between the true parent-child correlation and the foster parent-child correlation, which is $2(.52 - .19) = .66$. This is the same value as was obtained from comparison of siblings and unrelated children reared together. It probably underestimates the true proportion of genetic variance in IQ, for the same reason—selective placement by adoption agencies.

The IQs of adopted children show a significantly higher correlation with the IQs of their biological mothers, with whom they have had no social contact, than with their adoptive mothers or fathers. Studies of this correlation, however, are much less adequate than for other kinships. The largest, most recent, and technically most adequate study, the Texas Adoption Project, shows a correlation of .32 between the IQs of adopted children and their biological mothers' IQs. (Twice that correlation estimates the proportion of genetic variance = .64.) These same children show a correlation of only .15 with their adoptive mothers' IQs and of only .09 with that of their adoptive fathers'.

Finally, we should compare the correlation of unrelated children reared together (.16), who share only a common environment, with the correlation of MZ twins reared together (.88), who share a common environment as well as all of their genes. The difference between the two correlations estimates the proportion of genetic variance, which is .88 − .16 = .72.

Estimates of genetic variance differ slightly, depending on the age of the children involved in a particular study. Younger children's IQs reflect somewhat less genetic variance. As children mature and approach adolescence, their IQs increasingly reflect their genetic inheritance. Adopted children who have never had any contact with their biological parents show an increasing correlation between their IQs and the intelligence levels of their biological mothers as the children grow from infancy to late adolescence. It takes time for maturation to allow the individual's genotype to reach its full expression in the phenotype.

Heritability of Intelligence

The foregoing comparisons of the IQ correlations for various degrees of kinship, and whether children were reared in the same or different homes, are simple examples of how it is possible to get some idea of the relative influences of genes and environment on the development of intelligence. Differences among persons for a given trait measurement, like IQ, are quantitatively expressed as variance. In statistics and quantitative genetics, the variance expresses the total amount of variation—that is, individual differences—among persons in a defined population. Each kinship comparison that we looked at yielded an estimate of the proportion of the total IQ variance attributable to genetic factors.

Geneticists refer to the proportion of the total phenotypic variance that is attributable to variance in genotypes as the heritability of the trait. It is symbolized as h^2. Thus,

$$h^2 = V_G / V_P,$$

where V_G is variance in genotypes and V_P is variance in phenotypes, that is, the actual measurements of the trait, such as height, or IQ.

The various kinship correlations that we have just examined yielded values of h^2 of .74, .70, .66, .66, .64, and .72, giving an average h^2 of .69. This value comes very close to the values of h^2 estimated by more elaborate methods of quantitative genetics applied to essentially the same data. An average value of h^2 based on many different kinship comparisons is preferable to any single estimate of h^2, because, as was pointed out, any particular kinship correlation contains certain biases that will result in either an overestimate or an underestimate of h^2. For example, the correlation between MZ twins reared apart tends to slightly overestimate h^2, because although the MZ twins are reared separately, their environments are not as dissimilar as the environments of persons picked entirely at random from the population. And the correlation between unrelated adopted children slightly underestimates h^2 because of selective placement of adopted children, which results in those who are placed in the same home being slightly more alike genetically than persons picked entirely at random from the general population. Thus the biases that affect h^2 when it is determined from any given type of kinship correlations tend to cancel out when we average a number of estimates of h^2, each based on different types of kinship correlations.

Modern methods of biometrical genetics, however, do not obtain estimates of heritability in the simple way that I have just illustrated. Instead of obtaining a number of estimates of h^2 from each of a number of different kinship comparisons, and then averaging the different estimates of h^2, modern methods of analysis—made feasible by electronic computers—analyze all of the various kinship correlations simultaneously to get the most accurate overall estimate of h^2 that can be obtained from all of the data. This more elaborate methodology also takes into account the effects of dominance, assortative mating, and the correlation between genotypes and environments—all of which we have ignored in our simple calculations but which have different effects on different kinship correlations. If we had taken these other factors into account, there would be a greater uniformity of the estimates of h^2, although the average would still be very close to our estimate of .69.

When modern methods of biometrical genetics have been used for the analysis of a number of different kinships, the estimates of IQ heritability have ranged mostly between about .60 and .80, with a central tendency around .70. The variation in h^2 is due to a number of factors: (1) different sets of kinship data obtained in different populations, (2) a variety of mental tests that do not all have the same reliability, factorial composition, or heritability, and (3) differences in methods of estimating h^2 from the data, some methods taking more elaborate refinements into account, while others strive for the simplest genetic analysis that will explain the distinctive pattern of kinship correlations within the limits of statistical error.

There is a great deal of agreement among scientists regarding the heritability of intelligence. The experts are not concerned with arguing about any particular estimated value of h^2 within the whole range of most empirical studies, that is, between about .50 and .80. They all recognize the reasons for the variations in estimates of h^2 from one study to another. They are, however, generally in agreement concerning the very substantial heritability of intelligence and IQ.

Let's look at some fairly recent quotations from authoritative sources. A good place to begin is the latest edition of the *Encyclopaedia Britannica* (1975, Vol. 8, p. 1148):

> Concerning the extent of genetic determination in human intelligence, most investigations have yielded heritability estimates between 70–80 percent. Since such values are relative to the population studied and to the method of estimation, some disagreement should be expected. It seems most unlikely, however, that genotype contributes less than 50 percent of the variability and it is conceivable that the figure is close to 80 percent.

I have gotten a number of textbooks of genetics and psychology off the library shelf—books selected mainly for their recency or the prominence of their authors in the fields of genetics and psychology. What do these authors have to say about the heritability of intelligence? First, quotations from a number of geneticists.

> That the heritability [of intelligence] is large is a justifiable conclusion at this stage, although the precise value must remain in doubt for the various reasons given.—James F. Crow (1969)

> That differences between individuals in whatever qualities the IQ tests measure are genetically as well as environmentally conditioned is now securely established.—Theodosius Dobzhansky (1973)

> Gradually, however, it has been established that both genetic and environmental factors are responsible for the observed variance in normal, measured intelligence.—Curt Stern (1973)

> But in spite of . . . individual criticisms, the mountain of evidence taken together creates a generalization that no longer seems escapable: in and near the operational environment of the white middle-class culture, IQ has a strong underlying genetic component.—I. Michael Lerner and William J. Libby (1976)

The twin and other studies that we have discussed suggested a fairly high heritability for IQ. . . . All the data are consistent with a large heritable component for IQ.—L. L. Cavalli-Sforza and Walter F. Bodmer (1971)

This brief summary should demonstrate that, although much remains to be learned, there already exists a robust body of knowledge about the inheritance of intellectual abilities . . . the heritability of intelligence is very substantial and . . . assortative mating for various measures of intellectual functioning is high.—Gerald E. McClearn and John C. De Fries (1973)

The relation of intelligence testing to genetic analysis has immediate consequences. The two, of course, agree in showing, apart from exceptional and extreme situations, the primacy and preponderance of heredity in determining mental differences between individuals and communities.—Cyril D. Darlington (1978)

Here is what a number of well-known behavioral geneticists and psychologists writing textbooks on general psychology, intelligence, and individual differences have to say about the heritability of intelligence.

The heritability of IQ test scores is in fact very high . . . in the neighborhood of 80 percent.—Irving I. Gottesman (1972)

Taken as a whole, genetic influences on general intelligence appear quite substantial.—Lee Willerman (1979)

It would seem that all studies based on reasonably reliable data and fair-sized samples concur in indicating substantial genetic variance of at least 60 percent underlying individual differences in phenotypic IQ.—Philip E. Vernon (1979)

The data . . . permit two simple and unemotional conclusions: First, score on an intelligence test shows an impressive hereditary component. Second, the correlations of less than unity for monozygotic twins, and the small but positive correlations for pairs of unrelated persons living together, constitute equally impressive evidence that factors (environmental) other than genetic also influence scores on tests of intelligence.—Joseph D. Matarazzo (1972)

The fact that heritability of ability is substantial says only that the differences in individual oppportunity and environment among white American homes and schools of the past two generations have not been large enough to be the *chief* influence on standings in ability.—Lee J. Cronbach (1977)

Within populations of European origin, both the genotype and the environment demonstrably influence IQ, the former tending under present conditions to account for more of the individual variation in IQ than does the latter.—John C. Loehlin, Gardner Lindzey, and John M. Spuhler (1975)

The general conclusion to be drawn from all such information, to which there is considerable agreement, is that both heredity and environment contribute conditions determining the general intellectual status of individuals, as measured by intelligence tests.—J. P. Guilford (1967)

Clearly, genetic factors outweigh environmental factors in causing the wide range of intellectual ability found in human populations.—H. J. Eysenck (1979)

The general opinion of most authorities . . . seems to be that a substantial degree of genetic determination of measured intelligence can hardly be denied.—H. J. Butcher (1970)

There is very strong evidence that "normal" variation in intelligence as well as the more severe disorders such as phenylketonuria, are subject to hereditary influences. Intelligence is not inherited like money from a rich uncle, but IQ scores are strongly influenced by heredity.—Harry F. Harlow, James L. McGaugh, and Richard F. Thompson (1971)

With such general agreement among scientists, it is all the more amazing how the popular media have so often promoted the notion that the genetic inheritance of intelligence is a highly controversial issue. This is not to say that there are not a few dissenters who claim that genetics has nothing to do with IQ differences. But they are an extreme minority, as are those few who even today refuse to acknowledge the overwhelming evidence for biological evolution. Usually the substantive basis for their dissenting claims is fallacious or trivial, or will not otherwise stand up under critical scrutiny. Nevertheless the doubting Thomases occasionally serve a legitimate scientific purpose by pointing out formerly overlooked weaknesses in generally accepted data, exposing inadequately supported conclusions, or noting improper methods of analysis in some uncritically or prematurely accepted finding. There has never been perfect unanimity of opinion on *any* scientific issue. But that fact does not contradict the consensus of the vast majority of those scientists who base their conclusions on the preponderance of the evidence.

In reviewing the several most recent kinship studies, two behavioral geneticists at the University of Colorado have indicated a discrepancy between older and newer data. The most recent studies show higher correlations, by about .10, for DZ twins, which, when used with the correlation of .86 for MZ twins to estimate heritability, yield a lower value of h^2, closer to .50 than the older data's estimate of about .70. Other recently reported kinship correlations (nontwin siblings, parent-offspring) also differ from older studies in such a way as to yield estimates of h^2 closer to .50 or .60 than to .70. The Colorado investigators state, "Although we conclude that the new mental test data point to less genetic influences on IQ than do the older data, the new data nonetheless implicate genes as the major systematic force influencing the development of individual differences in IQ. In fact, we know of no specific environmental influences nor combinations of them that account for as much as 10 percent of the variance in IQ" (R. Plomin and J. C. Defries, "Genetics and Intelligence: Recent Data," *Intelligence* 4 [1980]: 15–24).

The discrepancy between the older and newer data is not yet understood and seems to have nothing to do with the quality or quantity of the data or the methods of analysis, although the newer data have not been subjected to as thorough biometrical genetical analysis as the data of older studies, about which there is now considerable agreement and which I have presented in the preceding paragraphs. The more recent data's DZ twin correlations of .62 and nontwin sibling correlation of .34 (as compared with the older studies' average correlations of .53 and .49, respectively) seem rather puzzling and anomalous. Although these new findings are not yet well understood, fortunately there are currently a number of large-scale kinship studies in progress, which should clarify the picture within the next several years.

Heritability of Intelligence versus Heritability of IQ

In discussing heritability, is there any point in drawing a distinction between the heritability of intelligence and the heritability of IQ scores? All studies of heritability are based on IQs or scores from similar tests of cognitive ability. IQs, or scores on any particular test, however, are only imperfect measures of intelligence. For one thing, tests do not have perfect reliability. In even the best tests, measurement error constitutes at least 5 percent of the test score variance, and it is usually closer to 10 percent. Also, any one test usually measures, to some extent, other factors more or less peculiar to the particular test, in addition to the general intelligence factor, *g,* which is common to all complex mental tests. There is good reason to believe that *g* is more highly heritable than the small specific factors peculiar to each different type of mental test. Then, too, children's IQs and other test scores fluctuate somewhat from year to year between early childhood and adolescence, whereas the individual's genotype for general intelligence does not fluctuate. These three sources of contamination in single test scores—measurement error, factorial impurity, and year-to-year fluctuation of test scores during childhood—can be taken into account statistically. When this statistical correction is performed, it raises the estimates of IQ heritability by at least 10 percent above what it is when the heritability estimate is based on a single IQ test given to individuals on a single occasion. If what we are mainly interested in is not just a particular IQ score, but the general mental ability that a person manifests over an extended period, the genetic part of the variance of that ability in the population is considerably greater than the environmental part.

Misconceptions about Heritability

Immutability of Trait

Probably the most common misconception about the heritability of IQ is that high heritability ensures immutability of IQ. This is false. High heritability of a trait does not necessarily make it unchangeable through environmental means—in individuals or in populations. On the other hand, the misconception that high heritability implies immutability has been so much warned against in recent textbooks as to leave the equally false impression that the heritability of a trait has no bearing whatever on its mutability by manipulation of the existing environment. So just what, in fact, does heritability imply about the susceptibility of a trait to environmental change?

Consider what heritability essentially indicates with respect to a trait. It indicates that proportion of the individual variation ("variance") in the trait that is caused by variation in individuals' genotypes. Since an individual's genotype is determined at the moment of conception and is not susceptible to environmental manipulation, the genotypic determinants of IQ are, for all practical purposes, immutable. So-called genetic surgery, which aims to directly alter single genes, is still in its infancy and is virtually out of the question for polygenic traits like intelligence. The individual variation that is contributed by the environment is the complement of the heritability, minus error variance; this is the environmental variance. For example, if the heritability of IQ is .70, and if there is .05 variance due to measurement error, the proportion of environmental variance then will be $1 - .70 - .05 = .25$. The environmental variance is that part of the variation among individuals' IQs that is caused by variations in all of the environmental influences that affect IQ to which they have been subjected throughout their development.

But now we must take a closer look at this environmental variance. Many geneticists prefer to call it nongenetic variance, because the term "environment" ordinarily has a narrower connotation than it requires in this context. People tend to think of "environment" as only the cultural and social surroundings a child is brought up in—the socioeconomic status of the child's family, the educational level of the parents, the number of books in the home, and the like. But the nongenetic variance actually includes all sources of variance not contributed by the genes, and this includes much more. What we ordinarily think of as an individual's environment is like the tip of an iceberg. The sum total of the environmental effects that go to make up the nongenetic portion of the IQ variance is largely unseen.

First of all, these nongenetic effects begin in the womb. The mother's age, health, smoking and drinking habits, nutrition, and number of previous pregnancies are a few of the many prenatal environmental factors. Perinatal factors—the circumstances surrounding the birth process—and the child's entire health history from birth on, the number of older and younger siblings in the home, and innumerable other factors, all contribute to the environmental variance. Any one of these influences may, on the average, contribute only a minute fraction to the total environmental variance. Hence they have been termed microenvironmental factors. But there are so many of these small influences that altogether they constitute a sizable proportion of the environmental variance. Because these microenvironmental influences are each so small and yet together so numerous, they are extremely difficult, if not impossible, to bring under our control. Yet widespread improvements in general nutrition and health care during the past century have had generally beneficial effects on children's growth rates, physical stature, and mental development. Because virtually everyone in the entire population has benefited about equally from these improved conditions, however, they have produced a rise in the overall population average on these physical and mental traits while scarcely affecting variation among individuals.

We can speak of these kinds of environmental conditions that affect nearly everyone about equally as the average environment. But the average environment does not show up in a heritability analysis, because it does not constitute any part of what we refer to as the environmental variance. In any given heritability analysis, the environmental variance is the result of the deviations of every individual's environment from the average environment in the population at that time. Thus the environmental variance—which is about 25 percent in the case of IQ—reflects only those environmental deviations from the population's average environment that are actually manifest in the population. The analysis does not and cannot tell us anything at all about potential but presently nonexistent causes of environmental variance in IQ (or any other trait). Even if the heritability of IQ were 100 percent, theoretically we might discover some entirely new factor—call it Factor X—which when introduced into a person's environment would raise his IQ by, say, 30 points. If we gave Factor X to some people but not to others, we would thereby create new environmental variance, and a proper heritability analysis would show that the IQ no longer had 100 percent heritability. Some of the total variance in IQs would then be attributable to the new Factor X, which now is a source of environmental variance. Factor X contributes to environmental variance only because some people in the population enjoy the benefit of Factor X, and therefore deviate positively from the average of all the environmental factors that actually affect IQ, while other people are deprived of Factor X and therefore deviate negatively from this average. But if now we give Factor X to everybody in the population and thereby raise everyone's IQ by 30 points, then no one will deviate from the average environment that affects IQ and the heritability of IQ will again be 100 percent.

In brief, the nongenetic or environmental variance reflects only those actually present environmental differences that affect IQ among persons in a specified population. Not all kinds of environmental differences will affect IQ, and of course those that don't are not reflected in the heritability analysis or the environmental variance. Differences in people's dietary habits are certainly an environmental difference, but such environmental variation in the United States is quite insignificant as far as the IQ is concerned, assuming that the dietary variation does not include malnutrition (see Chapter 5).

Thus, heritability analysis of IQ does not reflect the effect of the overall average quality of the environment. It can reflect only those environmental effects that are deviations from the average environment.

Knowing the heritability of IQ tells us absolutely nothing about as yet nonexistent environmental factors—biological or psychological—that might conceivably alter the IQ but that do not currently contribute to the variance of IQ.

Given the environmental factors that do, in fact, contribute to the 25 percent environmental variance in IQ, how much room does that give us for changing IQ by environmental means?

Assuming that we could identify and control all of the environmental factors that are responsible for the 25 percent nonheritable variance in IQ—a very unrealistic assumption indeed—we could make some fairly dramatic changes in people's IQs. If we could take the 20 percent of the population who experienced the least favorable environments for the development of intelligence, and give them instead the environments of the 20 percent of the population who grew up in the most favorable environments, their average IQs would be about 20 points higher. And if we could force the 20 percent of the population with the best environments to grow up instead in the worst environments, their IQs would be about 20 points lower. This calculation assumes that there is no correlation between people's genotypes for intelligence and their environmental conditions. If poorer genotypes for intelligence tend to occur more frequently in poorer environments for intellectual development, then moving the persons found in the worst environments to the best environments will not produce as large a gain in IQ. For the same reason, moving the people in the best environments to the worst would not produce so large a loss in their IQs.

We can appreciate the predominance of genes over environment in determining IQ variation by hypothetically giving to the 20 percent of the persons with the poorest genotypes for the development of IQ the genotypes of the 20 percent who are most favorably endowed. This would raise their IQs by an average of about 35 points—or about 75 percent more than the analogous environmental manipulation.

What if, by some magical stroke, we could completely wipe out all types of environmental variations that contribute to differences in people's IQs? Everyone would then have developed in whatever was the average environment. To what extent would this complete elimination of environmental variance make people's IQs more alike? In terms of averages, everyone with an IQ of, say, 80 would increase up to about 83, and everyone with an IQ of 120 would decline to about 117. In short, the difference between the two groups' IQs would be reduced only about 6 points. Such equalization of the environment for everyone thus would not greatly reduce individual differences in intelligence.

This hypothetical deduction is consistent with the finding that an assortment of children who are reared from infancy under quite uniform conditions still show as much individual differences in IQs as children picked at random from the general population. It would be hard to imagine how society could feasibly bring up children in more highly similar environmental conditions than those found in an orphanage or an Israeli kibbutz, where children are reared communally. Yet the variance of IQ in orphanages and kibbutzim is not appreciably different from what it is in the general population. Genetically unrelated children who are reared in the same home together from infancy differ, on the average, by about 15 IQ points (not including measurement error), which is barely less than the average difference between children picked at random from different homes.

Clearly, merely reallocating children to different macroenvironments among those already in existence would not have very marked effects on their IQs. Differences in the existing macroenvironments just don't make all that much difference in IQs. It is mostly differences in genotypes that make for IQ differences, along with a host of inadvertent microenvironmental factors which operate even within environments that are made as uniformly alike for children as would seem humanly possible.

Individual versus Population

It is often claimed that the genetic and environmental factors that shape the phenotype are so inextricably united as to make it completely impossible to determine their relative importance. This misconception arises from confusing two distinct things: (1) the development of a trait in a single individual and (2) differences in the trait among various individuals, measured as the variance.

To be sure, no individual develops any characteristic without some biological substrate traceable to genetic inheritance. And no individual develops without an environment. The very existence of an organism depends on both heredity and environment, without which there would simply be no organism. In this truistic sense, heredity and environment are indeed inextricable and both are equally important. Intelligence, like any other physical or behavioral characteristic of the individual, develops in a biological substrate through the individual's interaction with the physical and social environment.

But that is a quite different point from the question that heritability analysis attempts to answer. It is concerned not with how a trait develops in an individual, but with how much of the observed variation among individuals is a result of variation in their genotypes and how much is a result of variation in the nongenetic factors that have influenced the development of the trait. As we have seen in the preceding sections, the methods of quantitative genetics can give us an answer to this question. Trouble arises only when the answer and its inherent logical limitations are not properly understood.

Heritability is often said to be a population concept, without any relevance to individuals. This is both true and false. It is true only in three ways.

1. There is no way to determine the heritability of a trait from the study of a single individual.

2. Heritability is expressed in terms of variance—that is, differences between individuals—and these differences are expressed in terms of individuals' deviations from the mean or average of some specified population of which they are members. In practice, of course, we study just a sample drawn from some population. But the methods of statistical inference, if rigorously followed, permit us to generalize our conclusions from the sample to the population, with some specified probability of error.

3. The estimated heritability of a trait is dependent on certain characteristics of the population in which it is determined: (1) the amount of genetic diversity in the population and (2) the diversity of relevant environmental influences with respect to the trait in question. For example, a population in which there is very little environmental variation of the kinds relevant to mental development would show less total variation in IQ, but the heritability of IQ would be higher than it could be in the same population if there were increased environmental diversity. In other words, as the environmental conditions affecting IQ become more equal for everyone in the population, the remaining IQ variation, although it is less, is more a result of genetic differences. Thus, very high heritability does not necessarily mean that the trait in question is not susceptible to environmental influences. It could mean that there is very little variation among persons in the population in the environmental factors that influence the trait. These factors, then, will affect the average level of the trait in the population, but will not contribute much to the variance of the trait in the population, which will be largely genetic.

A good example of this is height. The known nutritional factors that can affect height are now so equally available to virtually everyone in industrially developed countries that very little of the variation in height is attributable to nutritional differences. The heritability of height has been determined to be about .95; that is, 95 percent of the variance in height is due to genetic variation. Weight, on the other hand, is much more sensitive to differences in dietary intake and other living habits. The heritability of weight is only about .75.

Now, the fact that heritability cannot be determined or interpreted without reference to a population should not be misconstrued to imply that it has no relevance to individuals. The logic of heritability analysis permits us to conceptualize an individual's phenotypic deviation (P) from the population's average phenotypic value as having two components: (1) the individual's genetic deviation (G) from the population's average genetic value and (2) the individual's environmental deviation (E) from the population's average environmental value. Thus, the individual's phenotypic deviation can be conceptualized as $P = G + E$. In the case of IQ, the value of G in this formula can be thought of as the average deviation from the population mean of IQ 100 of all individuals with a given genotype under all of the environmental conditions that exist in the population. In other words, G is the average effect, in all existing environments, of a particular genotype on IQ.

The full range of phenotypic values in the population corresponding to a given genotype is termed the reaction range of the genotype. The reaction range may differ for various genotypes; that is, the phenotypic expression of some genotypes may be more sensitive to environmental influences than others.

Similarly, the value of E in the formula $P = G + E$ can be thought of as the average effect of a particular environment on IQ for individuals of all the different genotypes in the population. The fact that we can directly measure only the phenotypic deviation P in any individual and cannot actually measure G or E, however, does not invalidate our conceptual model of the individual phenotypic deviation as being composed of the sum of a genetic deviation and an environmental deviation. We know that for IQ the genetic deviations, on the average, are considerably greater than the environmental deviations, such that the genetic variation in the population contributes about 70 percent of the total IQ variance and the environmental variation contributes about 25 percent, with the residual 5 percent of the variance due to measurement error.

It is theoretically possible to derive an estimate of an individual's genotypic value, if you have his phenotypic measurement and know the mean of the population of which he is a member and the heritability of the trait in that population. In the case of IQ, with a population mean of 100 and a heritability of .70, a person with IQ 130 would have a genotypic deviation of .70(130 − 100) = 21. The person's environmental deviation would be .25(130 − 100) = 7.5. Thus, not including measurement error, the individual's genetic and environmental deviations, plus the population average, add up to the phenotypic value of 128.5. Measurement error contributes the remaining 1.5 IQ points.

But this estimation of a person's genotypic value is merely an exercise in quantitative genetics. While it may have some instructive value theoretically, there is really no practical value in making such calculations. The reason is that there is nothing we could do with the theoretically estimated figures that we could not do just as well with the plain IQ scores. If we made these calculations for many persons, the rank order of the estimated genotypic and environmental values would be exactly the same as the rank order of the actual IQs we started with. The estimated genotypic and environmental values would show exactly the same correlation with any other variables as would the raw IQs themselves, so nothing at all in the way of statistical predictive power would be gained by using estimated genetic or environmental components. Now, if we could really know the true genetic or environmental values of a given individual, rather than just a statistical estimate of them, that would be a different story altogether. These would have predictive power independently of the IQ itself. Also, it should be realized that the estimated genotypic values in this case have a very wide margin of error. Estimated genotypic values are, on the average, only slightly closer to the true genotypic values (which we do not know) than are the IQ scores themselves.

Complications of Heritability Analysis

The picture of heritability analysis as presented thus far is somewhat oversimplified, because I have avoided five potentially complicating factors: assortative mating, dominance, epistasis, genotype-environment correlation, and genotype-environment interaction. They do not make a tremendous difference, but a technically sophisticated analysis must consider them. It is beyond the scope of this chapter to explain just how they are taken into account in heritability analysis. However, I can say enough about each of these factors to give readers some idea about how they can potentially complicate genetic analysis.

Assortative Mating

Positive assortative mating is the tendency for mates to resemble one another in certain characteristics. The degree of resemblance in a given measurable trait is expressed by the correlation between mates, which is referred to as the coefficient of assortative mating.

It so happens that, in our society, assortative mating is higher for intelligence than for any other trait. The average correlation between husbands' and wives' intelligence test scores in all the studies reported in the literature is + .43. Some of these correlations were determined in samples with a fairly restricted range of IQs, like college students, which would lower the average correlation. And of course, measurement error also lowers the correlation. Therefore, I estimate that after correcting for these factors that weaken the correlation coefficient, the true degree of assortative mating for intelligence in our total population is probably best represented by a correlation close to .50. (Height also shows a fair degree of assortative mating—about .30.) This means that husbands and wives are about as much alike in IQ as brothers and sisters. The average difference in IQ between spouses (as between siblings) is about 12 points (excluding meaurement error). In just slightly more than half of married couples, the male has the higher IQ, because men with very low IQs are less likely to marry than are women with a comparably low IQ, and women with very high IQs are less apt to marry than are men with the same high IQ.

Assortative mating in a population has two main effects: (1) it increases the total variance of IQ in the population and (2) it increases kinship correlations. Assortative mating *per se* does not affect the mean IQ of the population. Under the present degree of assortative mating for IQ, the total variance of IQ is some 10 to 15 percent greater than would be the case if the parents of the present generation had not assortatively mated for intelligence. Assortative mating thus favors the stratification of intelligence in the population. The increased genetic variance due to assortative mating is rather easily taken account of in heritability analysis. Assortative mating increases the heritability by increasing the genetic differences between families.

The fact that there is such a high degree of assortative mating for intelligence is of sociological as well as genetic interest. For one thing, it means that people put a higher value on this trait than on almost any other. People are particular about marrying someone whose level of intelligence seems to match their own. They may trade off a certain amount of intelligence, but not *too* much, for other desirable characteristics in their mates—personality, good looks, money, social position, and youth.

Obviously, people do not go around giving IQ tests to their prospective mates, and few tell others their IQ, even if they happen to know what it is. So how does the high degree of assortative mating for intelligence come about? Three main factors are operating.

First, most people have some fairly accurate notion of their own intelligence and can make equally accurate assessments of another person's intelligence on rather short acquaintance. We are especially alerted when we encounter persons who seem very different from ourselves in their general alertness, range of knowledge, understanding of things, developed skills, articulateness, and the like. Persons whom one perceives as intellectually deviating too unfavorably from one's self-estimate are ruled out as prospective mates.

Second, certain social institutions bring together persons of similar intelligence. The educational system is the primary agency in this. By the time children reach high school age they have already been considerably sorted out by intelligence levels. The brightest pupils are seldom in the same classes with the dullest, and the friendships—with others of either sex—that develop in high school already show a good deal of assortment for intelligence. High school dropouts tend to go with other dropouts. Those who do graduate from high school but do not go on to college tend to socialize with each other. Those who go on to college are sorted out even more in terms of scholastic aptitude. The ablest generally get into highly selective colleges where they are thrown together with others like them. And so on—all at the same time that young people are approaching marriageable age. Under these circumstances, a person's circle of acquaintances, from which he is apt to find a marriage partner, will have IQs that fall within a limited range of the total distribution of intelligence in the general population. The job market has a similar effect, bringing together people with more comparable levels of education, ability, competence, and interests. The place of work, like school and college, affords individuals the opportunity to observe and make better assessments of one another's capabilities in ways that might not be manifest in casual social encounters. Among the first things that a young woman wishes to know about a young man she is dating are the extent of his schooling and what kind of work he does. These are inexact but nevertheless fairly good indicators of intelligence level. If the woman is at the age of thinking seriously about marriage, the answer will usually make much more of a difference than anything she could discover about the man on the dance floor or at a cocktail party.

A third factor in assortative mating is much less important in the overall picture, but should be mentioned nonetheless. This is the fact that in middle- and upper-class families there are rather strong sanctions against marriage for persons of low IQ, say, below 80 or thereabouts. Middle-class parents of a child with an IQ markedly below average regard the prospect of his marriage with considerable anxiety, partly because of the more likely unpromising qualities of the marriage partner, whose IQ may not be much different, and partly because of the likelihood of a future burden to the family if there are offspring. Various inducements not to marry are often made, with the result that, in the white middle class, as we move down the IQ scale, the marriage rate declines rapidly below IQ 80 and is practically negligible below IQ 70. Indirectly this has the beneficial effect in each generation of "siphoning off" some of the genes for low intelligence and thereby slightly raising the average IQ of the middle-class segment of the population. Most matings between persons in the low range of IQ generally come from families of low socioeconomic status. Persons with IQs of 60 to 70 do not stand out as conspicuously different in a family or neighborhood where the average IQ is generally low. An incompetent or unemployable couple of low socioeconomic status who cannot support their own children do not threaten a financial burden for their own parents, because they can obtain welfare aid without the compunction or social stigma that would deter most middle-class families. This state of affairs promotes the social stratification of intelligence.

Dominance and Inbreeding Depression

Genetic dominance was referred to earlier as the fact that certain alleles (alternate forms of a gene) at a given locus are dominant over other alleles (termed recessive) at the same locus. A dominant allele combined with a recessive allele at the same locus has the same effect on the trait as two dominant alleles.

Probably some large fraction of the alleles that enhance intelligence are dominant, with the result that some proportion of the variance in IQ is attributable to the increment of intelligence that arises from the combinations of dominant and recessive alleles. These so-called dominance deviations make up the dominance variance. Quantitative genetic analyses estimate the dominance variance to constitute about 15 to 20 percent of the total variance in IQ.

The main effect of dominance is to decrease the correlation between parents and their offspring and between full siblings (including DZ twins). Dominance reduces the parent-offspring correlation slightly more than it reduces the sibling correlation. This fact, which can be explained by genetic theory, provides one means for detecting the presence of genetic dominance. Another means is the fact that the correlation between half-siblings (children with only one parent in common) is reduced by dominance more than is the correlation between full siblings. Without dominance, the correlation between half-siblings should be equal to just half the correlation between full siblings. A half-sibling correlation that is less than half the full-sibling correlation indicates the presence of dominance. For reasons too complicated to explain here, four times the difference between the full-sibling correlation and the half-sibling correlation estimates the proportion of dominance variance.

Probably the most dramatic evidence for the recessiveness of low intelligence is the phenomenon known as inbreeding depression. Everyone possesses recessive alleles at many loci on his chromosomes. When there are two such recessives at the same locus, they detract from the individual's intelligence, or at least they fail to enhance it. But that would involve one's receiving a recessive allele at the given locus from each parent. Fortunately, however, each parent's recessive alleles for any polygenic trait, like intelligence, are scattered more or less at random on the chromosome's loci, so there is little chance that very many of the recessive alleles inherited from one's mother and father will be matched up at the very same loci in one's own chromosomes. More often, at any given locus, a recessive allele inherited from the mother will be paired with a dominant allele inherited from the father, and vice versa. A recessive plus a dominant adds up to the same enhancing effect as having two dominant alleles at that locus. And so it is over many loci.

But if there is inbreeding, that is, mating between a man and a woman who are closely related to one another genetically—such as a brother and a sister, a father and a daughter, or first cousins—then there is a much higher probability that their recessive alleles will be at identical loci because these alleles were inherited by both mates from common ancestors only one or two generations removed. Consequently their offspring will inherit many more unfortunate combinations of two recessive alleles at the same loci than if their parents were genetically unrelated.

When the degree of inbreeding is so close as to be termed incestuous, as between father and daughter or brother and sister, the result can be catastrophic, not only for the offspring's intelligence but for other traits as well. Studies of the offspring from incestuous matings show a markedly increased rate of physical birth defects as well as mental deficiency. Nearly one-third of the offspring from such incestuous matings are too defective, physically or mentally, to be placed for adoption. They are usually cared for in institutions. It is not a surprising fact that a strong taboo against incest has existed in every human society throughout recorded history.

Lesser degrees of inbreeding, as between first cousins or second cousins, also involve some greater-than-ordinary genetic risk. Therefore, in many places the law forbids marriage between cousins. Studies have shown that the offspring of first- and second-cousin matings are somewhat physically smaller and have lower IQs (on the average, about 3 to 4 points lower) than children born to genetically unrelated parents. This remains true even after controlling for such factors related to children's IQ as the parents' social class, education, age, and occupation.

The results of a number of studies of the effects of inbreeding leave little doubt about the existence of recessive alleles for low intelligence and of dominant alleles for superior intelligence. It is a point of interest that according to the genetic theory of evolution, the genes for those traits which confer some advantage for survival in the process of natural selection tend to develop dominance. Thus the evidence for dominance of the alleles that enhance intelligence suggests that human intelligence is a product of our species' biological evolution through natural selection, which generally favored individuals who possessed more of this trait.

Epistasis

When the phenotypic expression of a gene at one locus in one of the individual's chromosomes is modified by a gene occupying a different locus on the same or another chromosome, the effect is known as epistasis. The effects of epistasis are practically indistinguishable from those of dominance, and in most genetic analyses the little variance contributed by epistasis gets thrown in with the dominance variance.

Its effect is to lower all kinship correlations, with the exception of MZ twins. Some geneticists are now beginning to entertain the possibility that epistasis has been underrated in past estimates of IQ heritability and that it may account for some part of the IQ variance we have formerly attributed to environment. Quite large epistatic effects have been found in some species of animals, which can be studied in controlled breeding experiments. But our present human kinship data, without such experimental control, afford virtually no possibility of figuring out the amount of variance in IQ contributed by epistasis.

Genotype-Environment Correlation

There is a correlation between genotypes for mental abilities and the environmental conditions that affect their phenotypic expression. A greater-than-chance number of children with genotypes for superior intelligence are born to parents who can provide a more favorable environment for mental development. And a greater-than-chance number of children with relatively poor genotypes for intelligence grow up in homes that afford little intellectual stimulation. The effect of this so-called genotype-environment (G-E) correlation is to make the bright brighter and the dull duller, thereby increasing the total variance of IQ. It also tends slightly to increase kinship correlations.

Estimates of the percentage of IQ variance accounted for by G-E correlation range from 0 to 20 percent, depending on the particular kinship data analyzed and the method of analysis. Some analyses include the contribution of G-E correlation as part of the genetic variance, and some include it with the environmental variance. Of course, it is not strictly either one or the other. But a certain part of it could justifiably be considered inseparable from the genetic variance, because some part of the G-E correlation is created by the genotype itself. To some extent the genotype fashions its own environment in such a way as to amplify its own phenotypic expression.

To understand this, it is useful to recognize three kinds of genotype-environment correlation, which are now termed passive, reactive, and active.

Passive G-E correlation is completely imposed by circumstances independent of the individual, such as being born into a favorable or unfavorable environment. The child has no control over his parents' socioeconomic status, their education or occupation, or their intelligence. In principle, this type of G-E correlation could be wiped out completely by taking all newborn babies away from their natural parents and randomly redistributing them to foster parents.

Reactive G-E correlation, however, would remain relatively unaffected by this maneuver. Children with different genotypes are treated somewhat differently because of their genotypic difference. A brighter child will stimulate more interaction and more sophisticated conversation from the adults and older children around him, and this in turn acts as "positive feedback" for the child's cognitive development. Parents unconsciously tend to give a brighter child more advanced, complicated, or demanding toys, and ask him to do things they wouldn't think of asking a less capable child. Teachers, too, behave differently toward children depending on their perceived abilities. Dramatic examples of this are to be seen in the cases of some unusually gifted children. Their parents or teachers go all out to cultivate the child's talent, in some cases even to the neglect of the other children in the family. The great cellist Pablo Casals displayed so great a musical gift as a child that his parents made great sacrifices to send him to the best music teachers they could find. And the great mathematician Karl Friedrich Gauss, the son of a bricklayer, was so mathematically precocious as a schoolboy that his amazed schoolteacher enlisted the services of a university student in mathematics to tutor the young Gauss, who while still in his teens was recognized as one of the world's greatest mathematicians.

Thus the social environment reacts differentially to different individuals, partly because of the differences in their genetic endowment, and this works to magnify the differences among phenotypes.

Active G-E correlation is completely beyond our control in any humane environment. It results from the individual's actively selecting and creating environmental conditions that reflect the individual's genotype. The musically gifted child spontaneously pays more attention to sounds and music, whether anyone wants him to or not. He carries musical phrases around in his head, sings to himself, goes over in his memory the music he has heard on the radio, and so on. The mathematical child is unusually fascinated by numbers and arithmetic manipulations, and amuses himself by juggling these, just as most children have fun kicking a ball or playing tag.

As a child, the noted Indian lawyer and politician Bhimrao Ambedkar was not allowed to attend his village school, because he was born an untouchable. But one day, out of curiosity, he peeked in the schoolroom windows. What he saw caught his fancy, and he went back to the window day after day, until he caught on to what the teacher was explaining at the blackboard. He thereby learned to read. From then on he could educate himself, and at age 15 he entered a contest and won a university scholarship based on written examinations at the University of Bombay. He graduated with a B.A. degree by the age at which most students begin college, and went on to obtain a law degree and a doctorate in economics by the age of 21. No one had to force education on him. His genotype was the crucial ingredient.

Hence a child's genotype provides stimulation for its phenotypic expression. Brighter children are more curious, they are eager to know more, to try out more things, to ask more questions, to read more. They seem brighter partly because they do these things, but they also do these things because they are innately brighter. It is well-nigh impossible to get innately low-IQ children, even in the most culturally advantaged homes, to develop the same kinds of interests and learning habits that one sees in children with high IQs. No matter how hard we may try to create the same environmental opportunities for all children, we could never, even under the most rigidly totalitarian system of control, be able to eliminate the environmental differences that persons fashion for themselves in accord with their own particular genotypes.

Genotype-Environment Interaction

G-E interaction is inferred when various phenotypes show different amounts of responsiveness, or even responses in opposite directions, to exactly the same environmental condition. An environment that is optimal for the phenotypic expression of one genotype may be less than optimal, or even detrimental, for the phenotypic expression of a different genotype. A rare pathological condition known as galactosemia, due to a single mutant gene, is a dramatic example of G-E interaction. Children with the normal gene for the metabolism of lactose or milk sugar thrive on milk. A child with the abnormal gene for galactosemia, however, cannot properly metabolize galactose; the metabolites break down incompletely, creating toxic substances that damage the brain. This can lead to severe mental retardation if milk is not eliminated from the child's diet.

Aside from such abnormalities, however, there is strangely little evidence that G-E interaction plays any part in normal variations in IQ. Apparently whatever environmental effects are good or bad for the phenotypic development of one genotype are equally good or bad for any other genotype, where IQ is concerned. This may seem surprising, and yet no one has been able to find any evidence, within the range of IQ from about 60 to 140, of any G-E interaction. The existing data are quite adequate to detect G-E interaction if it in fact existed. The simplest test for it makes use of MZ twins reared apart. One calculates the correlation between (a) the average IQs for every set of twins, and (b) the absolute differences in the IQs of every set of twins. A significant correlation between a and b would indicate the existence of G-E interaction. But this correlation, based on the existing data, is so close to zero as to be nonsignificant. Hence most geneticists have dismissed G-E interaction as an important source of IQ variance. G-E interaction is often held up by critics of IQ heritability as a possible source of error in the calculations. But the only evidence for G-E interaction I have been able to find with respect to any kind of ability is based on strains of rats that were specially bred for maze learning ability—"maze bright" and "maze dull" strains. Both strains, when raised in a stimulus-deprived environment, are almost equally poor at learning to run through a maze without going into the blind alleys. And both strains, when they are raised in an extremely enriched, stimulating environment, are almost equally good at maze learning. But when both strains are raised in an "average" environment (the usual laboratory cage), the "dull" strain is much slower at maze learning than the "bright" strain. That is a classic example of genotype-environment interaction. Nothing like it has yet been found in human mental ability.

The Burt Affair

For some years to come, no chapter on the inheritance of mental ability can ignore the unfortunate legacy of Sir Cyril Burt.

Burt, who died in 1971 at the age of eighty-nine, was an eminent and distinguished professor of psychology at the University of London. The first British psychologist ever to be knighted, he was especially well known as a pioneer in the study of the genetics of mental ability, having been the first psychologist to introduce advanced methods of quantitative genetics in this field, along with masses of various kinship data on IQ that he collected over the years in the London schools. For many years Burt's theoretical papers, research reports, and conclusions figured prominently in any discussion of mental inheritance. He was the leading authority in the field.

After Burt's death, I pulled together all of the published results of his studies on the genetics of mental ability and systematically arranged all of the various kinship correlations in a series of nine large tables. When the whole of Burt's reported results were thus arrayed, certain peculiarities—certainly errors of some kind—became apparent in the figures. The most bizarre of these numerical anomalies had already been noted by Leon Kamin, a psychologist at Princeton and an ardent antihereditarian. Burt had reported exactly the same correlation of .771 for MZ twins reared apart in three different papers based on twin samples of twenty-one, thirty, and fifty-three twin pairs. The samples were presumably cumulative, with more twins being added to the original collection in each report. Even so, the probability of obtaining exactly the same correlation to three decimal places each time is virtually nil. I turned up a total of no less than twenty similar anomalies in Burt's reports. Burt went on purportedly cumulating kinship data throughout his long career, and after about 1955 the numerical anomalies in his reports seem to compound. As a result of such discoveries, within a few years after Burt's death he was accused of fraud by antihereditarians and by his long-time opponents. These sensational accusations received a lot of play in the popular press, especially in Britain, where Burt had long been a public figure.

Nothing definite could be proved, however, because the anomalies in Burt's reported kinship figures were so peculiarly unsystematic and senseless as to look more like the careless errors of an old man than like calculated fraud. Indeed, some of the anomalies in the figures were rather transparent copying errors, such as reversing, transposing, or substituting digits. Such numerical carelessness, if that is what it was, stood in puzzling contrast to Burt's elegant style of writing, his high level of technical sophistication in genetics and statistics, and the extreme rarity of theoretical and conceptual errors in his work. But the question was no longer really of any great scientific importance, because all of the kinship correlations of greatest value in genetical research had been replicated by many other investigators both before and after Burt's publications. And they all lead to essentially the same conclusions as Burt's. By this time the total deletion of Burt's empirical legacy would scarcely make an iota of difference to any general conclusions regarding the heritability of intelligence, so much greater is the body of more recent and better evidence.

None of Burt's kinship data, however, should now be included in any summaries or calculations of IQ heritability. It is all under a cloud of suspicion, since at least half, and probably more, of his purported data on fifty-three sets of MZ twins reared apart—the largest single collection of such data in the entire literature—has been convincingly claimed to be fraudulent: sheer fabrications of Burt's imagination!

The Burt puzzle was pieced together several years after Burt's death, by his biographer, Leslie Hearnshaw, a noted historian of psychology (*Cyril Burt, Psychologist,* Cornell University Press, 1979). Ironically, Burt was convicted by his own personal diaries and correspondence files, which were given to Hearnshaw by Burt's sister. There could not be found a shred of evidence that Burt had collected any new data on MZ twins reared apart since about 1952, after he retired from his professorship. Yet he went on writing articles on twins and the heritability of IQ, supposedly adding more and more cases to his twin collection, as late as 1966. In the last year of his life, in personal correspondence with Sandra Scarr, a psychologist at Yale, he reported the IQs of three more sets of MZ twins reared apart, twins whom he had presumably just found. There was never any evidence of their existence, and when I visited Burt at about the same time that he was writing to Professor Scarr, he never mentioned his new finds to me, even though a major topic of our conversation was genetic research on twins.

Hearnshaw's biography of Burt and his detective work in exposing Burt's deceptions is fascinating but sad—the story of a genius gone awry. Strangely, Burt, in his old age, really had no need to prove any point for which there was not already substantial evidence from other studies. Apparently he could not bear to see others outshine him in the field in which he had so long been the kingpin. The fear of falling from his high status and being regarded as a scientific has-been in his old age was probably too great a threat to his ego. His personal vanity was considerable, according to many of his former associates. So he began simply making up new ''data'' and writing articles about them, to create the impression that he was still making important contributions on the frontiers of science. During the last twenty years of his retirement he published more than 200 articles—an astounding output for a scholar at any age.

Hearnshaw's excellent biography of Burt reveals extenuating circumstances in Burt's old age that may allow future generations to settle on a more sympathetic attitude toward him. But the extenuating circumstances, probably interacting with flaws in Burt's character, in no way mitigate the end result: that all of his massive purported data on inheritance of mental ability is suspect and must now be treated as worthless. There is no certain way to clearly separate the authentic and the fraudulent data. It all has to be disregarded for any scientific purpose. It seems impossible to imagine any worse fate for a scientist's reputation, unless it were that his overall conclusions were wrong to boot. Unfortunately, it is not an extremely rare thing in science for bold falsehoods to be promulgated. Whether or not it involves intentional deceit is seldom asked, let alone established. Dishonesty in science usually cannot be clearly disentangled from stupidity or gullibility or technical incompetence. These, however, have never been invoked as excuses in Burt's case. Even his severest critics conceded he was intellectually brilliant, a skeptical and exceedingly penetrating critic of other scholars' work, and a sophisticated master of the technicalities of psychometrics, statistics, and quantitative genetics. Alas, his scientific integrity finally succumbed to overweening vanity.

4

Are Tests Colorblind?

THE MOST FREQUENT and vehement attack against mental tests of all kinds is the charge that they are culturally biased against racial and ethnic minorities and the poor. This claim is often seen in popular articles. Recently it has figured prominently in a number of court cases in which mental tests, or the uses or users of tests, were on trial. Last year, in a lengthy legal battle over the use of IQ tests in the public schools of California, the judge handed down a decision that outlaws the use of IQ tests for the placement of black and Hispanic pupils in special classes for the educable mentally retarded. The judge's main argument was that the IQ tests are culturally biased against these minority groups.

The issue is an extremely important one for both the users of tests and the persons tested. Are the observed racial differences in average test scores a result of biasing defects and artifacts in the tests? For all the legitimate uses of tests in schools, and for selection of applicants to colleges, in armed forces training programs, and in civilian jobs, are the tests as accurate and as useful for blacks and other minorities as they are for whites?

There are objective means for properly answering these important questions. Most popular claims of test bias, however, are based on fallacious and indefensible notions of what constitutes bias in mental testing. I shall thus first point out the fallacious notions about bias, and then I shall explain what bias actually consists of, and describe the methods for discovering test bias wherever it actually exists. Finally, I shall summarize the results of numerous investigations that have applied these methods to the most widely used standardized tests.

Fallacious Notions of Test Bias

Egalitarian Fallacy

The simplest notion that has dominated claims of bias is what I term the egalitarian fallacy. This is the idea that if a test shows a difference in average scores between any racial, ethnic, or social class groups, it must therefore be a biased test. According to this notion, an unbiased test should reveal reliable differences between individuals, but it should not show differences between the average scores of different racial or social groups in the population, or between the sexes. Virtually all legal cases concerning minority-group discrimination by tests, in which the courts have ruled that the tests were biased, are based solely on the fact that the minority group's scores averaged lower than the majority group's. The rulings of the courts on test bias have been mainly based on the egalitarian fallacy.

The fallacy in this criterion of bias is that it assumes the answer to the point in question. It makes the wholly unwarranted assumption that there are no differences (and can be no differences) between population groups—blacks and whites, rich and poor, males and females. There is no scientific justification for this sweeping assumption. Assumptions have a proper place in science, to be sure, but proper assumptions concern merely formal logical and definitional matters, not questions of empirical fact. To argue that a test is biased simply on the grounds that it shows a difference between groups is tantamount to claiming that our yardsticks are biased because they show a difference in height between men and women.

By the same token, the absence of a group difference in average test scores cannot, by itself, be evidence that the test is not biased for the groups in question. The test may be biased so as to make the groups appear equal in whatever the test purports to measure, when in fact they are different.

The idea that a group difference (or the lack of a difference) indicates bias (or the absence of bias) is now completely rejected by all the experts who do research on bias in mental tests.

Culture-bound Fallacy

The most common argument presented by test critics when asked to back up their claims of culture bias consists of pointing out particular test items that are "culture-bound" or "culture-loaded." Hence I term this the culture-bound fallacy. It is a fallacious argument, first of all, because the fact that a test item is culture-loaded does not necessarily mean that the item is biased for the particular groups in question; and second, because all the evidence indicates that psychologists cannot pick out truly biased items merely by inspection. In several studies, white and black psychologists have been asked to pick out the items of a test that they thought were the items that either most disfavored or least disfavored blacks, when compared with whites. Neither black nor white psychologists could pick out such items any better than chance. Biased tests or biased items simply cannot be identified by subjective impressions based on the external appearance of the test or item or on judgments of their culture loading. Bias can only be detected by objective statistical techniques applied to actual data.

The culture-bound fallacy is essentially a failure to distinguish between the concepts of culture loading and bias. The distinction is absolutely crucial for any intelligent discussion. Arguments that tests are culturally biased against minorities thrive on obscuring this distinction.

The Meaning of Culture Loading

"Culture loading" refers to the specificity or generality of the informational content of a test item, as contrasted with the item's demands for educing relationships, reasoning, and mental manipulation of its elements. Test items can be ordered along a continuum of culture loading in terms of the range of cultural backgrounds in which the item's informational content could be acquired. The answer to an item may depend on knowledge that could only be acquired within a particular culture, or locality, or time period. The opportunity for acquiring the requisite bit of knowledge might be greatly less in some cultures, localities, or time periods than in others.

The ordering of items on the culture-loadedness continuum is based on inspection of the items and subjective judgment. But there can be considerable agreement among several judges in the rank ordering of items on the continuum. The extreme end points of the continuum could be labeled "completely culture-free" and "completely culture-loaded." Of course, these are the hypothetical extremes at which no actual test items would be found. But that does not invalidate the concept of a continuum of culture loading. Physicists conceive of elasticity as a continuum on which different materials can be usefully ordered, even though there are no materials that are either perfectly elastic or perfectly inelastic. In designing problems whose essential feature is some form of relation eduction or problem solving, modern test constructors generally try to use content that is common to a wide range of cultural backgrounds. But items can be found, especially in some of the older tests, in which the difficulty level of the item is much more a result of its culture loading than of its demand for the eduction of relationships. Here, for example, is an extremely culture-loaded item that would be a reasonably valid measure of relation eduction for at most about a dozen of my closest relatives but for no one else:

Manis is to Martha as Leo is to
    (a) Lois (b) Lydia (c) Lou (d) Lucille.

The relation eduction here is very simple: husband-wife, uncles and aunts. The item would probably be fairly correlated with mental age and IQ among all the preschool children in my extended family, but it would be most surprising if this item showed any correlation with mental age or IQ among our next-door neighbors' children. The information required to educe these relationships is simply unknown to them.

Here is a much less culture-loaded item in which the demand for relation eduction is practically zero, but it is a highly culture-loaded item relative to most other items in standard tests:

Romeo is to Juliet as Tristan is to
    (a) Carmen (b) Elizabeth (c) Isolde (d) Marguerite.

Here is a narrowly culture-loaded question that would be a reasonably fair "odd man out" type of item for anyone who had lived for a time in London but would be an exceedingly poor item for everyone else, although New Yorkers might have a slight edge over, say, Californians.

Cross out the one name that does not belong with the others: Central Park, Green Park, Holland Park, Hyde Park, Regents Park.

Here is a much less culture-loaded item, but it is still more culture-loaded than many:

Author is to *novel* as *composer* is to
    (a) *book* (b) *work* (c) *symphony* (d) *statue* (e) *piano*.

Here is a much less culture-loaded item:

60 is to 30 is to 15, as 20 is to 10 is to __.

The greatest intellects of ancient Greece, such as Plato and Archimedes, would have had no trouble with this last item but could not get any of the previous items, which indicates that the content of those items is also temporally restricted. The degree of culture loading of some items can change from one decade to the next.

Notice also that culture loading *per se* has nothing to do with the item's difficulty. Very difficult items can be based on informational content that is practically universal in human experience or in which the information content is trivial compared with the reasoning required by the item. For example, continue the series:

$$X\ 0\ 0\ 0\ 0\ X\ X\ 0\ 0\ 0\ X\ X\ X\ 0\ 0\ \underline{\qquad}.$$

This item does not depend on *knowing* anything; it depends on seeing the relationships among the elements.

There are other items in which the contents of the item are of such trivial importance to its level of difficulty as to render the item's culture loading very low. Consider the following question, on which we know the percentages of a large representative sample of 9-year-olds in the United States who select the different alternative answers:

A pint of water at 50° Fahrenheit is mixed with a pint of water at 70° Fahrenheit. The temperature of the water just after mixing will be about:

Answers	% of 9-year-olds
20° F	4
50° F	2
60° F	7
70° F	5
120° F	69
I don't know	12
No response	0

The majority of 9-year-olds can add 50 + 70, and most could divide 120 by 2 if it were presented to them just as a problem in arithmetic computation. But the logical reasoning aspect of the problem is beyond them, and they fail to see the physical absurdity of the answer 120. Some critics of tests would argue that the children who fail this item do so because they have had less experience with thermometers than children who get the right answer. Yet the same reasoning demands can be built into items with informational content that is universally available to experience. And if we alter this simple temperature problem to make it a little more complex without increasing its culture loading, it is failed by more than half of the adult population:

> If you mix one pint of water at 50° F with two pints of water at 80° F, what will be the temperature of the mixture?

Here is another item with even less culture loading, consisting of simple arithmetic, which can be shown to be a trivial part of the problem as compared with its reasoning aspect:

> John is twice as old as his sister Mary, who is now 5 years of age. How old will John be when Mary is 30 years of age?

Over 20 percent of adults fail this item, but nearly all who fail show that they can do the arithmetic calculations by giving the answer "60" and by answering correctly the simpler item: "Mrs. Jones bought a loaf of bread for 30¢ and a bar of candy for 5¢. How much did she spend all together?"

Here is an item that is passed by 50 percent of the adult population. It does not seem a very culture-loaded item, and those who have not driven motorboats in lakes or rivers are probably not disadvantaged by the item's content, although it is undoubtedly true that rich people are more likely to own a motorboat than poor people.

> A motorboat can travel 5 miles an hour on a still lake. If this boat travels downstream on a river that is flowing 5 miles per hour, how long will it take the boat to reach the bridge that is 10 miles downstream?

"Culture-reduced" tests try to minimize culture loading by not using words, letters, numbers, or even pictures of familiar common objects. They consist of only simple elements—lines, curves, circles, and squares—and they involve such universal concepts as up/down, right/left, opened/closed, whole/half, larger/smaller, many/few, full/empty, and the like. Quite complex problems involving relational reasoning can be made up of such elements—for example, figural analogies, figure series completion, and matrices. Such tests are near the opposite extreme on the culture-loading continuum as compared with tests involving specific factual knowledge or scholastic content.

Standardization Fallacy

This is the mistaken notion that because a test was devised by psychologists who are members of a particular racial group or social class and the test was standardized on a sample of persons from the same segment of the population, the test is thereby biased against every other group. This idea is expressed in many statements by psychologists, educators, and sociologists. Here are some typical examples from the literature:

> Persons from backgrounds other than the culture in which the test was developed will always be penalized.

> IQ tests are Anglocentric; they measure the extent to which an individual's background is similar to that of the modal cultural configuration of American society.

> Blacks have been overlooked in devising questions for tests and were not included in the population used to standardize the figures used for the interpretation of test scores.

> Aptitude tests, standardized (or "normed") for white middle class children, cannot determine the intelligence of minority children whose backgrounds differ notably from that of the "normal" population.

The fallacy is not that a test standardized in one group might not be biased for some other group, but the dogmatic claim that it is necessarily biased against any other group simply by virtue of its standardization on a different group.

The claim that groups outside the test's standardization population will inevitably score lower than members of the standardization population is flatly refuted by evidence. Raven's Progressive Matrices Test was devised by two Englishmen, J. C. Raven and L. S. Penrose, and standardized on samples from England and Scotland. Yet Eskimos living in the icy wastes above the Arctic Circle score on a par with the English and Scottish norms. The Wechsler Intelligence Scales, devised by David Wechsler, a clinical psychologist at New York University, were standardized on samples of the United States population. Yet large representative samples of the population of Japan average 6 IQ points above the U.S. "norm" on nonverbal IQ, which is based on the nonlanguage parts of the test that need no translation or other alteration to be appropriate for the Japanese. A new standardization sample of American children in 1972 scored 6 IQ points higher on the old Stanford–Binet IQ test that was originally standardized in 1937. This contradicts the claim made by one critic that test scores decline as time moves away from the moment when the test was standardized—an extreme example would be a test written in Middle English.

Standardization has two aspects: (1) item selection and (2) standardization or "norming" of the total test scores. Items for a particular test are selected from a much larger pool of items devised to measure whatever the test is intended to measure. All items in the pool are tried out on large samples, and items are selected in terms of certain item statistics that tell how difficult (percentage failing) the item is in the standardization population and how well the item discriminates between persons whose scores on the whole test are in the top 27 percent and those whose scores are in the bottom 27 percent. Items are selected so as to represent all levels of difficulty in fairly evenly graded steps, from easy items that are failed by only 1 percent of the population to items that are failed by 99 percent. Items that do not discriminate well between high and low scores on the whole test are discarded, because such items evidently do not measure the same trait that is measured by the test as a whole.

The finally selected items are assembled into the final test and the frequency distribution of raw scores (the number of right answers) is compiled. This frequency distribution of scores is the basis for the test's norms. It permits the conversion of raw scores into some more meaningful form, such as percentiles, standard scores, or IQs.

The item selection aspect of test construction could conceivably result in the selection of different items for one population than for another. When the test is intended for use in different cultural groups, the item selection procedures should be applied to each group separately and only those items should be retained which meet the same optimal standards for selection in the different groups. One way of investigating bias in a test is to repeat the item selection procedures for the minority group that had not been included in the original standardization and determine how many of the items would have to be discarded for that group, using the same statistical criteria that were applied in the original standardization. This has been done with tests that were originally standardized on whites. When the item selection procedures were applied to blacks, usually all of the items met the same statistical selection criteria for both groups. In other words, the same items would have been selected from the total item pool if the test had been devised originally for blacks instead of for whites.

The conversion of raw scores to percentiles, IQ, or other standardized scores is not changed in any fundamental way whether they are based on the white population or the white and black populations combined. Individuals' scores will retain the same rank order in either case, and the percentage of blacks scoring above or below the white median (or any other point on the scale of scores) will remain unchanged. The numerical values of the standardized scores are shifted slightly by including the two populations in the standardization procedure, but the change in scale is of no essential significance—it's like shifting from a Fahrenheit to a Celsius thermometer.

In summary, a test is not necessarily biased just because some groups get lower scores than others, or because the items are culture-loaded, or because the lower-scoring group was not included in the standardization sample.

The True Meaning of Bias

"Bias" means a systematic error of measurement or estimation. The error can be positive (the true value is consistently overestimated) or negative (the true value is consistently underestimated).

Bias should be distinguished from random error. When we average a large number of values containing random error, the positive and negative errors, being unsystematic and therefore of equal frequencies and magnitudes, tend to cancel each other, so the average value more closely approaches the true value the more cases we include in the averaging. There are two types of random error: measurement error and sampling error. Measurement error is random error in a single measurement, such as a person's IQ score, and is also loosely termed the unreliability of the score. Sampling error is random error in some statistic (for example, the mean or average) based on a sample drawn at random from a population. A random sample seldom perfectly represents the whole population from which it was drawn, and statistics calculated on the sample will deviate to some extent from what the value would be if it were based on the whole population. The amount of deviation—underestimation or overestimation—in such a case is termed sampling error. It can be decreased simply by drawing larger random samples.

When we speak of a test as biased for a group, we mean that the scores for the group consistently underestimate or overestimate the true values. This bias is in addition to any random measurement error, which infests all tests scores to some extent. More simply, a test can be said to be biased for a group when any given score obtained by an individual in that group does not have the same meaning as the very same score obtained by an individual in another group. The two groups in question might be different racial groups, different socio-economic levels, different sexes, or any other category of persons in the general population.

The Detection of Test Bias

The key question, then, is how we can objectively recognize when a test is biased. Numerous statistical methods have been used. I shall describe a few of the most important methods in a nontechnical way, avoiding the mathematical formulations that are needed by psychometricians or statisticians for their actual application or precise interpretation. Following the description of each method, I shall summarize the main findings of the studies that have applied the method to well-known standardized tests given to majority and minority (usually white and black) samples.

A biased test yields scores that mean something different for persons of one group than for persons of another group, even when two persons from different groups have *identical* scores on the test. Therefore, the detection of bias consists in looking for properties of the test that indicate that the same scores may mean different things for different groups. For convenience, we can divide these indicators of bias into three broad categories.

1. *Situational bias,* that is, conditions in the test situation, such as the race, language, or manner of the tester, that could differentially affect the test performance of persons of different races or cultural backgrounds.

2. *External indicators of bias,* that is, the relationship of test scores to other variables external to the test or testing situation. A biased test is likely to show significantly different correlations with some external variable for the majority and minority groups. The most important external indicator of bias is the test's predictive validity in the two groups in question, that is, how accurately the test scores can predict some external criterion of consequence, such as scholastic performance, college grades, or success on the job.

3. *Internal indicators of bias,* that is, psychometric properties of the test and test items, such as the test's reliability, the rank order of item difficulty, the intercorrelations among subtests, the factor composition of the test, and the shape of the function relating the probability of passing any given item to the person's total score on the test. If such psychometric features of a test behave differently in the majority and minority groups, it is evidence of bias. For one thing, it could indicate that the same total score is made up of different admixtures of abilities in the two groups and that therefore the same score could mean something rather different for persons from different groups.

Situational Bias

Race of the Tester

It is a popular claim that the lower average test scores of blacks are due, at least in part, to the fact that the tests are usually administered by a white tester. Blacks, it is argued, would feel more comfortable with a tester of their own race and, as a result, would perform better on the test.

Fortunately, there has been considerable research on this issue—thirty independent studies—and there can be little doubt about the conclusions. The studies, for the most part, consist in having two or more black and two or more white testers administer a given test to groups of whites and blacks, so that persons of each race are proctored by testers of each race. The overwhelming conclusion from all these studies is that the race of the tester has inconsistent and negligible effects on the mental test scores of whites and blacks. The observed average racial difference in scores cannot be attributed to the race of the tester.

Language and Dialect of the Tester

It is also argued that blacks from poor backgrounds speak a kind of dialect and are less familiar with the Standard English used in verbal tests and test instructions, even when there is a black tester.

Studies show that black children from an early age comprehend Standard English at least as well as, and usually better than, Black English. Highly verbal, individually administered tests that depend on understanding the tester, such as the Stanford–Binet IQ test, have been translated into Black English and administered to black children by black testers who are adept in the dialect. The scores do not differ from those obtained when the test is given in Standard English. Also, blacks score about the same, relative to whites, on nonverbal tests as on verbal tests. The consensus of researchers on this topic is that blacks are not penalized by the use of Standard English in test items or test instructions.

Bilingual Groups

The language of the test, however, does make a difference for groups, usually immigrants, who speak a foreign language or are bilingual, with English as their second language. Many Hispanic children, American Indians, and first-generation Asians speak their native language at home and come into contact with Standard English only in school. The fact that all these groups obtain lower scores on verbal than on nonverbal tests, and on reading tests than on arithmetic tests, strongly suggests that their different language background may handicap their performance on verbal or language-loaded tests. Scores on such tests for persons from different language backgrounds should be regarded as suspect and should be supplemented by nonlanguage tests. Even then, great care must be exercised to ensure that the test instructions are fully understood. This can usually be determined by including such easy test items that anyone who understands the test instructions would have no trouble getting the right answers. There are a number of very suitable tests for non-English-speaking persons, and it is psychometric malpractice not to use these when language problems are suspected. The verbal tests, of course, may well have more short-term validity for predicting scholastic performance or other behaviors that depend heavily on a knowledge of English. But in such cases, the test users must be careful not to extend the interpretation of the verbal test scores beyond their relevance to behavior requiring familiarity with English. Even this limited interpretation should not be extended more than a year into the future, because, given adequate opportunity, there can be rapid gains in language mastery.

Tester's Attitudes and Expectations

The manner in which the tester gives instructions, the tester's expectations about the subject's test performance, the incentive or rewards for doing one's best, and the like, could conceivably affect blacks and whites differently, to the disadvantage of blacks. Studies have been devised to find out whether these factors make a difference. Tests are given with and without motivation-inducing instructions, or in a friendly, warm, and casual manner versus a formal, cool, and aloof manner, with and without praise and encouragement throughout the testing. Moreover, the order of items is altered, interspersing easy with difficult items, to prevent any consistent feeling of difficulty or failure on the subject's part. Even money incentives and rewards have been used to improve performance, paying subjects for every item passed. Tests have also been given with and without time limits, and preliminary practice tests have been given, to see if blacks would benefit from practice more than whites.

It turns out that all these experimental manipulations of the testing conditions produce very little or no effect on the scores, and they produce even less effect on the average difference between blacks and whites or between different social classes.

A dozen studies have been done to determine whether the teacher's or tester's preconceptions of a child's ability level or expectation of test performance would influence his actual test scores. The results consistently show no significant effect of these prior expectations by teachers or testers on children's IQ test scores. This is not to say that most teachers cannot make fairly accurate estimates of their pupils' IQs after they have had them in class for a few months. But if a teacher is given false information about a child's IQ, it does not seem to affect the child's actual test performance. Also, teachers generally put little stock in a child's test score if it seems seriously discrepant with their own impression of the child's ability. In the case of markedly deviant children, such discrepancies between the teacher's impression and the test scores warrant further investigation by the school psychologist.

Bias in Test Scoring

Individually administered intelligence tests, such as the Stanford–Binet and the Wechsler scales, involve rather subjective scoring of many items—the subject's answers to vocabulary, general information, and verbal comprehension questions, and the rating of the quality of his attempts at copying geometric figures, and the like. Although there is a high degree of agreement among different scorers, the question arises as to the possibility of some systematic bias, probably unconscious, in the scoring of tests when the scorer knows the race or other background characteristics of the individual whose test he is scoring.

Studies have shown a significant "halo effect" in scoring answers of borderline or ambiguous correctness. That is, if such a response occurs in a test in which there are clearly many correct answers making for an overall high score, the scorers will tend to give some borderline answers the benefit of the doubt and score them as "pass"; but if the very same ambiguous response occurs in a generally poor test record containing many clearly failed items, scorers tend to score it as "failed." However, the one study of this type of "halo effect" scoring bias in the test records of a black child and a white child, with black and white scorers, showed no significant effects of the race of the children or the race of the scorers.

Miscellaneous Situational Effects

Other conditions that studies have shown to be of negligible effect on the test scores of blacks and whites or of different social classes are the sex of the tester, test anxiety, motivation, and self-esteem.

In summary, research has not found any features of the testing procedure that tend to bias the test performance of different racial groups and social classes.

External Indicators of Test Bias

Predictive Bias

As was emphasized in Chapter 1, mental test scores are of no real importance in their own right. They gain importance only because they can be indicative of a person's performance on other criteria that *are* of great practical importance, such as success in school or on the job. When the correlation between scores on a particular test and some external criterion of practical importance is well established in a certain population, the test can be used to predict performance on the criterion. Reviewing a bit of Chapter 1, the test is said to have predictive validity, which is quantitatively indexed by the coefficient of correlation between the test scores and some measurement of performance on the criterion, such as teachers' marks, college grade-point average, work supervisors' ratings, or some objective assessment of actual proficiency on the job.

Thus, in most actual uses of tests, the scores are used as a predictive index based on the tests' validity coefficient for the criterion of concern. A person's test score is entered into a mathematical prediction equation (technically termed ''regression equation''), which yields a statistical prediction, that is, a best estimate of the person's standing on the criterion. (There is some estimated ''margin of error'' in these predictions.) The test's validity coefficient—the correlation between test scores and the criterion—is the crucial ingredient in the prediction equation.

The reader will be reminded of the bare essentials of the predictive use of test scores by referring again to Figure 3 on page 21. The exact position of the prediction line is determined mathematically from the actual data on samples of persons who have taken the test and whose performance on the criterion has been assessed. The position of the prediction line is the crucial issue as concerns test bias.

Prediction is biased if persons from different populations (e.g., blacks and whites) who obtained the same test score do not, on the average, perform the same on the criterion. In other words, bias exists if one and the same test score actually predicts different levels of criterion performance, depending on the person's group membership.

What this means in terms of Figure 3 is that the prediction line is in a different position for members of one population than for members of another. The prediction line as determined for the one population, therefore, does not give equally valid predictions if it is used to predict the criterion performance of persons from the other population. There will be some consistent underestimation (or overestimation) in the predictions for the second group. On the other hand, if scores are unbiased, the prediction line will be one and the same line for both populations. That is, any given score will have the same meaning with respect to the criterion (i.e., it will predict the same level of performance) for any persons obtaining that score, regardless of their group membership.

Hence, one important method for detecting bias is to determine the position of the prediction line separately for the two (or more) populations of concern, and then see if the positions differ significantly in any way. If the prediction lines' positions are found to differ significantly, the test scores are considered a biased predictor of the criterion for the two (or more) groups in question.

For example, suppose we are using SAT-Verbal scores to select college applicants. (For the sake of simplicity in this example, we shall not take high school grades into account, although in most colleges they are given more weight than the SAT scores.) In the previous year, say, we have determined the prediction line based on white students whose SAT-V scores and grade-point averages (GPAs) were on record in the college registrar's files. This year we have many black as well as white applicants. We want to select only those who are predicted to obtain an overall GPA of at least 2 (a C average), which is required to remain in college. We decide that a cutoff score of 465 on the SAT-V is reasonable, because, according to our prediction line, a score of 465 predicts a GPA of 2. About half of the students with an SAT-V of 465 obtain GPAs of less than 2 (and therefore are put on probation or flunk out), and the other half obtain GPAs of 2 or above. We use the same cutoff score of 465 for both white and black applicants, acting as if the scores would predict GPA equally well for both groups.

When we check up on this a year later, we find that all the white students whose SAT-V score was 465 obtain GPAs of 2 (grade C), just as we had expected from our prediction line. But all the black students whose SAT-V score was 465 obtained GPAs of 2.5 (C +). In other words, our prediction line, which was based on white students, didn't give an accurate prediction for blacks—it consistently underestimated their GPAs by 0.5, or half of a letter-grade level. This selection procedure, therefore, is biased against blacks, with the result that fewer blacks were admitted than should have been. We properly conclude that, if our selection procedure is to be equally fair to all applicants regardless of race, we cannot use the same prediction line for blacks that we use for whites.

So how can we make our method of selection more fair? What we can do is determine the prediction line separately for whites and blacks and use the appropriate prediction of GPA for each applicant depending on his race. If the slopes of the prediction lines are the same for both groups (that is, if the lines are separated but parallel), the predictions of GPA under this procedure will be equally accurate for blacks and whites alike and therefore would be considered fair to individuals of both groups.

This method of using test scores fairly is possible when the test has the same validity coefficient in both groups, because the slope of the prediction line is a function of the test's predictive validity. Therefore, the most crucial question is whether the test's validity is significantly different for the two groups.

Notice that the fair selection procedure just described carries no implication that the percentages of black and white applicants who are accepted (or rejected) will be equal. What it does mean is that the predicted GPAs of black and white applicants will be equally accurate; that is, the GPAs will not be systematically underestimated or overestimated (in relation to the actual obtained GPAs) for either blacks or whites. In that sense, the selection of applicants can be said to be colorblind.

Published Evidence

I have examined all the published evidence pertaining to the predictive bias of many different tests for blacks and whites—IQ tests used in schools, scholastic aptitude tests used for college admissions, specialized aptitude tests used for the assignment of recruits to different training programs in the armed forces, and ability and achievement tests used for personnel selection and promotion in business and industry. I shall first summarize all these results in a general way, and then briefly mention some specific widely used tests and the findings about their predictive biases in various settings in which these tests are most frequently used—in school, college, the armed forces, and employment selection.

General Conclusions

1. The first general conclusion is that, in the majority of studies, the prediction lines are not significantly different for whites and blacks. That is, there is no predictive bias. Any given test score, regardless of whether it is earned by a white or a black person, predicts the criterion with equal accuracy. The test can be characterized as completely colorblind, and the test scores can be used in the same way for members of both races. One and the same prediction line works equally well for both groups.

2. In a considerable number of studies, however, there is significant predictive bias when the prediction line based on the white sample (or on the combined white and black samples) is used to predict the criterion performance of blacks. Virtually without exception, however, the direction of the predictive bias in these cases is contrary to the popular notion that test scores underestimate the criterion performance of blacks. The consistent finding is that when there is significant predictive bias, the test scores overestimate the performance of blacks on the criterion when the scores are interpreted the same for blacks as for whites. This kind of bias in a selection procedure will result in more blacks being accepted on the basis of test scores than would be accepted if the predictive bias were totally eliminated. Thus, the studies have shown that when significant predictive bias is found to exist, it invariably favors the selection of blacks.

In terms of the prediction line depicted in Figure 3, in the most common type of bias there are actually different prediction lines for whites and blacks, with the black prediction line slightly below but parallel to the white prediction line. (Psychometricians term this "intercept bias.") Hence, if we use the white prediction line for predicting the criterion performance of blacks, whose true prediction line is below the whites', we overestimate the criterion for blacks. Equally accurate predictions for both whites and blacks can be obtained in this situation by basing the prediction for each person on the prediction line derived from his own racial group. More often, however, the selecting institution will simply use the white prediction line for both white and black applicants and give the blacks the selection advantage of the predictive bias.

3. Equally good prediction for blacks and whites can nearly always be achieved by using their separate prediction lines when the use of a single prediction line (based on whites or on whites and blacks combined) is shown to result in significant predictive bias. This is possible because the predictive validity of tests is the same for blacks as for whites. I doubt that there is any general finding in all of psychology to which there are fewer exceptions. A number of experts in psychometrics who have reviewed all of the validity coefficients of tests for blacks and whites ever reported in the entire research literature state that differential test validity for blacks and whites is simply nonexistent. Where predictive validity is concerned, tests that are valid for whites are equally valid for blacks.

4. If differential validity for whites and blacks is nonexistent, then why do a good many studies show predictive bias—the overestimation of blacks' criterion performance—when the white prediction line is used for both groups? Conversely, if the black prediction line were used for both groups, the predictions for whites would be biased—their criterion performance would be underestimated. The fact that test validity is the same for both groups means that each group's criterion performance can be predicted equally well from each group's own prediction line.

When the two groups do not have the same prediction line, it is invariably the case that the groups differ more on the criterion than can be accounted for by the difference in their test scores. It is commonly believed that whites and blacks differ more in their test scores, on the average, than in the criterion performance the test is used to predict. But this is not always so, especially when the criterion is intellectually demanding. Blacks and whites differ about as much, for example, in scholastic achievement as in IQ. When the average white-black difference on the criterion is nearly the same as the average white-black difference on the test, and if the test's predictive validity is not exceptionally high, then it is mathematically inevitable that the prediction lines will not be the same for the two groups: The black prediction line will lie below, but parallel to, the white prediction line. As already noted, this is a rather common finding.

The implication of this comes as a surprise to many. It means the test's validity as a predictor of the criterion for either group is not sufficiently good to predict so large a difference between blacks and whites on the criterion as actually exists. Improving the test's validity—that is, its ability to predict the criterion performance—for both groups would lessen its bias. The predictive validity can often be appreciably improved by using two or three different tests, and combining the scores in an optimal way. If the criterion performance involves abilities A, B, and C, and our predictor test measures only ability A, the test's predictive validity for this criterion will not be very high. We could improve the overall validity by using additional tests that measure abilities B and C. In some cases B and C will not be other abilities but non-cognitive traits of personality and character that also play a part in the criterion performance.

5. Thus, contrary to popular expectation, the elimination or re-duction of the only type of predictive test bias that is actually found, by further improving the tests' reliability and validity, would not tend in the direction of equalizing the percentages of black and white selectees in any nonquota selection procedure based on test scores, but would have just the *opposite* effect.

Specific Findings

1. *WISC and Stanford–Binet.*   The Wechsler Intelligence Scale for Children (WISC) and the Stanford–Binet Test are the two individually administered IQ tests that are the most frequently used by school psy-chologists for testing children who are referred to them by their teachers because of learning problems. In many states, a child's IQ on one of these tests is an essential part of the criteria for deciding whether or not he should be placed in a special class for slow learners or for the educable mentally retarded (EMR). Because of the higher percentage of black pupils who are referred for individual testing and are subse-quently placed in special classes, the WISC and Stanford–Binet have come under more suspicion and outright attack for being culturally biased than have any other tests used in the schools.

The legal battle in the case of *Larry P. et al.* v. *Wilson Riles, Superin-tendent of Public Instruction for the State of California* ostensibly hinged on the issue of racial bias in the WISC, which was formerly used in Cali-fornia schools as one of the criteria for assigning children to EMR classes, in which there is a much higher percentage of blacks than their percentage in the total school population. The district court ruled that the WISC is racially biased and enjoined the use of standardized intel-ligence tests for the identification of black children as EMR, or as a cri-terion for the placement of black pupils in EMR classes.

To explain the arguments on which the judge's decision in this case was based would require detailed discussion, which would unduly side-track the present summary. Legal decisions, of course, are generally based on a number of complex considerations of a social and political nature. In the *Larry P. et al.* case, little weight was given to the actual evidence concerning cultural bias (or actually the lack of it) in the WISC and Stanford–Binet and other IQ tests.

The fact is, on the basis of the existing research evidence, it would be much harder to make a case that the WISC and Stanford–Binet are biased against blacks than to make the contrary case. The validity coefficients of these IQ tests for predicting scholastic achievement are about the same for blacks and whites at every level of IQ. The presumption that a black child with an IQ of 70 or 75 (the criterion for placement in an EMR class) is scholastically more proficient than a white child with the same IQ is contradicted by recent studies which show that the scholastic achievement level of black children who are referred for individual psychological testing because of unusual learning difficulty in the classroom is as accurately predicted by the WISC IQ and Stanford–Binet IQ as in the case of white children who are referred for individual testing. In fact, the prediction lines of whites and blacks are not significantly different for either test. This means that a given IQ predicts the same level of scholastic achievement for a black child as for a white child. There are also other internal types of evidence, described in a later section, which indicate that these tests are not biased against blacks. A black child with a low IQ has the same problems with scholastic material as a white child with the same low IQ. The IQ does not misrepresent either child's scholastic ability. Whether or not a low-IQ child who is performing far below his classmates should or should not be placed in a special class is an entirely separate issue, with no bearing on the question of test bias.

2. *SAT.* The most widely used college entrance examination, which is required by most selective colleges in the United States, is the College Entrance Examination Board's Scholastic Aptitude Test, better known as the College Boards or the SAT (described in Chapter 1). No other test has been more extensively or thoroughly investigated for predictive bias in the white and black populations of college applicants.

The results of the many studies of bias in the SAT are very clear-cut and amazingly consistent, considering the range of colleges in which the studies were conducted. The SAT's validity for predicting college grades is about .50 for both whites and blacks. More of the reported validity coefficients are slightly higher for blacks. When SAT scores are combined with high school grades, the predictive validity is raised to about .60. This all means that the SAT can be used by college admissions officers with equal effectiveness for blacks and whites alike.

An important general finding is that for blacks SAT scores are a better predictor of college grades than are high school grades, whereas for whites high school grades are a slightly better predictor. The main reason is probably that grading standards in different high schools are more variable and less accurate indicators of academic performance for blacks than for whites. Blacks with strong academic aptitudes are at a greater advantage when college selection is based on the SAT rather than high school grades.

Although the validity of the SAT is essentially the same for whites and blacks, in many studies the white and black prediction lines do differ slightly. In all cases the black prediction line is below the white, which means that if separate prediction lines are not used (as they are not, in most racially integrated colleges), the common prediction line (based mostly on whites) slightly overestimates the grade-point average of blacks. The overestimation is greatest for the highest-scoring black students. Thus, contrary to popular claims, the SAT, in every case where it is a biased predictor, is biased in *favor* of blacks. Elimination of the predictive bias would result in the selection of *fewer* blacks, assuming the selection procedure was based solely on the SAT scores and did not take applicants' race into account. In recent years, when blacks and whites are equated for aptitude, proportionally more blacks than whites enter college.

The SAT has not been so extensively studied in other ethnic groups, so it is impossible to draw equally firm conclusions for them. The largest study involving Mexican-Americans, on four campuses of the University of California, showed that neither SAT scores nor high school grades systematically underestimates or overestimates the average GPA of Mexican-American students. But other studies have shown some predictive *over*estimation of Mexican-American grades by the SAT, usually a lesser degree of overestimation than in the case of blacks. The majority of studies find that the SAT is not a biased predictor of college grades for Mexican-Americans.

Studies of the SAT's predictive validity for college students from different socioeconomic (SES) backgrounds show no indication of bias disfavoring (i.e., *under*estimating) applicants of lower SES. The SAT does not consistently under- or overestimate college grades of students from a wide range of SES. In fact, if getting into college were based solely on SAT scores, the one group in the population that would show the largest percentage increase in college admissions would be the children of white blue-collar workers. The tests can "read through" the veneer of social class background to identify academic talent more objectively and accurately than teachers' marks or interviews by college admissions officers.

Students' high school records are a considerably more biased predictor of college performance, resulting in greater overestimation of college grades for minorities, than SAT scores.

3. AFQT and GCT. The use of tests in the armed forces reveals no more overall bias with respect to blacks and whites than is found for college selection tests. But the nature of the bias, when it is found, is somewhat different, not because the tests are so different, but because the criteria predicted by the tests are often very different from the criterion of college performance.

The tests most commonly used by the military are the Armed Forces Qualification Test (AFQT), designed to screen youths for enlistment in the armed forces, and the General Classification Test (GCT), used to assign recruits to different specialized training courses.

The AFQT and GCT are essentially tests of general mental ability, and are better predictors of general job performance than any other single test. That is because the general ability factor enters into nearly every type of job performance and especially in job training, even when the training does not appear to involve anything very "intellectual." Comparisons of the bottom one-third, middle one-third, and top one-third of recruits on these measures of general aptitude show, for example, that when they are trained on tasks such as visual monitoring, rifle assembly, missile preparation, phonetic alphabet learning, and map plotting, the low-aptitude recruits need two to four times more training time, two to five times more training trials, and two to six times more prompting in these various tasks than the middle- and high-aptitude recruits.

The placement of recruits in the most appropriate training programs in terms of their tested aptitudes is estimated to save the armed forces more than $400 million per year. The random allocation of recruits to different training courses would result in a much higher failure rate and the need for retraining in other programs than when assignments are based on test scores. Hence a great economy in military training is made possible by aptitude tests. Specialized aptitude tests, used in combination with tests of general ability, slightly improve prediction of performance in certain training programs that call for special abilities, such as mechanical aptitude, numerical ability, motor coordination and dexterity, and response to visual or auditory stimuli.

General ability tests do not predict performance on many armed forces jobs quite as well as they can predict school or college grades, mainly because general cognitive ability is less important in jobs that call for other kinds of ability. The less the intellectual demands of the job, the less well does a general ability test predict performance.

Predictive bias of AFQT and GCT scores for blacks and whites is generally slight or nonsignificant for most training criteria. When it is found, however, it takes the form of white and black prediction lines that are nonparallel and therefore cross each other. Invariably this results in two kinds of predictive bias when race is not taken into account: blacks scoring below the black average on the AFQT or GCT are underestimated, and blacks scoring above the average are overestimated in job training and performance, relative to whites. This predictive bias can be eliminated by using separate prediction lines for each racial group.

4. *GATB.* The most widely used and most carefully researched test battery for employment selection in civilian jobs is the General Aptitude Test Battery (GATB) developed by the U.S. Employment Service. This battery of twelve tests measures nine different aptitudes which, in various combinations, have useful predictive validity for literally hundreds of different civilian jobs, from semiskilled to professional.

For some years, the U.S. Department of Labor has conducted studies of bias in the prediction of job performance of blacks and whites from their GATB scores. Thousands of persons in some thirty different occupational classifications have now been studied. In not one of these studies is there a significant difference in the predictive validity of the GATB composites for whites and blacks. However, when the same prediction line is used for whites and blacks, the GATB scores in some cases slightly overestimate blacks' job performance. (Underestimation of black job performance by the GATB is never found.) Consistently, when there was any indication of predictive bias in different job categories, it favored blacks—that is, more blacks than whites who passed the GATB selection cutoff actually failed on the job.

The studies of Hispanics and Asians on the GATB involve too few subjects for any reliable generalizations.

Studies of blacks and whites based on many other employment selection tests in a wide variety of occupations show results very much in line with the results described for the GATB. When significant predictive bias is detected, it is invariably the case that the test scores overestimate blacks' actual performance on the job. This is even more clearly in evidence when the criterion is assessed by some more objective means than supervisor ratings of job performance, such as a work-sample test or a job-knowledge test. Blacks tend to fall just as far below whites on work sample and job knowledge assessments as on aptitude test scores.

Childhood Test Scores as a Function of Age

As childen mature physically, their mental capabilities also grow, and this is reflected in the regular increase in raw scores (i.e., number of items passed) on all tests of general mental ability. A graphic plot showing the gradual rise in raw scores as age increases is called a mental growth curve. We can also plot mental growth curves for single test items, by showing the percentage of children who can pass the item at each year of age from early childhood to maturity. Good mental test items yield a growth curve showing a smooth regular increase in the percentage of children passing the item at each successive year of age.

What has this to do with test bias? Just this: if a test or individual test items showed these regular mental growth curve characteristics in population A but not in population B, it would indicate that the test is biased against population B.

When such mental growth curves, both for total test scores or for single items, are plotted for white children and black children on standard IQ tests, both groups show highly regular mental growth curves. The only important difference is that the black growth curve lags behind the white. Thus there is no indication of test bias in terms of this criterion. At any given age, in the range above age 2, a smaller percentage of black than of white children pass any given item in the test. If we determine the age at which about one-half of black children can pass an item, we find that the same item is passed by about one-half of white children who are 10 to 20 percent younger. Thus the average black 10-year-old performs on these tests about like the average white 8- or 9-year-old. Yet standard IQ tests and their individual items reflect the smooth, regular growth curves of mental ability equally well for blacks and whites. If this were not found for a particular test, it would constitute a very strong argument that the test was biased. But the finding of regular growth curves for blacks and whites on a given test, by itself, does not prove the absence of bias, because the test could be measuring something different in the two groups and both things could show regular growth curves. Height and weight and physical strength, for example, all show growth curves that resemble the mental growth curve. Hence the mental growth curve criterion of test bias, to carry much conviction, must be supplemented by other evidence that the test is measuring the same thing for the groups in question. Such evidence is sought in the pattern of the test's correlations with a host of other diverse variables. If the test's correlations with a variety of other variables is the same for both groups, there is a strong presumption that the test measures the same trait equally well in both groups and that the test scores have the same meaning in both groups.

Kinship Correlations of Test Scores

If a test shows different kinship correlations for two groups, it is a strong indication of bias, unless, of course, the difference in correlations is due to some statistical artifact such as a markedly restricted range of scores in one group. An unbiased test should show the same correlations between twins, or siblings, or parents and children, or any other kinships, for different populations. Also, the average absolute difference (the difference regardless of sign) in test scores between kins should be the same in different groups.

This is what we find in comparing kinship correlations and absolute differences between kins in test scores of whites and blacks. On a number of mental tests, the correlation between siblings is the same for blacks and whites, as is also the average absolute difference between siblings. The same thing is true for twins. Thus, with respect to kinship correlations and differences, our standard tests behave as we should expect if they are not biased for blacks or whites. This in itself does not necessarily prove the absence of bias, because the bias could conceivably affect the scores of all kins to the same degree. On the other hand, if kinship correlations and absolute differences between kins were *not* the same for both racial groups, it would be definite evidence of bias. Note that such a method for detecting bias can prove the presence of bias if there is a significant difference between the groups, but it cannot prove the absence of bias if there is not a significant difference. It is like the case of proving that a suspected burglar is guilty by showing his fingerprints on the stolen goods, whereas the absence of fingerprints would not prove that he is innocent. Tests are in the same position in terms of the kinship criterion of bias—the evidence does not prove them "guilty," and so they are accorded the presumption, but not proof, of "innocence."

Internal Indicators of Test Bias

There are a number of characteristics of tests themselves, aside from the total score, which should reasonably be expected to differ from one group to another if, in fact, the test is culturally biased. I shall describe several of these characteristics, selecting only those that do not require very complicated statistical reasoning.

Internal Consistency Reliability

A test's reliability coefficient tells us how internally consistent the test is in whatever trait it measures. It is related to the degree to which all the items comprising the test are correlated with one another. Clearly, a test that is culturally biased against a particular group should be more likely to have lower reliability for that group than for a group against which it is not biased. A significant difference in reliability coefficients is indicative of bias.

Comparisons of the reliability coefficients of a number of widely used tests in large samples of blacks and whites show no appreciable or consistent differences, hence no indication of bias.

Item Discriminability

Item discriminability means how well a single item discriminates between high and low scorers on the test as a whole. Usually the top and bottom 27 percent of persons in the total score distribution are compared on the percentage passing the item. A good item shows a much higher percentage of high scorers than of low scorers who pass it.

Items differ considerably in discriminability. It is an important finding that when the diverse items of an IQ test are rank-ordered for discriminability in a white sample and in a black sample, the rank order is the same for both groups. This means the items that best discriminate between groups of high and low intelligence among whites are the same items that best discriminate among blacks. In other words, all the items behave in the same way in both groups. This would seem unlikely in a culture-biased test, unless it could be convincingly argued that all of the diverse items in the test are equally culture-biased.

We can also examine how well each of the items of a test discriminates between groups of children who differ by, say, two years in age. We find that the items that best discriminate between high- and low-ability groups are also the same items that best discriminate between older and younger children, and they are the same items for blacks as for whites. Again the items behave the same in both racial groups.

Finally, we can determine how much each item discriminates between groups of blacks and whites in terms of the percentage of each group that passes the item. It turns out that the items that discriminate most *between* blacks and whites are the same items that best discriminate high- and low-ability groups *within* each racial group. This combination of findings would seem highly improbable for a culture-biased test. If the racial discriminability of the items were due to cultural bias, we would then have to explain why the cultural differences reflected in each item so closely parallel the ability differences and age differences found within each racial group. There is no theory of cultural differences that would predict such a finding. The finding, however, is what would be expected with test items that are not culturally biased, but measure with equal accuracy in both the black and white populations.

Rank Order of Item Difficulty

This is one of the best methods for identifying biased test items. The difficulty level of an item for a given group is indexed by the percentage of all persons in the group who pass the item, which is technically termed the item's p value. Thus, relatively easy items have large p values, and difficult items have small p values. An item of average difficulty for the group has a p value of 50; that is, 50 percent of the group pass the item and 50 percent fail.

The test in question is given to large representative samples of two subpopulations, usually whites and blacks. The p values of each item in the test are determined separately for each group. The items are then rank-ordered in difficulty (p values), from easiest to hardest, for each group. The ranks of the two groups can be lined up side by side, for example:

<table>
<tr><td></td><td colspan="2" align="center">*Rank Order of Difficulty*</td></tr>
<tr><td align="center">*Item*</td><td align="center">*In Group A*</td><td align="center">*In Group B*</td></tr>
<tr><td align="center">a</td><td align="center">1 (easiest)</td><td align="center">1 (easiest)</td></tr>
<tr><td align="center">b</td><td align="center">2</td><td align="center">4</td></tr>
<tr><td align="center">c</td><td align="center">3</td><td align="center">2</td></tr>
<tr><td align="center">d</td><td align="center">4</td><td align="center">5</td></tr>
<tr><td align="center">e</td><td align="center">5</td><td align="center">3</td></tr>
<tr><td align="center">etc.</td><td align="center">etc.</td><td align="center">etc.</td></tr>
</table>

We can then see to what extent all of the test items maintain the same rank order of difficulty for the two groups. The degree of similarity between the groups in the rank order of their item p values can be quantified by calculating the rank-order correlation between the two sets of ranks. The rank-order correlation can range from 0 (no greater similarity than chance) to 1 (perfect correspondence in ranks). Correlations above .95 represent a very high degree of similarity in the order of item difficulty. Items that differ markedly in rank order in the two groups can be suspected of bias. That is, the item is too easy or too difficult for a particular group in relation to all of the other items in the test. Items that maintain the same rank order of difficulty in two groups can be presumed to be measuring the same ability in both groups.

Notice that an *overall* difference between groups' item p values, such that one group has almost uniformly lower p values on all items, will not lower the rank-order correlation.

Any test item for which different groups have had markedly unequal exposure or opportunity for learning would be considered a culture-biased item, and its rank order of difficulty would differ significantly between a group for which it is culturally biased and a group for which it is not.

We have found some extreme examples of such culturally biased items in the Peabody Picture Vocabulary Test (PPVT) when it was administered to schoolchildren in England and the results were compared with those obtained on children of the same age in the United States. The PPVT consists of 150 plates, each bearing four pictures. The tester states a word that is represented by one of the four pictures, and the subject is asked to point to the appropriate picture. Certain words are clearly culture-biased for comparing children reared in England with children reared in the United States. For example, the word "thermos" has a strikingly different rank order of difficulty in England than in the U.S. "Thermos" is an American trade name for what the English call a "vacuum flask." Similarly, "bronco" is an easy word for American children, but is unknown to a much larger percentage of English children of the same age. In England, "caboose" means a ship's kitchen, and hence many English children fail the PPVT item that requires pointing to the last car on a train. Certain words are biased in the reverse direction—they are relatively easier for the English than for Americans. For example, "bannister" and "goblet" are relatively easy items for the English. Enough of these item biases go in opposite directions so that they nearly balance out, and English children and white American children of the same age obtain about the same total score, on the average.

A very different finding emerges when we compare American black and white children attending the same schools. Overall they differ about 15 IQ points on the PPVT. But the PPVT items are obviously so culture-loaded that we might expect certain items to reveal cultural differences between blacks and whites by showing marked differences in rank order of difficulty, as was found in comparing English and American children. It turns out that the rank order of item difficulty is almost exactly the same in both racial groups, although blacks show a consistently smaller percentage passing than whites on every item of the PPVT. There are no markedly deviant items—the rank-order correlation of item p values between blacks and whites is .98, a very high correlation indeed. For comparison, the rank-order correlation of PPVT item p values between males and females all of the same race is also .98. In other words, the relative difficulties of the highly culture-loaded PPVT items differ no more between whites and blacks than between males and females of the same race, whether white or black. Whatever cultural difference between blacks and whites on the PPVT is revealed by comparing the rank order of item difficulties is no greater than the cultural difference between males and females of the same social background. A few PPVT items show significant sex differences in p values—for example, "casserole" and "parachute."

The vocabulary subtest of the Stanford–Binet IQ test shows comparable results, with a rank-order correlation of .98 between the item difficulties of blacks and whites. Again, blacks show consistently lower p values on every word. This suggests either that blacks have an overall smaller vocabulary than whites of the same age or that all the words in the vocabulary test are about equally culture-biased. But it seems puzzling that such a diverse assortment of words should reflect such uniform differences in cultural exposure to the words.

If a cultural difference can make for such results, it should be possible to make up a vocabulary test that is equally culture-biased in favor of blacks, yet preserves the same rank order of difficulty of the items in black and white samples. The Black Intelligence Test (BIT) was an attempt to create such a test. It is a multiple-choice vocabulary test consisting entirely of black ghetto slang. Blacks obtain higher scores on this test than do whites. But the test shows extreme cultural bias in terms of the rank order of item difficulties, which correlate only .52 between blacks and whites, as compared with the correlation of .98 for the Peabody Picture Vocabulary Test, .94 for the Wonderlic Personnel Test, .96 for the Wechsler Intelligence Scale for Children, .98 for Raven's Progressive Matrices, and .98 for the Stanford–Binet vocabulary subtest—all tests on which blacks average the equivalent of 15 IQ points lower than whites. The lower vocabulary scores of blacks probably reflect their overall smaller vocabulary, as indicated by a study in which a count of the total number of different words of *any* kind used by groups of black and white primary school children revealed that the black children use only half as many different words as white children of the same age.

What makes a cultural difference hypothesis especially untenable is that the rank order of item difficulties is so very similar even in tests composed of extremely diverse types of items. The items of the Stanford–Binet test between ages 3½ and 5½, for example, are of all different types, as shown in Table 4, along with the percentages of white and black 4-year-olds passing each item. The rank-order correlation between the whites' and blacks' item difficulties is .99, with a larger percentage of whites passing every item. The items of the Wechsler Intelligence Scale for Children are about as diverse as those of the Stanford–Binet, and show a similarly high rank-order correlation of item difficulties for blacks and whites. On the average, blacks do not perform significantly better than whites on any of the 161 items of the WISC.

With tests composed of such heterogeneous contents and diverse types of items, the importance of these findings is that they are almost impossible to reconcile with the cultural difference explanation of the white-black difference on mental tests, which argues that whites and blacks have had differing degrees of experience and familiarity with the informational contents of the tests. But it seems so improbable that the diverse kinds of experience or familiarity called for by these highly varied items would all diffuse across the racial-cultural boundary in an order that exactly corresponds to the order of difficulty of the items among whites, and to the order of diffusion across age boundaries among whites and among blacks, and to the order of diffusion of information from brighter to slower children of the same age within each racial group. No one has ever posited any cultural difference of such a nature that could be responsible for such results.

Determining the rank order of item difficulties in each racial group, of course, is a means for assessing the validity of popular claims of cultural bias in specific test items. For example, a favorite target of test critics is the WISC Verbal Comprehension item:

What is the thing to do if a fellow (girl) much smaller than yourself starts to fight with you?

TABLE 4
Stanford–Binet Test Items and Percentage Passing
by 2,526 White and 2,514 Black 4-year-olds

		% Passing	
Item	Description	White	Black
III-6, 1	Identify the larger of 2 balls.	89%	71%
III-6, 3	Match pictures of animals.	95	80
III-6, 4	Name common objects in pictures.	91	81
III-6, 6	Answer either "What do we do when we're thirsty?" or "Why do we have stoves?"	81	50
IV,1	Picture vocabulary: Name the objects on 14 of 18 cards.	47	23
IV,2	Child is shown three objects (e.g., car, dog, shoe); one is hidden; child must then name the hidden object.	79	67
IV,3	Opposite analogies: e.g., "Brother is a boy, sister is a _____." (Must answer 2 out of 5 correctly.)	59	35
IV,4	Picture identification: e.g., "Which one do we cook on?"	69	41
IV-6, 2	Opposite analogies II. (Same as IV, but must answer 3 out of 5 correctly.)	34	12
IV-6, 3	Object similarities and differences: pick out object in picture that is different from others.	60	32
IV-6, 5	Follow instructions: e.g., "Put the pencil on the chair, go over and shut the door, and bring the box over here."	61	41
IV-6, 6	Answer either "What do we do with our eyes?" or "What do we do with our ears?"	49	31
V, 1	Must add at least 2 features to incomplete drawing of a man.	27	11
V, 3	Must know meaning of 2 of the following: *ball, hat, stove.*	57	32
V, 4	Copy a square. (Must have "square" corners.)	15	5
V, 6	Construct a rectangle from 2 triangular cards.	9	6

Those who point to this item as a prime example of culture bias in the WISC argue that black children are typically taught to "fight back," and therefore the keyed correct response (which is "not to fight back") runs counter to their cultural values. Yet it turns out that this item is slightly easier for blacks, relative to all the 160 other items in the WISC, than it is for whites! Removing this item from the WISC would penalize the black subjects. This is one more illustration of the great fallibility of subjective judgments of item bias.

Culture-loaded versus Culture-reduced Tests

As was explained at the beginning of this chapter, test items can be arranged subjectively along a continuum of culture loading, ranging from highly culture-loaded items to very culture-reduced items. There is a high degree of agreement among judges when they are asked to differentiate items that fall in the upper and lower extremes of this continuum—when items are judged as the "most cultural" and "least cultural" in informational content. Culture-loaded and culture- reduced experimental tests have been composed entirely of items taken from many standardized IQ tests and classified by a large number of judges as "most cultural" and "least cultural."

If the average difference between blacks and whites on standard IQ tests is a result of the cultural content of these tests, we should expect to find a considerably larger average white-black difference on the experimental test composed of the items judged as "most cultural" as compared with the experimental test composed of the "least cultural" items. In fact, however, just the opposite is found. Blacks at every socioeconomic level score significantly better on the "most cultural" than on the "least cultural" test. This is true even when the difficulty levels of the most and least culture-loaded tests are made to be exactly the same for whites. For example, here are two items that a large number of judges agreed to assign to the "most" and "least" cultural categories, respectively:

ABYSMAL ::

(a) bottomless (b) temporal (c) incidental (d) matchless

A hotel serves a mixture of three parts cream and two parts milk. How many pints of cream will it take to make 15 pints of this mixture?
(a) 5 (b) 6 (c) 7½ (d) 9 (e) 12

For blacks, the first item is easier than the second; for whites it is the reverse. The relatively better performance of blacks on the items generally judged to be the more culturally loaded in most standard tests is a typical finding. It comes as a great surprise to those who have always assumed, without any evidence, that the generally lower test scores of blacks are due to cultural bias.

How can we explain this surprising finding?

If we examine the items that are classified by judges as the "most" and the "least" cultural (when these items are matched in difficulty), we notice one, and only one, rather systematic difference between them. The most culture-loaded items usually call for some specific bit of information which the subject has to have acquired before taking the test and which, in the test situation, he simply has to recall from memory. The difficulty level of such items depends mostly on the rarity of the bit of information called for, such as knowing a particular uncommon word or little-known fact. The least culture-loaded items, on the other hand, generally call for some kind of reasoning or problem solving that must be done in the test situation itself. The difficulty level of such items depends on the complexity of the mental operations required to arrive at the solution. Usually these are the most highly g-loaded items of any test—items of the type that led Spearman to characterize g as relation eduction, logical inference, and abstract reasoning, regardless of the specific item content that is used to elicit these cognitive processes.

Verbal versus Nonverbal Tests

It seems plausible that verbal tests, being dependent on a specific language, would allow more scope for cultural bias to creep in than would be the case for nonverbal tests. Blacks who most often speak Black English, and who are accustomed to syntax different from Standard English, might therefore be especially handicapped by verbal tests.

A thorough survey of all published studies comparing the average difference between whites and blacks on verbal and nonverbal tests of every kind reveals that, contrary to the expectation of the cultural-difference argument, the groups differ significantly less on verbal than on nonverbal tests. All other ethnic minority groups in the United States—Mexican, Indian, Puerto Rican, and Asian—perform relatively better on nonverbal than on verbal tests. This should not be surprising, considering that English is the second language for many members of these groups.

My study of all this literature, however, leads me to conclude that the verbal-nonverbal distinction is not of fundamental importance. The greater white-black difference on nonverbal than on verbal tests is merely a consequence of the fact that many verbal tests call more on memory, whereas nonverbal tests require more complex mental manipulation of rather simple elements to produce the correct answer. These contrasting characteristics suggest a difference in the g loadings of verbal and nonverbal tests. It is the test's g loading—its dependence on reasoning or inference—rather than whether it is verbal or nonverbal that determines how much it discriminates between whites and blacks. When verbal and nonverbal items are matched on both difficulty and g loading in the white population, blacks perform equally on the verbal and nonverbal items. Mexican-Americans, however, still perform less well on verbal tests under these conditions. The verbal-nonverbal distinction is much more important than the g-loadedness of items for groups in which English is a second language. Their lower verbal scores, as compared with nonverbal scores, are more clearly related to the language factor than to differences in the tests' g loadings.

Factor Analysis of Tests in White and Black Samples

Factor analysis is a complex mathematical method for reducing a large number of tests to a smaller number of factors; that is, more fundamental dimensions of ability that account for the intercorrelations among all the tests. A factor analysis begins with the intercorrelations among a number of different tests, and from these are determined the primary ability factors that account for the individual differences in scores on all the tests in the battery. The number of factors is usually far fewer than the number of tests. For example, the Wechsler Intelligence Scales consist of eleven different subtests. Factor analysis extracts only four factors from these eleven subtests: g, the general ability factor common to all of the tests; V, a verbal ability factor found largely in the verbal tests; P, a performance factor found mainly in the nonverbal tests, and M, a short-term memory factor found in digit span memory and in problem arithmetic (because the elements of a problem have to be retained in memory until it is solved).

If a battery of highly diverse tests were culturally biased against one group, it would be unlikely to show the same pattern of intercorrelations among the tests, and hence the same factorial structure, as are found in a group for which the tests are not considered culturally inappropriate. Therefore, we can use factor analysis to detect test bias. If factor analysis fails to reveal the same factors in two cultural groups, the tests entering into the factor analysis may be suspected of cultural bias. Even when the factors are the same in both groups, if any particular test shows a markedly different factorial composition in one group than in the other, it would be suspected of bias.

A number of quite large and diverse batteries of standardized tests have been subjected to factor analysis in both white and black samples. What all of these analyses show, virtually without exception, is that exactly the same factors emerge from the white and black test data. Moreover, there is a high degree of similarity between blacks and whites in the sizes of the factor loadings on the various tests. For example, the tests that show a high g loading for whites also show high g loadings for blacks. The larger and more representative the samples, the greater seems to be the similarity between the factor analyses based on them.

The results of factor analyses of numerous tests in black and white samples afford the possibility of checking an interesting hypothesis about average white-black test score differences originally suggested by Charles Spearman in 1927. Spearman had noticed in a battery of diverse tests that the magnitude of the average difference between whites and blacks varied from one test to another, and rather closely corresponded to the varying sizes of the tests' g loadings. The largest white-black differences were seen on the tests that were the most g-loaded. This was a potentially important observation, because, if it were further substantiated, it would mean that the white-black difference in test scores is mainly due, not to specific cultural factors in this or that test, but to a general factor that all ability tests measure in common, some more than others.

I have investigated Spearman's observation in several large-scale factor analyses of test batteries given to whites and blacks. In no case have the data contradicted Spearman's hypothesis, and in most cases there is a high degree of correspondence between various tests' g loadings and the magnitudes of the average white-black differences on the tests. In short, Spearman's hypothesis is strongly borne out by the data.

As mentioned earlier, a test item seems to elicit g according to the cognitive complexity of the item's demands. With this basic concept of the nature of *g* in mind, we tried a simple experiment using the forward digit span (FDS) and backward digit span (BDS) subtests of the revised Wechsler Intelligence Scale for Children (WISC-R). The reader will recall that in FDS, the tester reads off a string of digits at the rate of one digit per second, and the subject immediately repeats the string of digits. The test begins with a series of three digits, and the length of the series is increased by one digit until a length of series is reached for which the subject fails to recall the series correctly in two tries. The length of the longest series the subject can recall is termed his or her forward digit span. In BDS, the tester again reads off a series of digits, but now the subject must repeat them back in reverse order. The longest series the subject can repeat in reverse order is his or her backward digit span.

It would seem implausible to claim that the BDS test is any more culture-loaded than the FDS test. The essential difference between FDS and BDS is their difference in complexity, although it is only a small difference, because, as mental test items go, BDS is not very complex. But BDS requires the subject to transform the input series—he must mentally reverse the sequence of digits before ''reading'' them out. In short, BDS takes more mental work than FDS, and all subjects, without exception, can recall a longer series of digits forward than backward.

The FDS and BDS tests, in addition to the WISC-R Full Scale IQ, were obtained from 622 black and 622 white children drawn from elementary schools in California by a random sampling procedure.

Now, if BDS elicits more *g* than FDS, as we hypothesized, then we should expect a higher correlation between BDS and IQ than between FDS and IQ, because the Full Scale IQ is a good index of *g*. This is what was found, in both racial groups—BDS correlates about twice as much with IQ as does FDS. Now, if the average IQ difference between whites and blacks is essentially a difference in *g*, as Spearman had conjectured, then these groups should show a greater average difference on BDS than on FDS. This, in fact, is what was found. The average white-black difference on BDS is about double the difference on FDS, and this difference is still seen between whites and blacks classified into upper, middle, and low socioeconomic levels. The difference in the *g* loadings of FDS and BDS thus reveals an average difference between blacks and whites which cannot be accounted for by culture bias or socioeconomic status.

We have corroborated this finding in other experimental tests that are devised to differ markedly in *g* loadings. Tests of rote learning and memory, for example, have quite low *g* loadings and also show less difference between whites and blacks than any other types of mental tests. Yet these tests call for as much attention and motivation as any others; but they require little transformation or mental manipulation of the input. They emphasize learning and memorizing by repetition, in contrast to thinking and reasoning.

Analysis of Errors

If the specific errors made on tests differ between groups, we may suspect cultural bias. Errors can be most objectively analyzed in multiple-choice items. When large groups of black and white children fail a multiple-choice test item, we can determine whether they picked the same or different distractors (incorrect answers), and we can compare the percentage of whites and blacks who picked each of the several distractors.

When this kind of distractor analysis was made for large samples of age-matched black and white children who had been tested on the highly culture-loaded Peabody Picture Vocabulary Test and the nonverbal culture-reduced Raven Progressive Matrices, there was no difference between blacks and whites in their choices of distractors for the vast majority of the items that were failed. There are large differences in the "popularity" of different distractors—some "pull" many more errors than others. But those blacks and whites who fail an item show the same percentages of choices on the several distractors.

But there are some items on which blacks and whites differ in their predominant choice of distractors. We examined these distractors carefully and discovered an interesting thing. Some errors are more "sophisticated" than others. That is, more complex mental manipulations of the problem elements (but not complex enough to get the correct answer) lead to the selection of different distractors. For such items, older children (of either race) make different errors than younger children: The older children select the more "sophisticated" distractors. But the most interesting finding is that when groups of black and white children of the same age differed in their choice of distractors, the difference was the same as that found between younger and older white children. The distractors most commonly chosen by black children are the same distractors that are most often chosen by white children about two years younger. Thus the choice of distractors seems to be more related to mental age than to racial-cultural background. It appears as if the black children developmentally lag one to two years behind their white classmates in the elementary school years.

All of the features of test performance, such as different choice of distractors, that were found to discriminate significantly between white and black children of the same age could be simulated by comparing groups of older and younger children of the same race. Moreover, all of the tests' discriminating features between blacks and whites are *wiped out* when the test records of black children are compared with those of white children who are about two years younger. Thus the racial differences in test performance look much less like what we would expect from differences in cultural background than from a difference in overall rates of mental development. The evidence for this hypothesis seems more compelling when we look at the results of tests that are specially intended to reflect developmental trends.

Developmental Tests

The Gesell Figure Copying Test (FCT) consists of ten simple geometric forms such as circle, cross, square, triangle, rectangle, diamond, cylinder, and cube, each printed on the upper half of each page of a test booklet. The figures are arranged in increasing order of difficulty, from a circle to a three-dimensional representation of a cube. The child is given a pencil with eraser and asked to copy each figure, taking as much time as needed to make the copy look as much like the model as possible. The test's difficulty level makes it most suitable for children between the ages of 3 and 12. Performance is scored by how closely the child's copy of each figure approximates the model.

The remarkable thing about this test is that a child typically copies each figure in the sequence at practically an adult level of performance—up to a point where the next figure in the sequence presents great difficulty. The child may copy the circle, cross, square, triangle, and crisscrossed rectangle perfectly, but fail miserably in trying to copy the next figure in the sequence—a diamond shape. Typically the child fails every figure following the first failed figure. The child tries, erases, and tries again, but the drawing remains peculiarly distorted in its most essential features, often scarcely resembling the model.

As children mature, they can correctly copy more of the figures in the sequence. For example, children need a mental age of about 7 to copy the diamond, of about 9 to copy the cylinder, and of about 12 to copy the cube. It is extremely difficult to teach children how to copy the figures that they cannot spontaneously copy. Even when a child can be taught to copy one of the more advanced figures, it does not improve performance on an easier figure that the child couldn't copy correctly.

This highly developmental task—which, incidentally, is an excellent measure of *g*—has nothing essentially to do with motor skill or perception. A child's difficulty with a particular figure reflects the child's inability to conceptualize the essential features of the figure, such as the fact that sides of the diamond are straight lines, two opposite angles are acute and the other two are obtuse, and the vertical axis is longer than the horizontal axis. The child must be able to analyze the figure into these characteristic features to be able to copy it. His copying performance is guided by the accuracy of his concept of the figure.

This concept with respect to each figure seems to undergo a typical progressive change as the child mentally matures, from early to later childhood. These progressive changes are seen in the copying efforts of children at different ages. Certain distinctive distortions and difficulties in copying a given figure are common at certain ages, and the difficulties qualitatively change with age.

The Figure Copying Test has been given to thousands of elementary school children—white, black, Mexican-American, and Asian-American. Although there are large group differences in total score on the FCT, children of every group show the same developmental sequence of difficulties, regardless of their cultural backgrounds. But these developmental landmarks are reached by different groups at different ages, on the average. At any given age Asian (Chinese and Japanese) children score highest, followed closely by whites, then Mexican-Americans, and lastly blacks. The differences between certain groups are considerable. For example, black children in the fourth grade (ages 9–10) perform on a par with Asian children in the first grade and slightly below white children in the second grade. Mexican-Americans, although socioeconomically lower than any other groups tested, score about halfway between Asians and blacks and nearly on a par with middle-class white children. It would seem most difficult to account for all these effects in terms of differences in cultural background *per se.* There is no feature of performance that distinguishes, say, the average 10-year-old black child's drawings from the average 8-year-old white child's. This looks more like a general developmental difference than like a cultural difference.

The Swiss psychologist Jean Piaget devised a number of varied developmental tests that are especially revealing of a child's stage of mental development. The tests are simple tasks, using familiar objects, that call for judgment, mental manipulation, and reasoning about things that are universally available to observation.

One example is the test of the child's concept of the horizontality of liquid. The child is shown an upright bottle of red liquid, then is shown a full-size drawing of the empty bottle tilted 45 degrees from the vertical position, and is given a red crayon and asked to draw the red liquid in the tilted bottle. Most children below age 8 or 9 draw a line that is parallel to the bottom of the bottle, while older children more often correctly draw a horizontal line, showing an understanding of the concept that the surface of a liquid remains horizontal regardless of the position of its container. It is interesting that many children less than 8 years of age do not improve their incorrect drawing even after being shown the liquid in the actual tilted bottle.

This test was given to large samples of three ethnic groups in grades 1 to 3 (age 6–8) in California schools. The percentages passing the test were as follows: Asian, 43 percent; white, 35 percent; black, 13 percent. Nine other Piagetian tests of other basic concepts were given to the same groups. Blacks performed less well than whites and Asians on every test; Asians exceeded whites on seven of the ten items. The group differences on these tests are of slightly greater magnitude than those found with most standard tests of general intelligence. It has been shown in factor analyses of Piaget's tests that they are exceptionally good measures of Spearman's *g*. Although the Piagetian tests tend to magnify the white-black difference by about 20 percent, compared with the difference in Stanford–Binet IQ, they tend to diminish differences between whites, Mexicans, and Indians; and Asians and Arctic Eskimos surpass urban white children of the same age.

5

Environmental Influences on IQ

In CHAPTER 3 WE SAW that, according to most studies, about 70 percent of the population variance in IQ is attributable to genetic variation, and at least 5 percent of the variance is due to measurement error, which leaves about 25 percent of the IQ variance to be accounted for by environmental factors. A large number of studies have tried to discover the nature of the environmental factors that contribute to IQ variance. Many important facts have been learned from these studies, but mysteries about the environment remain. It is difficult to pin down all of the environmental factors that contribute to the nongenetic variance in IQ.

Prenatal, Perinatal, and Neonatal Factors

Biologically, the existence of an individual begins at the moment of conception. Environmental influences begin at the same time. How important are the prenatal influences on the developing embryo and fetus in terms of the child's later IQ?

There are many factors that could conceivably affect the brain's development during gestation and thereby affect the child's later intellectual development: the mother's health, including her nutrition and smoking and drinking habits during pregnancy, her age and the number of previous pregnancies, the interval since her last pregnancy, blood type and Rh incompatibility of mother and fetus, her history of X-ray exposure, and her red blood cell count, to list a few.

Besides all these factors that can act during gestation, there are many so-called perinatal factors—all the things that might be involved in labor and delivery: duration of pregnancy, induction of labor, duration of labor, forceps delivery, Caesarian section, breech birth, weight and condition of the placenta, premature separation of the placenta from the womb, anoxia (oxygen deprivation) at birth, birthweight, and many others.

In the past decade, the National Institutes of Health conducted the most elaborate and comprehensive study ever attempted to assess the effects of prenatal and perinatal factors on children's later IQs. The study also looked at neonatal factors—conditions of the infant during the first year of life—that might affect the child's later IQ, including illness, trauma, abnormalities, and infant tests of sensory-motor development. This large investigation, known as the Collaborative Study (reported by S. H. Broman, P. L. Nichols, and W. A. Kennedy, *Preschool IQ: Prenatal and Early Developmental Correlates,* Erlbaum Publishers, 1975), involved 26,760 children in various regions of the United States (approximately 45 percent white, 55 percent black), whose mothers were enlisted in the study during pregnancy. The children were periodically examined up to age 8 years. At age 4 they were all given the Stanford–Binet IQ test to determine how much of the variance in IQ could be explained by all the prenatal, perinatal, and neonatal factors that had been carefully assessed during the pregnancy, the birth, and the infant's first year of life.

The study took into account all the variables I have already listed and many more; forty-five prenatal, thirty perinatal, and thirty-four neonatal factors were assessed. All these factors combined account for only about 3 to 4 percent of the total variance in IQ at 4 years of age. This is true for both whites and blacks. This does not mean that these factors, when extreme, are not important to a particular child's mental development. But the extreme conditions that could affect later IQ are so rare in the total population as to account for very little of the overall variation in children's IQs by age four.

The Collaborative Study also assessed 60 other variables concerning family background, including the mother's IQ and both parents' education, socioeconomic status, and mental and physical health.. When these 60 background variables were added to the 109 prenatal, perinatal, and neonatal variables, the whole composite of 169 variables accounted for about 25 percent of the IQ variance at age 4. Obviously, the family background variables account for much more of the IQ variance than do the other factors. But many of the background factors, such as mother's IQ and education, include genetic factors as well, so they really cannot give a correct indication of strictly environmental influences on variation in children's IQs.

What the Collaborative Study indicates most clearly is that very little of the total IQ variation among children, both white and black, can be attributed to the conditions of pregnancy, birth, or the infant's first year that investigators have been able to assess. Although any one or a combination of these factors, when extremely unfavorable for a particular individual, can have a severe effect on the individual's IQ, the average effect of all these variables as they normally occur in the population is very slight, amounting to less than 4 percent of the total variance in IQ.

Nutrition

The evidence from a number of studies indicates that the variation in nutrition within the U.S. population at present contributes no detectable amount to variance in IQ. However, prolonged severe malnutrition in the first two to four years of life, as occurs in some Third World countries, can stunt mental growth by as much as 20 IQ points or more. Investigators have found many such cases, although they are still a small minority, in such places as Africa, Central and South America, and India. But they have not found IQ-depressing degrees of malnutrition in any segment of the present U.S. population.

A relatively short period of up to six months of severe malnutrition in otherwise adequately nourished infants or children does not permanently affect their IQs. Even severe famine during the prenatal period and extending into the first few months of infancy has no significant effect on the average mental test scores of the victims tested in their late teens. This was shown in a study in the Netherlands. Parts of the population had undergone extreme famine near the end of World War II, conditions that resulted in a marked decline in average infant weight and a steep rise in the rates of fetal loss and infant mortality. Yet about 19 years later, some 20,000 young people who had been conceived and born under these dire conditions of malnutrition scored every bit as high on a nonverbal IQ test as a comparable population sample which had never been deprived of adequate nutrition. Thus, we can conclude that nutritional factors are not a significant cause of differences in IQ in our present population.

Birth Order

Birth order contributes a small but significant amount to IQ variance—about 1 or 2 percent. Each successive child born into a family has, on the average, a slightly lower IQ, by about .7 IQ point, than the previously born child. This birth-order effect is slightly magnified when the births are more closely spaced. A parallel effect is found for scholastic achievement as well. Also, there are disproportionate numbers of first-born among persons who are eminent enough to have biographical entries in *Who's Who* or the *Encyclopaedia Britannica.*

The birth-order effect is entirely nongenetic, because genetic theory offers no reason to expect order of birth to result in any systematic difference in genetic makeup. Each sibling receives a random half of each parent's genes, so there should be no genetic reason why siblings born later should average lower in IQ.

Strangely, single children (i.e., those without siblings) have slightly lower IQs than first-born children who have one or more younger siblings.

Scientists have not yet generally agreed on an explanation of the effect of birth order on IQ. While there can be no doubt of the reality of the effect, it is difficult to investigate because the effect is very slight; we would need enormous samples to detect it as statistically significant. This makes it extremely difficult to determine any specific environmental factors that are hypothesized to be responsible.

The most prominent and ingenious theory, proposed by social psychologist Robert Zajonc, argues as follows. The first child enters a family composed of two adults and receives their undivided attention. In addition, the "mental level" of the child's social environment is the average mental age of the two parents. The first child enjoys this advantage for at least nine months, usually longer. The second child entering the family must share the divided attention of the parents and also experiences a social environment with an overall "mental level" composed of the average mental ages of the two parents and the first-born child—a considerably lower average "mental level" than was experienced by the first-born. Moreover, the first-born child, being more mature and experienced, can act as a teacher to the younger sibling, which is advantageous for the older child's mental development and sense of initiative. And so on, with each successive child in the family. The theory neatly accords with most of the observed effects of birth order and spacing of births, and predicts the slightly lower average IQ of twins as compared with singletons. Twins elicit divided attention from their parents or older siblings, and their birth into a family more drastically dilutes the average "mental level" of the social environment—twins can hardly learn much from each other during their early development.

Some psychologists now believe that a purely psychological theory of the birth order effect is inadequate. They believe that prenatal biological factors must be a necessary part of the explanation. The capacity of the mother's womb to nurture the fetus may be somewhat depleted with each sucessive full-term pregnancy. Something of this sort is suggested by the finding that when parents adopt a child and then have a natural child of their own, the second child, although the mother's first-born, is reared psychologically as the second-born. But these children are not lower in IQ than the first-born children to parents who adopt a second child. Another suggestion that prenatal factors are involved is that more closely spaced pregnancies result in lower birth weight of the second-born child as well as slightly lower IQ.

Family Size

Since, on the average, the IQ of each successive sibling in a family is about .7 of an IQ point lower than the previous sibling's, larger families inevitably have a lower average IQ simply because of this birth-order effect. But, in fact, it is found that the average difference in IQ between different-sized families is about two times greater than can be accounted for in terms of the birth-order effect alone. This means that part of the variance in IQ involves differences in family size that are independent of the IQ variance contributed by birth order.

The independent contribution of family size amounts to a decrease in the average IQ of the family of about .7 IQ point for each additional child. But family size *per se* has no directly causal implications for IQ, as the birth-order effect does. The explanation lies in the fact that parents with lower IQ, lower educational level, and lower socioeconomic status have a larger number of children, on the average, than parents with higher IQ, higher educational level, and higher socioeconomic status. The intercorrelations among all these variables involve both genetic and environmental factors.

Some social scientists have worried about the negative correlation between family size and IQ—the fact that parents with below-average IQs tend to have larger-than-average families with below-average children. This state of affairs existing over many generations should produce a steady decline in the average intelligence of the population. This worry seems to be mitigated by the fact that a smaller percentage of persons with below-average IQ ever marry or have children at all. Hence there presumably would not be a disproportionately high birth rate in the below-average segment of the population when all persons—the childbearing and the childless—in that segment of the population are taken into account. Whether or not this supposed "balance of forces" is actually such as to prevent a decline in the average IQ of our population is examined more closely in Chapter 7.

Home and Family Environment

Countless studies show substantial correlations between various elements of a child's home environment and IQ scores. "Home and family environment" includes variables such as the neighborhood, the number of rooms in the home, the presence of such amenities as telephone, television, and phonograph, the number of magazines and books, the parents' educational and occupational level, family income, whether private music lessons or dance lessons are given to the child, membership in established organizations, and travel experiences. All these variables are highly correlated with one another and are usually subsumed under the single label of socioeconomic status. The best overall indicators of SES are the occupational level of the chief working parent and the educational levels (years of schooling) of both parents.

Such composite indices of SES show correlations of about .40 to .50 with children's IQs, which means they account for about 15 to 25 percent of the IQ variance. (SES correlates about .70 with the parents' IQs, which means IQ predicts about 50 percent of the variance in the parents' SES.) Some studies rightly include the parents' IQs as part of the child's environment, and this, added to the other SES indices, can raise the correlation with child's IQ to over .70. If we include assessments of how much time the parents devote to their children in reading, conversation, playing games, and so on, and also some estimate of the intellectual quality of the parent-child interactions, our composite measure of "environmental influences" may correlate as high as .85 with the child's IQ—seemingly accounting for more than 70 percent of the IQ variance!

But wait! How is that possible if our heritability analysis in Chapter 3 attributes only about 25 percent or less of the total IQ variance to nongenetic or environmental factors? A moment's reflection reveals this is really not too much of a puzzle. When children are reared by their own parents, all of the intercorrelations between the several environmental variables, the parents' IQs, and the children's IQs represent a confounding of genetic and environmental causes.

This can be most easily understood in terms of Figure 7. In this diagram, directly measurable or observable variables are represented by rectangles; indirectly measurable or inferable variables are shown as ovals. Correlation without causation is indicated by curved lines. Direct causal connection is indicated by straight lines, with arrows showing the direction of causation. Notice that the quality of the home and family environment, which includes parental behavior, is directly influenced by the parents' IQs. The double arrow between the environment and the child's IQ shows that both influence each other. A brighter child, because of his genotype, may show a greater-than-

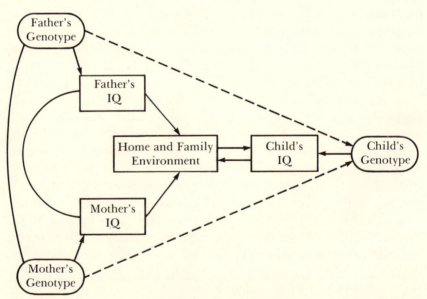

Figure 7. Diagram showing causal connections (straight arrows) and correlations (curved lines) between genetic and environmental factors that influence a child's IQ. In the case of an adopted child, the dashed lines should be deleted.

average interest in reading or in certain hobbies, causing the parents to provide more books and other equipment. Moreover, the intellectual quality of the parents' verbal and instructional interactions with the child are influenced by the child's manifest ability, which is reflected by IQ. A child's interaction with the environment thus acts like a positive feedback loop.

But notice the dashed lines going from the parents' genotypes for intelligence to the child's genotype for intelligence. This connection and the connection between parental IQs and the quality of the child's environment make it clear that the observed correlations between environmental indices and IQ are necessarily a mixture of environmental and genetic influences. This is unavoidable in any study based on children who are reared by their own biological parents.

For a proper study of the effects of the home and family environments on children's IQs, we obviously need a situation in which there is no connection between parent's and children's genotypes—that is, Figure 7 without the dashed lines. Only then will the correlation between environmental factors and child's IQ indicate the true causal influence of the environment, uncontaminated by any genetically mediated correlation between these variables. This is the situation we find when children are reared from early infancy in adoptive homes. Hence the most informative studies of environmental influences on IQ are studies of adopted children.

Adoption Studies

Adoptions are not arranged for the purpose of scientific studies, and so the evidence provided by them, although better than any other currently available, is not perfectly ideal from our standpoint, as it would be if the data could be obtained from a carefully designed experiment. We must keep in mind four main features of adoption studies that may bias the results.

1. Probably the most important feature is the ***restricted range of environmental variation*** among adoptive homes. Adoption agencies take great care in placing infants. They screen out prospective adoptive parents of low socioeconomic status, public welfare recipients, broken homes, or persons who show any signs of being mentally or emotionally unfit for the demands of parenthood. Consequently, couples who qualify to adopt a child are generally better-than-average parents and provide better-than-average environmental advantages for the adopted child. It would seem that the average adoptive home, including the quality of the parents, is superior to about 75 or 80 percent of homes in the general population, in the features deemed important by adoption agencies.

The result of this restriction of the range of adoptive environments is that it limits the size of the correlation that could be found between the measurable environmental differences among adoptive homes and the IQs of the adopted children. If children could be placed in foster homes selected purely at random from the total population, we should expect to find a somewhat higher correlation between environmental indices and foster children's IQs.

2. Second in importance, from our standpoint, is the *selective placement* of adopted children. Every adoption study shows some evidence of it. Agencies, whether intentionally or not, have a tendency to select infants who were born to brighter and better-educated young women for placement into homes with better-educated adoptive parents. This creates some degree of correlation between the child's genotype and certain characteristics of the adoptive home environment, which is influenced by the adoptive parents' IQ and educational level. Hypothetically, perfect selective placement could, of course, result in the same set of causal connections that occur when parents rear their own children, as depicted in Figure 7, because the child's adoptive parents would be perfectly equivalent to his biological parents. But in reality the selective placement we find in adoptions does not begin to approach that situation. Whatever small degree of selective placement does exist, however, would have the effect of slightly inflating the correlation between environmental indices and adopted children's IQ.

Even when selective placement is not admitted by the adoption agency, it can be detected in two ways: by finding a significant correlation between the IQ, education, or SES of the child's biological parents and the adoptive parents, or by finding a correlation between the IQ or educational level of the adopted child's biological mother and the IQs of the adoptive parents' biological children. When these correlations have been determined, they have always been very low—below .20. In general, the correlation between the IQs of biological and adoptive parents is less than .10. Thus selective placement is generally not a serious obstacle to drawing conclusions about the effects of home environment on IQ.

3. Probably the least important biasing factor in adoption studies, because of its small effect on the results, is the *absence of low-level IQs.* Agencies are cautious about placing infants who may be suspected of mental retardation either because the infant shows some neurological abnormality or because one or both of the biological parents are deemed mentally deficient. Such children are often reared in orphanages or placed in foster homes on a trial basis until they are old enough for a reliable assessment of their mental development. The most deficient children, therefore, seldom show up in adoption studies. The effect is to slightly raise the average level of the IQ of adopted children, who in most studies average about IQ 110. This is considerably above the average IQ of 100 in the general population, but not all of the 10 IQ points can be due to the early screening out of possibly subnormal children. Some part of the adoptive children's IQ advantage— probably about half—is brought about by their much better-than-average home environment and the beneficial influence on their psychological development from the couple who were specially selected for their good qualities as parents. But it is hard to know just what to make of the higher-than-average IQ of children in adoption studies, for the following reason, which may be the most serious biasing factor in adoption studies.

4. The sample of adoptees who take part in any study that involves IQ testing (usually both of the adopted child and the adopting parents and any of their biological children) may be biased because of *self-selection.* That is, the families taking part in such studies have volunteered to be tested and are therefore self-selected; they are not representative of *all* adopted children, as would be a perfectly random sample of all adoptees. Often a substantial percentage of the adoptive parents who were contacted by the adoption agency or by the investigators refuse to participate in such a study. How much bias this introduces into the test results is difficult to say. But the one aspect of the data that seems most likely to be affected is the average IQ of the self-selected sample. It is most likely that the average IQ is biased upward—just how much, we do not know. But all the evidence indicates that families who volunteer for IQ testing score higher than a randomly selected sample from the same population. Therefore, we should be cautious about putting too much stock in the average IQ reported in adoption studies where the participating families were self-selected volunteers.

Environmental Correlates of Adopted Children's IQ

Keeping all of these slightly limiting and biasing features of adoption studies in mind, we can now look at the main evidence they provide concerning the effects of family environments on children's IQs.

   The four largest adoption studies comprise a total of 1,000 adoptees. The adoptive homes are largely of middle and upper-middle socioeconomic status, but span a considerable range of SES, from blue-collar working class to professional and managerial. In each study, a number of environmental variables were assessed—aspects of the environment that I have mentioned as important causes of IQ variation in the population. The results of the four studies are in remarkably close agreement, so they may be summarized together. Statistical analysis shows that the overall environmental assessments, which include both adoptive parents' IQs and their amount of education, account for barely 5 percent of the IQ variance of the adopted children. Most of this percentage is contributed by the average IQ level of both adoptive parents plus the adoptive mother's amount of education.

Environmental Variables	% of IQ Variance
Adoptive parents' IQ	4
Mother's education	3
Father's education	2
Composite environmental index	5

The reason the first three percentages do not add up to more than 5 percent for the composite index, which includes various other aspects of the environment as well, is that they are not all independent. The different variables are all so highly intercorrelated that they overlap each other. The variances due to three completely uncorrelated variables would add up like this:

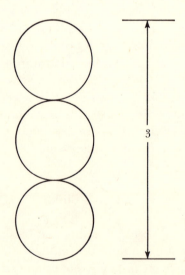

But three correlated variables would overlap each other and therefore add up like this:

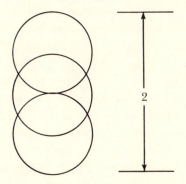

How can we interpret this environmental contribution of 5 percent of the IQ variance? What does it mean in terms of IQ points? One way of explaining it would be to say that the adopted children who are in the most favorable 1 percent of adoptive environments average about 8 IQ points higher than the average IQ of all the adopted children. Those in the least favorable 1 percent of adoptive environments would average about 8 IQ points lower than the overall average IQ of adopted children. Hence, the difference between the top 1 percent most favorable and bottom 1 percent least favorable home environments would amount to about 16 IQ points.

But this is most likely an underestimate of the full range of environmental effects on IQ in the general population, because extremely unfavorable environments are very rarely found among adoptive homes. A recent adoption study in France suggests that the difference between very high and very low socioeconomic environments may have a considerable effect on IQ. The investigators tested the IQs of the full and half-siblings of children who had been adopted into high SES homes. The biological mothers of these children were of low SES and had reared a sibling or a half-sibling of the adoptee. The high SES adoptees' average IQ was 110.6, whereas their nonadopted siblings averaged 94.7—a difference of about 16 IQ points. Again, we are not sure to what extent self-selection of families or other factors may have biased these results, which are based on only a small sample of twenty siblings. One might suspect that high SES parents would be more aware of relatively low intelligence in their adopted child and would be less apt to volunteer the child for IQ testing than would be low SES parents.

On the other hand, the evidence from adoption studies leaves no doubt of the genetic influence of the biological mother's intelligence on the adopted child. This can be seen clearly in the recent Texas Adoption Study, by comparing the IQs of the twenty-seven adoptees whose biological mothers had the lowest IQs in the sample with the thirty-four adoptees whose biological mothers had the highest IQs, out of a total of 455 mothers. The results are shown in Table 5. The most striking result is found in the percentages of adoptees with IQs above 120 and below 95. The extremes of IQ seem to be strongly affected by the biological mother's intelligence level.

Another interesting fact in adoption studies is that measurable aspects of the home environment account for less IQ variance as the children become older. The largest study based entirely on adolescent adoptees (adopted in infancy) found that a composite index of eight environmental assessments accounted for only about 1 percent of the total IQ variance. This led the investigators to conclude that all humane environments, ranging from "solid working class" to professional and managerial class homes, are functionally equivalent for stimulating children's mental development.

Whereas the correlation between the home environment and IQ decreases with age, the correlation between adoptees' IQs and their biological mothers' intelligence increases from early childhood to adolescence. This is further evidence of the importance of genetic factors in children's mental growth.

Table 5

IQs of Adoptees as a Function of Biological Mother's IQ

Biological Mother	Average IQ of Adoptive Parents	Adoptee's Average IQ	Percentage of All Adoptees	
			IQ 120 or above	IQ 95 or below
Low IQ: Average 89.4	110.8	102.6	0	15
High IQ: Average 121.6	114.8	118.3	44	0

Source: L. Willerman, "Effects of Families on Intellectual Development," *American Psychologist* 34 (1979): 923–929. Reprinted by permission.

Effects of Extreme Environmental Deprivation

The notion that the common social class differences in environment vary along a continuum of deprivation, with the environment becoming more "deprived" as we move from upper to lower SES, is a serious misconception. The environment of every SES level affords much more cognitive stimulation and opportunity for acquiring information (but not always the same *content* of information) than any child can fully utilize. It is an exceedingly rare occurrence when a child is found in an environment that provides too little cognitive stimulation and experience to promote normal mental growth. Such children, fortunately rare, have been reared under grossly abnormal conditions of social isolation, usually with little or no exposure to normal speech, and even with a restricted opportunity for normal experience of the physical environment.

Only a few of these cases of extreme isolation have been authenticated and carefully studied by psychologists. These studies are most instructive concerning the effects of extreme environmental deprivation—social and physical—on a child's mental development and IQ.

Probably the best known and most carefully documented of these examples is the famous case of "Isabelle," an illegitimate child whose grandparents apparently wanted to keep her and her deaf-mute mother hidden from the world. Isabelle was confined in a dimly lighted attic from birth until age 6½, when she was discovered and rescued from these unusual circumstances. Isolated since birth from everyone but her mother, she communicated only through gestures. When found by the authorities, Isabelle was totally incapable of speech and made only "strange croaking sounds." Her behavior was described as almost like that of a wild animal, displaying fear and hostility. In many ways she acted like an infant. So little was her experience of physical objects that her reaction to being handed a ball was typical of a six-month-old infant; on an index of social maturity she had a social age of 2 years 6 months. When first tested on the Stanford–Binet, she obtained a mental age of 1 year 7 months—an IQ of about 25. Obviously, Isabelle's extreme isolation from normal encounters with the social and physical environment had had a devastating effect on her mental development by age 6½. What would be the long-term mental consequences of such severe environmental deprivation?

Isabelle was removed to a normal environment and given special training. At first, her progress was slow and discouraging. But in a few weeks she began to "catch on," and her mental development then proved astounding. She advanced rapidly through the whole normal sequence of mental development seen in normally reared children between one and six years of age. Thus, Isabelle's rate of mental development was almost three times faster than the normal child's! She began to talk after about two months of training. Only nine months later she could read and write, do simple addition, and retell a story after hearing it. After another seven months her vocabulary was about 2,000 words and she was asking complicated questions. Within two years after she was found with a mental age of less than 2, she had advanced to a mental age of about 8. That's six years of mental growth in just two years! She appeared then as a bright, cheerful, energetic girl who spoke well and performed normally in school. Berkeley sociologist Kingsley Davis, who studied Isabelle and last saw her in her senior year in high school, reported then that she seemed to be a completely normal teenager.

After rapidly gaining her "normal" mental age by around 8½ years of age, Isabelle thereafter developed mentally at the same rate as the average child of her age. Professor Davis likened the extraordinary rate of Isabelle's early mental development to the rapid recovery of body weight in a growing child after an illness. During recovery, the child shows an extra fast rate of growth until he has attained normal weight for his age, whereupon further growth proceeds at the normal rate. The case of Isabelle thus shows this remarkable similarity between physical and mental growth.

The most important thing demonstrated by the case of Isabelle is that extraordinarily severe deprivation throughout the first six years of her life did not have an irreversible effect on her eventual mental development. As soon as she was placed in a good social and educational environment, she quickly developed and maintained the IQ level of the average child. We cannot know, of course, whether her eventual IQ would have been much higher had she not undergone the early years of deprivation. But we can safely conclude that such severe deprivation does not preclude the attainment of at least an average level of intelligence.

Effects of Schooling

I shall here be concerned only with the *direct* effects of schooling on individual differences in general mental ability as indicated by IQ.

Children with above-average intelligence generally perform better in school, and are more likely to graduate from high school, go on to college, and get high-paying jobs as adults. But these undisputed intercorrelations among IQ, scholastic performance, and eventual occupational status are not the primary issue here. What we wish to know is the effect of schooling. How much of the variation in people's IQs or general cognitive ability is the *direct result* of differences in schooling? Do people differ in IQ *because* of differences in their schooling? I am referring here to ordinary schooling and not to special programs expressly aimed at raising IQs.

An impressively comprehensive study addressing this question was conducted by a team of researchers at Harvard University (Christopher Jencks et al., *Inequality: A Reassessment of the Effect of Family and Schooling in America*, Basic Books, 1972). Without citing all the detailed evidence that these researchers bring to bear on this question, I here list their main conclusions.

1. *Preschool attendance* before age 6 has little permanent effect on cognitive development. Greater equality of access to preschool by all segments of American society would scarcely reduce the population variance in IQ. Jencks and his colleagues conclude that ''we cannot expect universal preschooling to narrow the gap between rich and poor or between whites and blacks. Universal preschooling might even widen the gap'' (p. 879).

2. *Elementary school attendance* makes a substantial difference on ordinary group-administered IQ tests, as shown by comparisons of children who have attended school regularly with children whose schooling has been interrupted for several months or more by circumstances that are unrelated to the children's own characteristics, such as war or teacher strikes. Children who are thus deprived of regular schooling show a loss of several IQ points. The loss is accentuated for black children as compared with middle-class white children, whose reading level and other scholastic skills improve even when they are not attending school, although the rate of improvement is slowed.

3. *High school and college* have smaller effects on IQ than elementary school. Pupils with higher IQs tend to remain in school longer and more often go to college. But if one compares pupils of the same IQ in, say, grade 8, who attain different amounts of schooling after grade 8, there is some slight IQ advantage to those who remain in school longer and go on to college. Jencks and his colleagues estimate from all the existing evidence that after early adolescence, each additional year of schooling and college boosts an individual's adult IQ about 1 point above the level predicted from the person's IQ in early adolescence.

4. *Differences in school quality* have very modest effects on IQ. Differences between elementary schools have a more potent effect on IQ than differences between high schools. The overall effect on IQ of six years' attendance in an elementary school that ranks in the top fifth of all elementary schools in quality, as compared with a school that ranks in the bottom fifth, is only about 5 IQ points. Thus, if all elementary schools were equally effective, the total IQ variance in the population would be reduced by about 3 percent or less. High schools have even less effect on IQ. The differences in quality between high schools contribute less than 1 percent to the total IQ variance of twelfth-graders.

In summary, amount of schooling, particularly at the elementary level, has some modest effect on IQ scores, whereas differences between schools have a barely detectable effect on IQ. Probably about 5 to 15 percent of the total IQ variance in the population is due to differences in the amounts of schooling people receive, while not more than 4 or 5 percent of the variance is due to differences in the quality of schools. In all, educational inequalities of one kind or another probably account for at most about 20 percent of IQ variance. Another way of expressing this is that the average IQ difference between the upper and lower halves of the IQ distribution in the total population is now about 12 IQ points; but if all educational inequalities could be eliminated, the average IQ difference between the upper and lower halves would be about 10.7 IQ points—that is, a reduction of 1.3 IQ points. The differences among people in IQ are evidently not much a result of differences in their schooling.

Experimental Attempts to Raise IQ

Because of the obvious relationship of intelligence to educational performance, psychologists and educators for many years have shown an interest in improving children's intelligence by directly controlling the environmental factors thought to be important determinants of mental development. The outcome of such efforts, generally, seems to be this: special environmental stimulation can, at least temporarily, raise children's scores substantially on certain IQ tests. But there is as yet no evidence of any appreciable or lasting change in the *g* factor that the IQ is intended to measure and that is the basis for the IQ's correlations with scholastic and occupational performance.

Despite more than half a century of repeated efforts by psychologists to improve the intelligence of children, particularly those in the lower quarter of the IQ distribution relative to those in the upper half of the distribution, strong evidence is still lacking as to whether or not it can be done, or to what extent. Probably no other topic in the whole history of psychology has commanded such vast funds for research, especially in the past twenty years. The evidence from these assiduous efforts warrants only the most cautious and tentative optimism concerning the capability of psychologists and educators to permanently raise the intelligence of humans by any manipulation of the environment.

Are the intelligence gains attained through experimental treatments as stable over time as nontreated IQ? Are the gains that may be statistically significant also of sufficient magnitude and permanence as to be individually or socially important?

In order to think more clearly about these issues, two important distinctions must be kept in mind.

First, there is the distinction between the IQ or any specific test-score measurement of intelligence, on the one hand, and the general intelligence factor, g, on the other. Performance on specific tests, and on some types of tests more than on others, is more amenable to alteration through experimental treatments than is g.

It is badly misleading to view individual difference in intelligence as consisting only of differences in the various *specific items* of knowledge and skill that compose the contents of any particular IQ test. As explained in Chapter 2, these content-specific features of tests are merely vehicles for the measurement of g. Performance on the specific vehicles and on other tasks closely resembling them is undoubtedly trainable. All organisms possessing a nervous system are capable of learning. But what is learned about the specific vehicles used for measuring g does not itself constitute g.

When one speaks of raising IQ, however, the implication (and hope) is that it is g that is being raised and not just performance on a particular test or others much like it. Intelligence test scores are important only because of their many educationally, occupationally, and socially important correlates, and these are largely a result of the g factor in all manifestations of mental ability. There would be absolutely no point in trying to raise intelligence if the only result was higher scores on IQ tests. The real hope is that it would result in a higher level of performance on all of the "real life" correlates of IQ, as would be the theoretically expected consequence of raising g itself.

Second, we should take note of the distinction between intelligence gain that is significant for the individual and gain that is significant for a population. A relatively small IQ gain of, say, 5 IQ points, would not be of much tangible consequence to an individual and may hardly seem worth creating the special conditions that may be needed to bring it about. I wouldn't give five dollars to have five more points added to my IQ, whatever it may be.

However, an average gain of even 2 or 3 IQ points (assuming, of course, it represents a gain in *g*) can be of great social consequence to a whole population, provided the entire distribution is moved up the scale. Because of the normal distribution of mental ability, a slight change in the population mean has marked effects on the proportions of the population that fall above a given high cutoff score on the IQ scale, or below a given low cutoff score.

Although a 5-point IQ gain may be meaningless to an individual, for a population a mean gain of 5 points would double the percentage of persons with IQs over 130 and would reduce by half the percentage with IQs below 70. The educational, social, and economic consequences of such a change for a population could be tremendous. Therefore, from a population standpoint, we should not belittle the potential importance of even a quite small IQ gain, provided there is good reason to believe it is a permanent change in *g* rather than a short-lived enhancement of specific knowledge and test-taking skills.

Typical Findings

There is now a considerable consensus among workers in this field about the typical findings from experimental attempts to raise intelligence. I am here excluding reports of the amelioration of abnormal developmental deficits in rare cases of extreme social isolation or resulting from the deplorable neglect found in some orphanages in certain Third World countries.

Most studies that have tried to raise IQs have focused on children from poor homes or on those whose IQs in later childhood are statistically predicted, on the basis of certain socioeconomic, racial, and parental characteristics, to fall into the lower half of the IQ distribution. Here are the main conclusions that can be drawn from these studies.

1. It is found that the IQs of younger children (preschoolers) are more malleable than those of older children. Those programs that begin intervention earliest (usually in infancy) and last longest (up to school age or beyond) have produced the largest IQ gains.

2. IQ gains appear most marked during the early childhood years in which the kinds of test items used for assessing IQ gains allow for the most direct transfer of specific learning from the cognitive materials and training procedures that are applied to the experimental subjects.

3. Virtually without exception, there is a partial or total "fade-out" of treatment-induced IQ gains within one to three years after the treatment. The experimentally treated subjects, after their early acceleration in IQ scores, generally gravitate back toward their normally expected level in later childhood.

4. The effects of the experimental treatment on important cognitive correlates of the IQ are much less pronounced and fade more rapidly than the IQ gain itself, in some cases not even leaving any residual trace of the treatment.

Probably the most intensive and prolonged intervention study ever attempted, extending from early infancy to school age, is the highly publicized study of black ghetto children in Milwaukee. These children were selected as being at "high risk" for mental retardation, because they had older school-age siblings who were diagnosed as retarded by the school authorities. These high-risk children, during the period from shortly after birth until school entry at age 6, were taken from their homes for eight hours every weekday and given constant and intensive treatment intended to stimulate their mental development. Probably few, if any, children have ever been reared under more intensive mentally stimulating conditions. Each child had a one-to-one interaction with a specially trained teacher during most of the child's waking hours, five days a week, for the first 5 or 6 years of life. The estimated cost was $30,000 per child. A control group of children selected from the same locality by the same criteria were reared by their own mothers and received no special treatment other than routine medical checkups.

The early average gain in IQ of the experimental over the control group was so impressive—close to 30 IQ points—that one psychologist referred to it as the "Miracle in Milwaukee." These children are now well along in elementary school, and at the latest report their mean IQ had already declined some 20 points. The experimental group, however, still had appreciably higher IQs than the control group. But there was *no difference* between the experimental and control subjects in reading achievement, which is the single most crucial ability for scholastic success at the more advanced levels of education. This is a most important discovery, because reading comprehension is very highly *g*-loaded in the general school population. We have found that reading comprehension is more highly correlated with IQ than is any other area of scholastic performance included in the complete battery of

Stanford Achievement Tests. And reading comprehension is more highly correlated with all other forms of scholastic achievement than is any other school subject. The fact that the extraordinary intervention provided in the Milwaukee project so strikingly raised IQs without showing any residual effect on reading achievement after these children had been in regular schools for several years suggests that the cognitive skills inculcated by the treatment program displayed only the relatively narrow transfer typical of trained skills, rather than the broadly general cognitive ability that characterizes *g*. Untreated children whose IQs are comparable to the artificially enhanced IQs of the experimental group normally attain much higher levels of reading ability in elementary school.

A similar study is now being conducted in North Carolina. A group of black infants considered to be at risk for subnormal intellectual development on the basis of their backgrounds (their mothers averaged close to IQ 80) were given intensive cognitive stimulation intended to promote intellectual development in a day-care center, five days a week beginning at a few weeks of age and continuing up to age 36 months, when the first results were reported. There was also a matched control group that received no special treatment, although the experimental and control groups both received medical care and nutritional supplements. By age 36 months, the Stanford–Binet IQs of the experimental and control groups were 95 and 81, respectively—a highly significant difference.

Because this intensive program of environmental stimulation employed about 300 different curriculum activities devised to enhance mental development, one wonders to what extent some of these activities resemble the vehicles for the measurement of *g* employed in the Bayley and Stanford–Binet scales that were used to measure the effects of the treatment. The Year II tests of the Stanford–Binet consist of three-hole form board, delayed response to a small object hidden under one of three boxes, identifying parts of the body on a paper doll, building a tower of four blocks, and picture vocabulary of common objects. The Year III tests include stringing beads, building a "bridge" with three blocks, copying a circle, and drawing a vertical line. It is hard to imagine that a preschool program aimed at stimulating cognitive development could avoid providing practice in skills that, although perhaps not identical to those in the Stanford–Binet, would result in a narrow transfer-of-training enhancement of Stanford–Binet test performance. One would like to see the results on other types of *g*-loaded tests with quite different item content.

There is one indication in this study that the enhanced IQs of the treated group may not have the same meaning that IQs generally have. It is the finding that these children's IQs show nearly a zero rank-order correlation with their own mothers' IQs, whereas the control group shows a correlation of .43, which is very close to both the theoretical expectation and the empirical findings of other studies of mother-child correlation for IQ. (Even adopted children who have had no contact with their biological mothers since birth show a significant correlation between their IQs and their biological mothers' intelligence levels.) The fact that the mother-child correlation completely disappeared in the experimentally treated group suggests that the IQ scores of these children may no longer be indicative of *g* but reflect only the specific effects of intensive training in skills highly similar to those included in the Stanford–Binet test for that age range. Whether the IQ gains shown by these children represent only a short-term enhancement of test scores or an authentic enlargement of *g* must be determined by future follow-ups in this ongoing study.

Any intervention program that aims to enhance intellectual development and bases its claims of success on a mean IQ difference between experimental and control groups must sooner or later come to grips with the problem of demonstrating that the experimental group's heightened IQs still have the same *meaning* as an index of general intelligence, with all the implied correlates of IQ, that has long been established for untreated children.

Project Head Start

The degree of environmental intervention made possible through Project Head Start was much less extensive and began at a much later age than the intensive experimental programs described in the preceding section. Therefore, it should not be surprising that the outcomes of Head Start were less impressive with respect to gains in IQ or scholastic achievement. Of course, the aims of Head Start were much broader than just raising children's IQs and scholastic achievement, and I am not here evaluating Head Start's attainment of its broader goals. Follow-up studies of the effects of Head Start reveal no lasting improvement in IQ or scholastic achievement *per se*, but indicate other long-term benefits involving improved health care and the fostering of social competence and more favorable attitudes toward school—as shown by significantly fewer Head Start than matched control children being placed in special classes, being retained in a grade, or getting in trouble for "problem behavior." These conclusions are elaborated in a recent book that comprehensively reviews the history and the results of Head Start (E. Zigler and J. Valentine, *Project Head Start: A Legacy of the War on Poverty,* 1979).

It may seem surprising that two decades of large-scale, well-supported experimental efforts to accelerate children's intellectual development with lasting effect have not yet conclusively demonstrated the desired outcomes. Without such a demonstration eventually, future historians of psychology may well liken this period to the era of alchemy in the history of chemistry. The analogy is not completely negative. Although the alchemists failed in their primary aim—to find the "philosopher's stone" that could transmute base metals into gold—their experiments nevertheless advanced the science of chemistry.

6

Social Class and Race Differences in Intelligence

T HE RHETORIC OF popular criticisms of mental tests promotes the belief that IQ tests discriminate mostly along the lines of social class and race. Here are two typical charges:

> The middle-class environment is the birthright for IQ test-taking ability.

> Aptitude tests reward white and middle-class values and skills, especially ability to speak Standard English, and penalize minority children because of their backgrounds.

In view of such claims, it will be worthwhile to look at how much of the total population variance in IQ is attributable to social class and race differences, as compared with differences among persons of the same race and social class, and even full siblings who share the same parents and home background.

We have some excellent data on this point, based on the most up-to-date and widely used individual IQ test, the revised Wechsler Intelligence Scale for Children (WISC-R). IQs were obtained on more than 600 white and 600 black children representing a random sample of California schoolchildren, ages 5 to 12. The socioeconomic status of each child's family, based on information obtained from the parents, was indexed on a scale from 1 to 10, which reflects such social class indicators as the educational and occupational levels of the parents. The

191

very same criteria for social class indexing were of course applied to blacks and whites alike.

By a statistical method known as the analysis of variance, it is possible to determine what percentage of the total variation (technically known as variance) among all of the more than 1,200 IQs in the whole random sample is associated with each of the several "sources" that contribute to the total variance in IQs. The percentages of variance contributed by each of the sources will add up to 100 percent, that is, the total variance.

Table 6 shows these percentages. Social class and race differences independently account for 8 and 14 percent, respectively, of the IQ variance, and their joint contribution constitutes only 30 percent of the IQ variance. Most of the IQ variance in the population exists within racial and social class groups; that is, there is much variation (26 percent) in average IQ among families who are all of the same race and social class status; and even more of the variance (39 percent) exists among full siblings reared together in the same family. This analysis, which is typical of many other studies of this question, completely refutes the myth that IQ tests show most of their discriminations between races and social classes.

The second column of figures in Table 6 shows that the average IQ difference between any two persons of the same race picked at random from different social classes (when SES is divided into ten classes) is 6 IQ points. Compare that with the average difference of 9 points be-

TABLE 6

Percentage of Variance and Average Difference in WISC-R IQ
Independently Associated with Race (White/Black),
with Social Class, and between and within Families

Source	% of Variance		Average IQ Difference
Between races (within social classes)	14		12
Between social classes (within races)	8	30%	6
Interaction of race and social class	8		
Between families (within race and social class)	26		9
Within families (siblings)	39	65%	11
Measurement error	5		4
Total sample	100		17

tween the median IQs of families that are all of the same race and social class. The average difference between whites and blacks of the same social class is 12 IQ points. A large difference? But notice that the average IQ difference between siblings in the same family is 11 points. The average difference in the IQs of the same person tested on two occasions a week apart is 4 points. And the average IQ difference between all possible pairs of individuals picked at random in the total sample is 17 points. The foregoing analysis helps to put social class and racial IQ differences into proper perspective.

When the same IQ data are plotted graphically, as in Figure 8, other typical features of such data are highlighted.

First, it is a common finding in many studies that the average IQ difference between whites and blacks increases at higher levels of socioeconomic status, as seen in Figure 8.

Second, most large-scale studies have found that the average IQ level of black children from the highest SES categories is about equal to

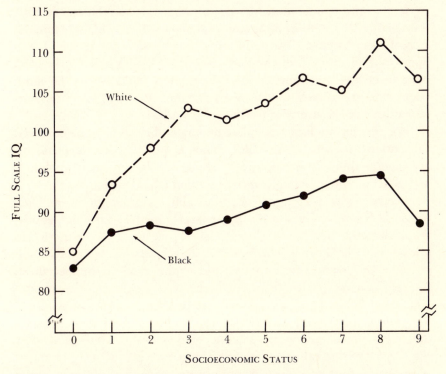

Figure 8. Average Full Scale IQ on the Wechsler Intelligence Scale for Children (Revised), for random samples of white ($N = 622$) and black ($N = 622$) California schoolchildren in ten socioeconomic categories.

the average IQ level of white children from the lowest SES categories, as seen in Figure 8.

Third, it is a routine finding that the IQ of the very highest SES level falls slightly below the next-to-highest SES level, as seen for both blacks and whites in Figure 8. There are speculations about the cause of this phenomenon. One is that the highest SES category includes more families with inherited status and wealth, while a much larger percentage of the next lower category have achieved their status by their own ability and are therefore actually more intelligent, on the average. But that is just a conjecture, and the matter has not been adequately investigated. The effect is of interest, however, because it has shown up at a high level of statistical significance in some very solid large-scale studies of the relationship of IQ to SES.

Social Class and IQ

In the white population, there is a rather low correlation, ranging from about .30 to .40 in most studies, between children's IQs and the SES of their parents. This is the usual finding not only in the United States but in every industrialized country where studies have been done since the invention of the first IQ test in 1905. In the adult population the correlation between persons' IQs and their own attained SES is much higher (.50 to .70).

We now have a fairly complete understanding of how the observed correlation between IQ and SES comes about. The key mechanisms are general ability (indexed by IQ), status attainment, social mobility, and genetic segregation and recombination (see Chapter 3).

General ability is an important factor, but certainly not the only factor, in SES attainment. Its effects are largely mediated through educational attainment. Children with higher IQs generally do better in school, like school better, stay in school longer, earn higher grades, and go on to college and to graduation, and acquire more of the specialized training and credentials often required for entry into high-status occupations. Thus IQ at high school age predicts both the educational and occupational levels attained by age 40, with a correlation of about .60. Educational and occupational level are the main indices of SES; they are related to other indices of SES such as income, neighborhood of residence, and, to a lesser degree, certain aspects of life-style, social attitudes, and interests. Even with a correlation of .60 between school age IQ and status attainment, there is still considerable IQ variation among persons all of the same SES.

A child's own IQ determines his adult *status attainment* to a much greater extent than does the SES of his parents. Because children's IQs are correlated no more than about .70 with their parents' average IQs, and only about .35 with their parents' SES, parents and their children, as well as siblings within the same family, can all differ quite markedly. Thus the average IQ difference between parents and children and between full siblings is about 12 IQ points (excluding measurement error). Almost one-half of the total IQ variance in the general population exists within families.

Therefore, in each generation we see a great deal of *social mobility,* with young adults moving into different social strata from that of their parents. More than 50 percent of children move to different SES categories as adults—some higher and some lower than the SES of their origin. The fact that very little of this social mobility is a result of their family's SES is shown by the often divergent social mobility of siblings from the same family. The correlation between brothers' adult occupational statuses, for example, is only .30, as compared with the correlation of .60 to .70 between individuals' IQs and their own occupational status. Also, it is found that sons who attain higher status than their fathers have higher IQs, on the average, than their fathers, and sons who attain a lower status than their fathers tend to have lower IQs than their fathers. This is true even when the IQs of both the fathers and their sons were obtained when each was in the eighth grade.

The substantial correlation between SES and IQ in the adult population and the fact that a good part of the correlation exists within families leads inescapably to the conclusion that some part of the SES differences in IQ are linked to *genetic differences.* It is exceedingly improbable that all of the intergenerational social mobility found associated with IQ would be linked only to the nongenetic component of IQ variation. Therefore, there can be little doubt that genetic differences in intelligence are associated with SES. There is just no way that the mechanisms of intergenerational social mobility could separate the genetic and nongenetic factors entering into adult status attainment. A predictable consequence of a genetic component in SES IQ differences is the finding that the IQs of children reared since birth in an orphanage show almost as high a correlation with the SES levels of their biological fathers, whom they have never known, as do children who were reared by their own parents.

Thus, high and low SES parents, on the average, have somewhat different genotypes for the development of intelligence. But, as I explained in Chapter 3, because of Mendel's principles of segregation and recombination of alleles, parents cannot pass on their genotypes to their offspring, but pass on only a random half of their genes. Consequently, there is a great deal of variation, in IQ and other genetically conditional traits, among all the offspring of any pair of parents.

The two main results of these Mendelian mechanisms are of great social importance: (1) the average IQ differences between children from different social classes are only about half as large as the average IQ differences between adults of different social classes, and (2) in each generation the full range of IQs is found among the children born within every level of SES.

Thus the laws of genetics actually work against the hardening of social classes into castes and promote a great deal of intergenerational social mobility through the agency of the genetic components of intelligence and other traits related to individual status attainment.

Mental tests, by reading through the veneer of social class background, can identify abilities wherever they occur, and thus may act as a leavening agent for the social mobility of able youngsters from lower SES backgrounds. That this in fact happens is shown, for example, by the finding in England that a greater percentage of children of the working class were steered into the college preparatory curriculum when selection was based on IQ and objective achievement tests instead of on teachers' marks and recommendations; the opposite was true for middle- and upper-class children, whose appearance, manners, and educational aspirations apparently biased teachers' marks and recommendations in their favor. Objective tests, especially those of the culture-reduced variety, can identify academic talent in children from every social background. They act as instruments of social justice by cutting through the biases that may infest other avenues of educational and occupational advancement, such as teachers' grades, interviews, letters of recommendation, and family connections.

Race Differences

Race differences in intelligence are much harder to understand, scientifically, than SES differences. As was explained in the preceding section, the mechanisms through which SES differences in intelligence come about—educational and occupational selection—are quite explicit and easily observed. The causal chain linking SES and IQ is not at all hidden. But scientists do not have this advantage in their study of racial variation.

In general terms, scientists are agreed that racial variation, at least in physical characteristics, is a product of the evolutionary process. It is a difficult and often controversial matter, however, to trace the roots of any particular racial differences. The least mysterious differences are the obvious physical features, such as skin pigmentation, which are explainable in terms of their selective advantage to survival in the contrasting climatic conditions in different parts of the world.

Behavioral differences between racial groups have less obvious causes and leave much room for contention among those who study them. This has been especially true regarding the observed racial differences in mental ability. Their scientific analysis is further complicated, and often hindered, by the fact that so many people have been brought up with a commitment to the belief that observed behavioral differences between human races—especially if they involve mental ability of any kind—cannot have a biological basis. These persons tolerate only those explanations that invoke differences in social and economic privilege, educational disadvantages, or culture-biased tests. They express righteous indignation at any suggestion of looking further than the immediate environment or the recent past for a fuller understanding of racial variation in ability.

That this is an unreasonable and scientifically unwarranted stance becomes clear if we take a broad view of racial variation as a biological, evolutionary phenomenon. It will be seen that there is no rational basis for the *a priori* assumption of racial equality in any trait, physical or behavioral.

Social and Biological Meanings of Race

Socially, we usually have little trouble recognizing a person's race, based on overall physical appearance. If a group of persons were asked to classify racially the various people they observe on the streets of any large city in the United States, there would undoubtedly be very much agreement among their classifications. And if the persons so classified were asked to state their racial background, there would be high agreement with the observers' classifications. This is the social meaning of race used by the proverbial "man in the street." It is also the form of racial classification used in the vast majority of studies of racial differences in IQ.

Social classification of race is closely, although not perfectly, correlated with biological criteria of race. The chief difference is that the biological criteria do not divide races up into distinct *types,* but view races as population groups that vary continuously in a large number of genetic characteristics. Where the boundary lines are drawn, and how many are needed to divide the human species into racial groups, are not intrinsically given by nature, but are a matter of taxonomic convention and vary depending on the purpose of classification. We can make a great many small subdivisions, in which case some racial groups will show relatively few genetic differences between them. The three largest racial subdivisions—Caucasoid, Negroid, and Mongoloid—are simply groups that show a great many genetic differences, probably more than would exist between any other three large subdivisions one could make of the whole human species.

Races are now viewed, from a scientific standpoint, as breeding populations that differ in the frequencies of various genes. All present-day races are one species—*Homo sapiens*—and are interfertile. However, they are said to be different breeding populations in the sense that the frequency of matings within each racial population is much greater than the frequency of matings between the populations.

For many millennia the major racial populations have been relatively isolated from one another reproductively, by geography or culture. As a result of genetic isolation and evolutionary divergence brought about by differences in climate and other selection pressures in the natural and cultural ecology that affect survival, the major racial groups show intragroup similarities and intergroup differences in numerous genetically controlled morphological, serological, and biochemical characteristics. That is, they differ genetically in physical features, blood types, and body chemistry.

The genetic differences that affect complex systems of the organism are all products of the evolutionary process. Different races have evolved in somewhat different ways, making for many differences among them. A few of the many physical characteristics found to display genetic variation between different races are body size and proportions, hair form and distribution, head shape and facial features, cranial capacity and brain formation, blood types, number of vertebrae, size of genitalia, bone density, fingerprints, basic metabolic rate, body temperature, blood pressure, heat and cold tolerance, number and distribution of sweat glands, odor, consistency of ear wax, number of teeth, age at eruption of permanent teeth, fissural patterns on the surfaces of the teeth, length of gestation period, frequency of twin births, male-female birth ratio, physical maturity at birth, rate of infant development of alpha brain waves, colorblindness, visual and auditory acuity, intolerance of milk, galvanic skin resistence, chronic diseases, susceptibility to infectious diseases, genetic diseases (e.g., Tay Sachs, sickle cell anemia), and pigmentation of the skin, hair, and eyes.

There are also behaviorial differences between races, but their genetic basis is often disputed, and cultural factors are the usual explanation. But in many animal species there are also races or subspecies that are interfertile and do not differ any more in terms of the conventional taxonomic criteria for classification as subspecies than do human races. Yet they undeniably show behavioral differences, whether they are born and raised in their natural habitat or in captivity. Two subspecies of gorillas—the mountain gorilla and the lowland gorilla—differ in behavior. There is certainly nothing in biology that precludes behavioral differences between subspecies (termed ''races'' in the human species).

Modern ethologists regard behaviorial traits as being subject to biological evolution, just like physical traits. An animal's behavior can be a more important aspect of its adaptation to the environment than its physical characteristics, and can play an important role in the evolution of the physical structures that mediate behavior, principally the brain.

As a general principle, then, we should expect to find genetically conditioned behavioral differences between human races that show many other signs of evolutionary divergence. Such a general principle, of course, by itself proves nothing about any particular difference between any particular racial groups. But it absolutely contradicts dogmatic adherence to the doctrine which denies that behavioral differences between human racial groups could have an evolutionary and biological basis, insisting they must be exclusively the result of cultural conditioning and environmental circumstances acting in the present. This dogmatic extremist view does not allow the possibility that diverse environmental or cultural conditions of the remote past could have created genetic behavioral differences that persist down to present generations, long after the original conditions that were instrumental in producing them have ceased to exist. We know from experimental behavioral genetics with animals that the capacity for acquiring almost every behavioral characteristic, including the general capacity for learning, responds to selection. Natural selection is one of the principal mechanisms of evolutionary change, as explained in the following section.

Evolutionary Divergence

From the viewpoint of evolutionary theory, it seems extremely improbable that any genetically conditioned characteristics, physical or behavioral, dependent on several or more genes, would have the same distributions of genotypes in all human populations. Geographical and cultural isolation of breeding populations over many generations results in cumulative differences in gene pools. There are four specific evolutionary mechanisms involved in the genetic differentiation of populations: gene mutations, random genetic drift, selective migration, and natural selection.

Mutation and ***genetic drift*** are random processes occurring at single gene loci, and consequently they are not major causal factors of racial differences in polygenic traits, that is, continuous traits, like height and intelligence, which are determined by a number of genes. The larger the number of genes involved in a trait, the less is the probability that random changes, or genetic drift, occurring at individual loci would all happen to act in the same direction to produce a consistent difference between populations.

The theory of genetic drift, however, permits calculations concerning the relative degree of genetic isolation between populations, based on the number of gene differences that would occur by random drift alone, without considering the greater systematic and directional differences brought about by selection. From such evidence, geneticists have estimated the "divergence times" or extent of genetic separation between the three major races as about 14,000 years between Caucasoid and Mongoloid, 42,000 years between Mongoloid and Negroid, and 46,000 years between Caucasoid and Negroid. These estimates are based on the observed differences in the frequencies of neutral genes, that is, genes for which there is no evidence of selection. The divergence time is the time that genetic drift by itself would take to make the frequencies of neutral genes differ between the major races as much as they do at present. In other words, this means that the three major racial groups have been separated long enough and completely enough to permit a purely random genetic drift in gene frequencies, a drift equivalent to some 2,000 generations of complete separation between the Negroid and the other two races, and about 700 generations of complete separation between the Caucasoid and the Mongoloid.

However, these differences due to drift would be expected to have little explanatory significance for racial differences in polygenic traits that have been subject to natural selection.

Migration per se is probably not a major factor in producing population differences in polygenic traits. But migration often involves selection, either of the original migrant population or of subsequent generations. Having to cope with the challenges of an alien environment affords new opportunities for selection to alter the gene pool of the migratory groups. Migration from a tropical to a temperate climate, for example, could produce a selection pressure on any gene involved in the traits of foresight, planning, and prudence needed to survive long winters. Plagues, famines, and other catastrophes, which often accompanied migrations, produced genetic "bottlenecks" in human populations. A large migratory population would be drastically reduced for a few generations to a small, highly selected breeding group, with statistically different gene frequencies from those of the parent population, which then grows again into a large population. Such bottlenecks can result in marked changes in the gene pool within a fairly short period, depending on the severity of the selection.

Natural selection is by far the most potent evolutionary mechanism responsible for the major differences between human races, especially in polygenic traits. When a complex phenotypic characteristic, physical or behavioral, is influenced by a number of genes, all the genes are selected simultaneously, because selection acts directly on the phenotypes.

The rapidity of selection for the relevant genes depends both on the severity of the selection pressure on the phenotypes and on the heritability of the characteristic, that is, the proportion of phenotypic variance due to genetic variation.

We know that cranial capacity, a crude index of intelligence, has increased greatly over the five million years of human evolution, almost tripling in size from the earliest fossil information of *Australopithecus* to present-day *Homo sapiens*. The greatest development in the brain was of the neocortex, especially those areas serving speech and manipulation. Tools found with fossil remains indicate that increasing brain size was accompanied by the increasing sophistication of work instruments, and along with this development are also found artistic drawings on cave walls.

In the latest one or two million years, the strongest selection pressure in humans has been for behavioral traits of increasing complexity, accompanied by the increasing size and complexity of the cerebrum, which controls the higher mental functions, making possible such intelligent operations as comparing, analyzing, separating, seeing relationships, classifying, counting, abstracting, conceptualizing, recalling, imagining, and planning. These abilities all came about through selection of the behavioral advantages for survival they afforded in meeting environmental challenges.

It seems highly probable that such powerful and subtle selective pressures have also operated, to some extent, differentially upon the various subgroups of the human species that have been genetically separated for thousands of generations. In evolutionary perspective, it should not be surprising if certain behavioral traits, with their genetically conditional physical underpinnings in the nervous system, differ among human races. If certain of our psychological measurements did not reflect some such differences, they would seem quite suspect because, in principle, evolutionary behavioral differences are practically certain to exist.

We can now only speculate about the possible causes of evolutionary variations in mental ability. Perhaps most important was the necessity of cooperation. In prehistoric times the hard struggle for survival made it imperative that people band together, cooperating as a group in hunting and warfare. Also, the invention of new tools and weapons afforded a selective advantage to those individuals and tribes who were the most adept in learning to use them. Each new invention divides the population into those who can and those who cannot master its use, and gives a selective advantage to those who can.

Population size is an important factor in the selective advantage of invention. The larger the group, the greater the number of exceptional individuals most likely to make discoveries and inventions. New inventions and novel variations of existing tools and their correlated skills are less likely to arise in the relatively small and culturally isolated groups characteristic of primitive societies. Moreover, when an innovation does occur, and especially if it is a great advance beyond the existing knowledge or skill at the time, it cannot be perpetuated unless some substantial number of the group can take it up. Depending on its degree of novelty and complexity, they would have to be the more exceptionally able individuals, and, given the normal distribution of abilities, more such able individuals would exist in a larger population. Hence, an invention by only one exceptional member of the group could take on selective significance for some substantial number of the population.

Inventions and discoveries involving tools, weapons, skills, and knowledge about the environment create greater salience of individual differences in abilities, which then become important factors in selective and assortative mating. As one moves from relatively primitive to relatively advanced societies, individual differences in cognitive ability become more conspicuous and more consequential in many ways that can affect an individual's ''fitness'' in the Darwinian sense, that is, the probability of leaving surviving progeny. In a number of early human societies mating was a prerogative of the ablest and most esteemed males, each of whom had many females, while many less esteemed males had no mates.

Evolutionary rates for certain traits could differ considerably among groups with different mating customs or different degrees of selective mating for various traits. In considering natural selection for abilities in humans, one must consider what proportion of a population is regarded by its members as subnormal or in any way undesirable from the standpoint of selective mating. This will of course depend to a considerable extent on the cognitive complexity of the cultural demands made by the society. Inordinate difficulty in learning to read, for example, would be of no consequence in an illiterate society, but could be an important factor in selective mating in societies that put great emphasis on literacy.

Even a very slight reproductive advantage can have marked genetic consequences on the time scale of human evolution. It has been calculated that a rare gene in the population, which confers only 1 percent reproductive advantage (that is, those who possess the gene leave behind 1 percent more progeny than those who do not possess it), will increase the percentage of carriers of the gene in the population from 1 percent to 99 percent in 1,000 generations, assuming that the same degree of reproductive advantage is maintained throughout this period.

Increased population size also decreases the degree of inbreeding and gives rise to more new genetic combinations which are the grist for natural selection.

Primitive societies consisted of hunter-gatherers, and for obvious ecological reasons their breeding groups remained relatively small in numbers. The advent of agriculture permitted population densities a thousand times greater, thereby magnifying the selection factors for cognitive abilities associated with a larger population. Also, agriculture probably placed a higher premium on intelligence than did hunting and gathering, in terms of abilities for counting, measuring, planning, mastering the environment, and a greater complexity of social, political, and economic organizations. Various subpopulations of the world differ by thousands of years in the time since they gave up hunting and gathering for agriculture, and some contemporary groups have never taken up agriculture.

Thus, in general terms, human evolutionary history and the relative isolation of various populations for thousands of generations would justify the expectation of genetic differences between populations in a host of characteristics including those in which selection pressures have acted differentially on behavior. These behaviors are polygenic traits in which population differences are *statistical* rather than typological. That is, these genes exist in *all* human populations, and vary only quantitatively in the relative frequencies of different alleles.

It seems most improbable that some of the genetic behavioral differences that have resulted in the course of evolution would not be among the observable differences between contemporary races.

A contrary view would have to argue one of four propositions:

1. The selection pressures in all long-term isolated populations in the course of human evolution have been identical for all groups for all abilities.
2. Even if there had been different selection pressures for different components of ability, these components would average out to the same value in their combined effects on performance in every population, provided there is equality of opportunity for the development and expression of abilities.
3. There is only one general ability that has any genetic basis, and that is a highly plastic capacity for cultural learning which is genetically equal in all populations and becomes differentiated only through environmental and cultural influences.
4. Even if there are genetic differences in ability between populations, they are so completely obscured by cultural and environmental influences that there is zero correlation (or even a negative correlation) between the various racial phenotypes and the underlying genotypes.

Arguments 1 and 2 have the disadvantage of being extremely improbable. Number 3 is contradicted by the factor analysis and genetic analysis of mental abilities, which reveal a number of distinct abilities under relatively independent genetic control. The fourth point seems more debatable, as it depends so much on the methods for measuring abilities and the extent of the cultural differences between the groups in question. This is actually the crux of the so-called IQ controversy.

Modern students of racial differences have seemed most reluctant to point out aspects of particular cultures as being in themselves in any way indicative of differences in mental abilities. The one eminent scientist in recent years who has written on the subject is John R. Baker, an Oxford biologist and a fellow of the Royal Society (*Race,* Oxford University Press, 1974). Baker notes that racial groups have differed quite strikingly in the degree to which they have developed "civilization," as judged in terms of a list of twenty-one criteria ordinarily regarded as signs of civilization. And they differ correspondingly in the degree to which complex cognitive abilities are manifested or demanded in various societies. The Arunta language of Australian aborigines, for example, conveys only the concrete; abstract concepts are not represented, nor is there any verbal means of numeration beyond one or two. Baker further notes that these criteria of cultural and intellectual advancement rank-order existing races much as do standard tests of mental ability when applied to representative members of these racial groups who have been reared under similar conditions of civilized life. But of course one can always argue that the environmental conditions have not been similar enough—and so we are back to the crux of the IQ controversy.

Racial Differences in Neonatal Behavior

Although no direct correlation between infants' behavior and later mental ability has been found, the study of behavioral differences among infants of different races is instructive because cultural and environmental explanations for the differences are virtually ruled out.

Certain rather consistent behavioral differences show up between babies of different races when they are only a few hours, days, or weeks old. This is true even when the mothers of different races have been matched on age, income bracket, number of previous children, extent of prenatal care, and the types and amounts of drugs administered during childbirth. And the infants are observed while still in hospital, before they could have been conditioned by their mothers.

Daniel G. Freedman, a behavioral geneticist at the University of Chicago and the leading investigator of ethnic behavioral differences in infants, provides a fascinating account of his findings in *Human Sociobiology* (Free Press, 1979). Chinese and Caucasian newborns, for example, differ markedly in temperament. Caucasian babies cry more easily and are harder to console. Chinese babies are more placid and "stoical." Placed face down in their cribs, Chinese babies were observed to remain in that position, with their faces buried in the bedding, whereas Caucasian babies immediately struggled to turn their faces to one side. When a small piece of cloth was placed on the baby's face, the typical Caucasian baby immediately struggled to remove the cloth by swiping his hands and turning his head, but the typical Chinese baby remained impassive, showing few overt responses. Japanese babies behave similarly, and Navaho Indian babies are even more "stoical" than the Chinese and Japanese. African and black

American neonates, on the other hand, are much more reactive and more advanced in muscular coordination; when only a few days old, they can perform motoric acts that are not seen in Caucasian and Asian babies before several weeks of age. Black infants also show more mature brain wave patterns than Caucasians. Newborn Australian aborigines and Africans placed in the prone position can lift their heads and look around, whereas Caucasian and Asian infants are unable to do this until they are about one month old.

Although these behavioral differences among neonates of different races may have no long-term significance for later cognitive development, they do seem to confirm our expectation, based on general evolutionary principles, that long-isolated populations will differ genetically in ways that can cause differences in typical behaviors.

Race and Mental Ability

While there is a considerable consensus among scientists today that genetic variation in mental abilities among races is not only possible but even likely, because of the divergent evolutionary trends mentioned previously, there is little consensus indeed when the discussion focuses on comparisons between any particular racial groups. It then becomes the most contentious of all subjects on the contemporary scene.

To question the doctrine of the genetic equality of human races in mental abilities is to violate what is unquestionably the most powerful taboo in the twentieth century. To have the question raised about any *particular* population seems outrageous to many. Many others who would try to keep an open mind are made to feel uncomfortable, as if they had committed a breach of etiquette.

Yet questioning is precisely what scientists *must* do if they are to further our understanding of the undisputed observed differences between certain races in mental test scores and all their educationally, economically, and socially important correlates. Were it not for these important correlates of IQ both within and across racial groups, the IQ would be much less often attacked than it is. There would be little controversy over the measurement of any characteristics showing individual differences and racial differences that have no obvious socially important correlates, for example, blood pressure. Yet the scientific problems of studying the genetics of racial differences in blood pressure are remarkably parallel to the IQ question. Blood pressure is a metric characteristic that shows substantial heritability within racial groups, but it is also affected by dietary habits and environmental stresses, in which there are both individual and group differences.

The study of racial variation in *any* characteristic, physical or mental, is surely not "racism," although some egalitarian dogmatists like to give it such a label. Since the holocaust of the Jews during Hitler's Nazi regime, with its politically inspired racist doctrine of Aryan supremacy, the well-deserved offensiveness of the term "racism" has been extended far beyond its legitimate meaning.

The scientific study of mental or behavioral differences between races, openly recognizing the possibility that genetic factors may play a role, cannot be called racist. It would be just as illogical to condemn the recognition of physical differences between races as racist. There are some people who would urge that such matters should not be studied at all, that certain questions are better left beyond the pale of scientific investigation. Although I respect this sincerely expressed opinion, I have not yet heard any arguments for it that compel consent. Those with opposing philosophies on this issue should announce their stands explicitly, so they can then agree to disagree on fundamental premises and each go their separate ways. It would help to clear the air.

IQ in White and Black Populations

Blacks are the largest racial minority in the United States. They differ more from the white majority in average IQ than any other sizable minority group. So it should not be surprising that white-black differences in IQ and other test scores have received the major share of study. Much of the motivation for research on black-white IQ differences in recent years has stemmed from the nation's concern with the seemingly intractable differences in scholastic performance under fairly equal instructional conditions, and from the relatively large percentage of black youths (more than three times that of whites) who fall below the minimum mental qualifications for induction into the armed forces, even when they are equated with white youths in amount of schooling.

The study of white-black differences is not an exclusively American phenomenon. In surveying the literature, it is a striking fact that the study of racial differences in mental abilities has focused much more extensively on sub-Saharan Africans and populations of African descent than on any other groups. Bibliographies of research on other races are extremely scant by comparison.

Because of the technical and theoretical difficulties and uncertainties in the cross-cultural testing of abilities, where language, customs, values, and the ways of life differ radically between the groups being compared, most investigators find it more interesting to study racial groups that share a common culture in terms of language, formal education, and types of employment. The major racial groups in the United States, at least in recent decades, come close to these criteria of a common culture.

Let us review briefly the main findings of research on the white-black IQ difference.

Magnitude

Nationwide, the average white-black IQ difference is close to 15 points, varying from 10 to 20 points in different regions of the country. With the white average scaled at IQ 100, the black average falls at IQ 85. There is considerable overlap between the IQ distributions of the two populations, with 12 to 16 percent of blacks exceeding the white average. As far as we can tell, the full range of IQs in the white population also exists in the black. IQs as high as 200, which is about as high as IQs ever go, have been reported for black as well as white children. And of course, no race ensures immunity from severe mental deficiency, which afflicts a small fraction of every population.

Figure 9 is a fair representation of the present IQ distributions of whites and blacks in the United States. The distributions are divided up by lines at 15-point intervals. Each interval is termed a "standard deviation," which in the case of most present-day standard IQ tests is 15 points. Figure 9 illustrates some of the statistical consequences of a mean difference of one standard deviation between two distributions of scores that each approximate the so-called normal distribution, as depicted here. The percentiles indicate the percentage of each distribution with IQs below a given level. (Of course, 100 minus the percentile is the percentage of IQ scores falling above a given IQ.) The percentiles are accurate for the normal curve, but may correspond only approximately to the actual population distributions, which most probably have slightly different standard deviations and deviate slightly from the normal curve at the extremes beyond ± 2 standard deviations.

When the two racial distributions of IQs are viewed in this manner, we can understand the great disparities in the percentages of whites and blacks who are selected, for whatever reason, from a segment of the IQ scale that deviates above or below one or more standard deviations from the average IQ of either group. For example, in some states the law does not allow schoolchildren to be placed in special classes for the educable mentally retarded (EMR) unless their IQ on an individual test is below 70, in addition to other criteria including consistently failing school work in regular classes. Referring to Figure 9, we see that the expected percentages of whites and blacks falling below IQ 70 are about 2.3 percent and 15.9 percent, respectively—a ratio of about 1 to 7. An IQ of about 115 is near the minimum required for admission to highly selective colleges. Referring to Figure 9, we see that

DISTRIBUTION

IQ	White	Black	PERCENTILE White	Black
145				
130			97.7%	99.9%
115			84.1%	97.7%
100			50.0%	84.1%
85			15.9%	50.0%
70			2.3%	15.9%
55			0.1%	2.3%
40				

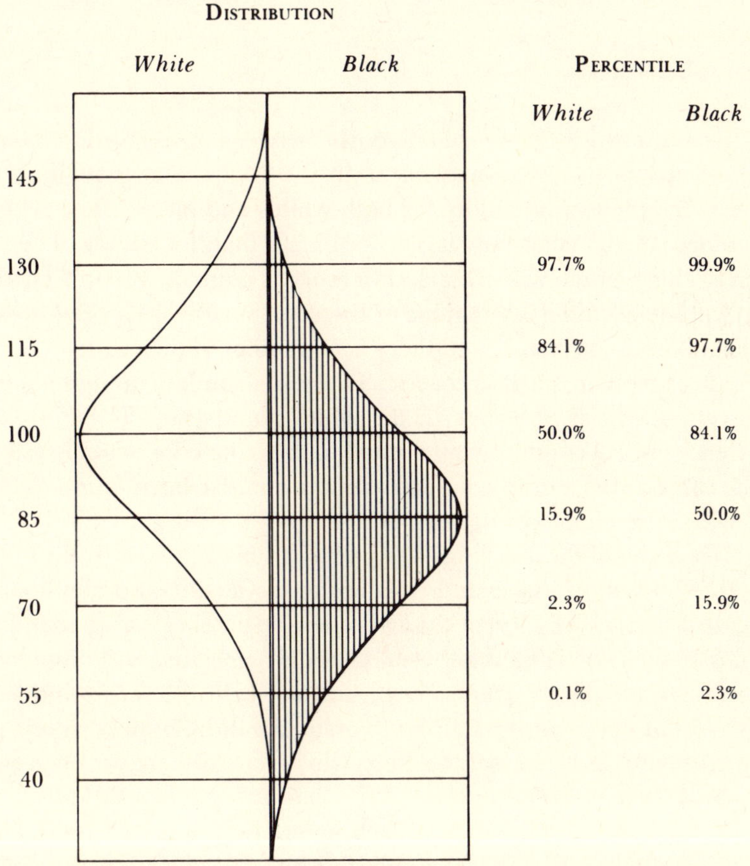

Figure 9. White and black IQ distributions represented as normal curves, showing the percentile ranks of a given IQ in each distribution. (The percentile rank is the percentage of the total distribution that falls below a given IQ score).

the percentages of whites and blacks scoring above 115 are also 15.9 percent and 2.3 percent, respectively—again, a ratio of about 7 to 1. Special programs for the academically "gifted" in many school systems select only students with IQs above 130, for which the white and black percentages are 2.3 percent and 0.1 percent—a ratio of 23 to 1. These percentages will of course vary somewhat from one school or community to another, because the average IQs of whites and blacks deviate from the overall national average in different regions, communities, and neighborhoods.

We should note some of the conditions associated with varying differences between the black and white IQ distributions.

Geographical Region

The nationwide testing of all youths between ages 18 and 26 for induction into the U.S. armed forces in the 1960s reveals regional differences in intellectual ability for both whites and blacks. The regional differences are considerably larger for blacks than for whites. The variation of the average white-black difference is equivalent to about 10 to 20 IQ points in different regions of the country. Blacks score lowest in the South and Southeast, and there is a gradient of increasing scores as one moves further north and west. There is a similar, though less pronounced, gradient of scores in the white population. These regional differences in IQ cannot be attributed to differing educational systems, as the same pattern of regional differences has also been found in black and white preschool youngsters.

This regional variation in IQ appears to be mostly a result of past selective migration associated with economic factors and employment opportunities with different educational and intellectual demands. A good part of the variation between states is associated with population densities in rural and urban areas, and agricultural versus industrial employment opportunities. Urban versus rural differences in test performance are a universal finding wherever tests have been used throughout the world.

The present-day American black population is not of 100 percent African ancestry. Probably the only full-blooded black Africans in the United States today are African exchange students. Studies based on the analysis of blood types which have different frequencies in African and Caucasian populations indicate that the average American black has received about 20 to 25 percent of his or her genes from Caucasian ancestors. Determinations of the percentage of Caucasian admixture in blacks in different parts of the country show that the amount of Caucasian admixture follows much the same regional gradient as IQ variation, going from the Deep South, with close to 10 percent Caucasian admixture, to the North and West, with about 20 to 30 percent, and the Northwest with as high as 40 percent.

Since practically all the Caucasian genes in the American black gene pool were introduced during the period of slavery, the present regional variation is undoubtedly due to selective migration. The fact that IQ and amount of Caucasian admixture in blacks parallel one another in geographical distribution, and that both of these variables more or less parallel the regional variations in the IQ in the white population, suggests only that similar selective factors have operated in the migrations of both populations. The correlation between amount of Caucasian admixture and the average IQ of blacks in different regions is a highly ambiguous fact with regard to interpretation. A similar association is also found between amount of Caucasian admixture, as indexed by skin color, and socioeconomic status. Because these facts could be the result of any one or any combination of several possible causes, no scientifically warranted conclusions can be drawn from them concerning racial genetic differences in IQ, except the weak conclusion that these facts do not contradict a genetic interpretation.

Age of Subjects

Tests devised for assessing the behavioral development of children under age 2 cannot be called intelligence tests, if by intelligence we mean the general factor common to performance on all complex cognitive tasks in the age groups above 3 or 4 years. Tests of whatever kind administered at below 2 years of age show very little or no correlation with cognitive tests given in later childhood and beyond.

Several carefully constructed infant tests provide reliable measures of early neuromuscular and perceptual maturation and coordination. In these functions, black infants are considerably advanced compared with white infants—up to about 15 to 18 months of age. This infant precocity in motoric development has been noted in a number of studies of African infants, as well as in blacks in the United States. In terms of a developmental quotient, with a standardized mean of 100 and standard deviation of 15 (like the IQ scale), the black-white average difference during these early months is of the order of 10 to 30 points.

The largest differences on record favor African infants and black American infants in poverty areas of the South.

By 2 years of age, the white-black developmental gap disappears. As the test content becomes more highly *g*-loaded with each succeeding year of age, the mental growth curve of the average white child overtakes that of the average black of the same age. By age 4 to age 5, the average difference between the groups amounts to about 15 IQ points. Probably the same amount of difference between the white and black averages would be found as far down the age scale as the *g* factor can be measured. The white-black IQ difference increases steadily from about age 2 to age 5, probably because the test becomes a better measure of *g* as the complexity of the items increases at higher age levels.

The average black IQ deficit does not change beyond age 5 for the vast majority of the black population. There are exceptions to this in some extremely deprived groups, found in certain small black communities in the rural South. But in most places the white-black IQ difference remains constant at every age level beyond age 5. This general finding casts some doubt on one of the main pillars of environmentalist explanations of the black IQ deficit—the ''cumulative deficit'' hypothesis, which holds that environmental disadvantages act like compound interest in producing a cumulative deficit in blacks' intellectual development. But one must wonder why environmental disadvantages do not continue to cumulate beyond age 5, when children begin school and are just becoming aware of the social milieu that is presumed to contain many of the ingredients that depress black IQ and scholastic performance. The fact that the 15-point black deficit remains stable after age 5 means that its causes, whatever they might be, must be sought in factors whose influences are already fully established before school age.

Nature of the Tests

As noted in Chapter 4, the average white-black difference is not equivalent to 15 IQ points on every kind of test. The white-black difference does not exist for all mental abilities, but mainly for conceptual and abstract reasoning, rather than learning and memory. The only feature of various tests we have discovered that is quite consistently related to the size of the white-black difference is the test's *g* loading, regardless of its item content, whether it is verbal or nonverbal, culture-loaded or culture-reduced, individually or group administered, oral or written.

The Scientific Search for Causes

The plain fact is that at present there exists no scientifically satisfactory explanation for the difference between the IQ distributions in the black and white populations. The only genuine consensus among well-informed scientists on this topic is that the cause of the difference remains an open question.

True, many people, including a good many scientists, hold strong ideological convictions or social sentiments on this issue. This militates against open questioning. It makes investigation uninviting. It biases interpretation of evidence. And it imposes a double standard of criticism of research and of its acceptability for publication by scientific journals, depending on whether the findings are perceived as supporting or contradicting popular views. It is hardly an atmosphere conducive to scientific consensus. Few other research topics in science are so unfavorably encumbered.

But even after we cut through all the extrinsic obstacles, we are still left with crucial problems and unknowns of an intrinsic scientific nature which legitimately prevent a scientific consensus on any given theory and compel the conclusion that we do not yet have a bona fide scientific explanation for the white-black difference in intelligence. In my extensive study of this whole topic, I have not been able to find any marshaling of evidence that could reasonably warrant the passionate beliefs that so many people hold concerning the cause of the IQ gap. Perhaps if any body of evidence were truly compelling, there would be no need for passionate beliefs.

Science thrives on opposing theories and competition among theories. Theories and hypotheses are the scaffolding for scientific knowledge. Scientific controversy can involve dispute over facts (that is, observations, measurements, events, statistical analyses of data) or dispute over theory and the hypotheses that flow from it, or both.

Scientists try to arrive at a consensus on some of the facts that must be taken account of in a given domain of scientific interest. They then formulate a theory that can comprehend the already established facts and logically and rigorously generate hypotheses that, in principle, can be empirically falsified. In this way, appropriate tests of a hypothesis can result in its rejection and thereby in the discovery of new facts. Unfortunately, hypotheses are often mistaken for accepted explanations by many of the public.

The discovery of objective knowledge is the real aim of scientific investigation, not the creation of theories *per se*. Theories are just the tools used in acquiring objective knowledge of nature, and as such they lead us to look where we might not have looked otherwise; they highlight important relationships that might otherwise go unnoticed; and they sometimes generate predictions that are counterintuitive and violate all common sense. But the main purpose of a theory is to lead us to objective facts that we did not know before. The discovery of some facts also enables us to do certain things that we could not do before. One indicator of the success of scientific endeavor is the undisputed results of its technological application, its power to cause events of practical consequence in the real world, whatever the value judgments we may make about them. By these criteria, the social and behavioral sciences have not yet been notably successful.

One of my chief aims has been to help advance our scientific understanding of the causes of psychological race differences by showing that it is, in fact, an unsettled question for which our present evidence cannot justify the pretense of a definitive answer. As goad and grist for scientific action, I have proposed a counterhypothesis to the popular belief in exclusively environmental or cultural causation, and have tried to show that a hypothesis involving genetic factors, in addition to environmental, is not only necessary as scientific scaffolding, but also more plausible than the strictly environmental hypothesis.

I do not hold with those who argue that in the absence of established knowledge we should publicly pretend there is no question, or assume as true that which we would like to believe. On this point, Bertrand Russell aptly stated what should be our guiding principle:

> Ethical considerations can only legitimately appear when the truth has been ascertained: they can and should appear as determining our feelings toward the truth, and our manner of ordering our lives in view of the truth, but not as themselves dictating what the truth is to be.

Inadequate Explanations of the White-Black IQ Difference

The present state of affairs in the study of the observed racial inequality in IQ (and all its correlates) can be characterized in three main points:

1. Many, if not all, of the most popular cultural and environmental explanations have been found inadequate by a preponderance of evidence. This forces those who insist on purely environmental explanations to hypothesize causes that are often purely *ad hoc;* that is, they are not derived from any general principles, but are merely devised for the single purpose of accounting for a specific phenomenon. Moreover, as most of the testable environmental hypotheses are found inadequate to bear the burden of a strictly environmental explanation, ever more vague or remote causes are hypothesized which are virtually untestable empirically.

But scientific ingenuity may eventually invent a way to test what seems a currently untestable hypothesis, and so a momentarily untestable hypothesis should not be dismissed out of hand. The only scientifically useless hypothesis is one that cannot be tested even *in principle*. I once heard a speaker declare, for example, that the white-black difference in IQ is a creation of science itself, which, being the invention of a white racist culture, is inevitably destined by the inherent nature of its methods to disprove racial genetic equality. Such an argument rules out scientific effort. Science has proved to be the most dependable means that people have yet devised for increasing our knowledge and understanding of natural phenomena.

2. The existing evidence severely limits the kinds of environmental causes that can be at all plausibly hypothesized.

3. A genetic hypothesis (which does not exclude environmental causation as well) is highly plausible in view of both the general evolutionary principles outlined previously and the well-established genetic component in individual variation in mental test scores. The trouble is, however, that a genetic hypothesis of race differences in IQ has not yet been put to even a halfway rigorous test by any techniques of genetic science. Nor has anyone yet figured out how to do so within the normal social and ethical constraints.

Because *human* populations are involved, and because human babies, in order to become truly human, must be reared by other humans capable of transmitting language and culture in the broad sense, the sheer technical problems in the bona fide genetical study of behavioral racial differences are truly tremendous. But *in principle* the genetic hypothesis is testable. It is therefore not scientifically useless. (Whether or not it is socially important is a separate question and one on which opinions differ.)

If it were a comparable question in plant or animal genetics, getting the answer would be a relatively trivial problem methodologically, because of the possibilities for complete control of the environment and for experimental breeding and cross-breeding, with true randomization of the mated pairs. Without these possibilities of experimentation in human genetics, we have to make do with much less powerful techniques, using naturalistic rather than experimentally controlled data. The consequence of this handicap, so far, has been weak inferences and inconclusive findings.

So that is where we stand at present. Those who would like a more satisfying answer will have to wait.

Let us now look at the most common environmental explanations of the average white-black IQ difference.

Socioeconomic Status

Only about 10 to 15 percent of blacks in the United States exceed the white median on indices of SES. Also, as pointed out in the first part of this chapter, there is a correlation between SES and IQ, within each race. The juxtaposition of these two facts is commonly given as an explanation for the black-white IQ difference. But it is totally inadequate.

As we saw in Table 6 and Figure 8, the white-black IQ difference shows up within every SES level and, in fact, increases at the higher SES levels. Equating the races on family SES reduces the average IQ difference between black and white children to 12 IQ points, as compared with the 15-point difference when the groups are not equated for SES.

But even this 3-point reduction in the mean difference cannot all be attributed to environmental factors. Because SES indicators, such as amount of education and occupational level, are correlated with IQ, and some part of this correlation involves genetic factors, then, when we equate blacks and whites on SES, we equate them to some extent as well on the genetic factors associated with SES. So nothing about environmental influences is proved by controlling SES in white-black IQ comparisons. If middle-class blacks are compared with middle-class whites, for example, the black group will be much more highly selected than the white group on whatever other traits and abilities are correlated with SES, so that we may be comparing, say, the upper 20 percent of blacks with the upper 50 percent of whites.

The objection is often heard that equating the groups on SES does not equate for *all* environmental influences. I don't know of anyone who has ever claimed that it does. But it does equate for those features of the environment that we mean by SES—education, occupation, income, and the like. And those aspects of the environment have *not* been shown to account for an appreciable part of the racial IQ gap.

If SES were the main factor in ethnic group differences in IQ, we should expect the rank order of different ethnic groups' mean IQs to be the same as their rank order on indices of SES. But this is far from being the case. For example, in a very large nationwide study it was found that on a composite of twelve SES and other environmental indices, the American Indian population ranks about as far below black standards as blacks rank below those of whites. Within each ethnic group these indices are correlated with IQ and scholastic achievement. But it turns out that Indians score *higher* than blacks on tests of intelligence and scholastic achievement, from the first to the twelfth grade. On a nonverbal reasoning test given in the first grade, before schooling could have had much impact, Indian children exceeded the mean score of blacks by the equivalent of 14 IQ points. Similar findings occur with Mexican-Americans, who rate below blacks on SES and other environmental indices, but score considerably higher on IQ tests, especially of the nonverbal type. Thus the IQ difference between Indians and blacks, and between Mexican-Americans and blacks, turns out opposite to what one would predict from the theory that ethnic group differences in IQ merely reflect SES differences.

Culture-biased Tests

The claim that tests are biased against blacks was discussed in Chapter 4, and I have examined the evidence much more comprehensively in my book *Bias in Mental Testing* (Free Press, 1980). The vast majority of present-day standardized tests of intelligence, scholastic aptitude, and achievement consistently fail to behave psychometrically in the ways we should expect if, in fact, they were culturally biased with respect to whites and blacks. The differences reflected by the tests are real, in the sense that the lower scores of blacks do not merely reflect artifacts or defects in the tests themselves. A strictly cultural explanation of all the observed psychometric features of the white-black differences in test performance is restricted to the rather implausible hypothesis that there is some broadly pervasive factor in the black culture that not only depresses black performance, relative to white, on all types of tests, but depresses in direct proportion to the tests' *g* loadings within each racial group, and affects a variety of psychometric features of tests in ways that perfectly mimic average age-group differences and high-low IQ differences of same-age children within each racial group. It would also have to be hypothesized that the many real-world criteria that standardized tests predict with equal accuracy for blacks and whites—scholastic achievement, college grades, rank in armed forces training programs, and job performance in a wide variety of occupations—are just as biased as the tests. It is hard to imagine what kind of cultural factors would produce this particular complex pattern of effects, which are quite unlike those found in other groups from different cultural backgrounds. As two sociologists who examined all this evidence commented: "Even if one postulates a vague but broad kind of 'experience' that behaves in exactly this manner, it should be evident that it would represent but a thinly disguised tautology for the mental functions that IQ tests are designed to measure" (R. A. Gordon and E. E. Rudert, "Bad News Concerning IQ Tests," *Sociology of Education* 52 [1979]: 174–190).

Motivation

Blacks appear no less motivated or cooperative in taking tests than other groups. On specially devised tests of attention, speed, and persistence, and on tests of rote learning and memory, which call for as much effort as most IQ tests, blacks perform about as well as whites. These tests are fairly sensitive to motivation, as shown by changes in test performance according to whether highly motivating or nonmotivating instructions precede the tests. Blacks and whites are affected equally by these conditions. Such tests show little or no average difference between blacks and whites, because they are specially devised to minimize dependence on the abstract or complex cognitive functions that characterize *g*.

It should also be noted that black youngsters do not show lower educational aspirations or poorer self-concepts or self-esteem than white youngsters.

Educational Inequality

The educational system cannot be held directly accountable for the lower black IQ, because the full 15 IQ points difference between whites and blacks is already there by age 5, prior to formal schooling, and for the vast majority of the black population the IQ does not show a decline throughout the twelve years of school attendance.

After more than twelve years of complete racial integration of the schools and classrooms in some communities, as in Berkeley, California, the average white-black difference in test scores is the same as it was when the races were largely *de facto* segregated by neighborhood schools. Attempts in recent decades to equalize or even do more than equalize education for blacks and whites have had no consistently detectable effect on the IQ gap.

Verbal Deprivation

It is a popular notion that blacks do less well on IQ tests because they are "verbally deprived," with less exposure to language and the subtleties of verbal communication. In Chapter 4 it was noted that blacks, on the average, perform at least as well on verbal as on nonverbal tests, and often slightly better. This would seem to contradict the verbal deprivation explanation of lower test scores.

We can find out something about how verbal deprivation would, in fact, affect scores on various kinds of tests, by looking at the studies of the most verbally deprived individuals we know of: children who were born totally deaf. These children do score considerably below average on verbal tests, as expected. But they perform completely up to par on the nonverbal culture-fair type of tests. Their performance, then, turns out to be just the opposite of the supposedly verbally deprived blacks, who usually score higher on verbal than on nonverbal tests.

Teacher Expectancy

Another factor popularly cited as a possible cause of the black IQ deficit is teacher expectancy—the notion that a child's test score tends to reflect the level of performance expected by his teacher, with the teacher's expectation often based on prejudice or stereotypes. Numerous studies of teacher expectancy, however, have failed to establish this phenomenon, either as a general effect on any child's IQ or as a contributing factor to the lower IQs of blacks.

Malnutrition

Severe malnutrition, especially protein deficiency, during prenatal development, infancy, and childhood, can impair mental as well as physical growth. Such impairments have been found in the nutritionally most deprived children in Africa, Asia, and South America. However, there are no comparable findings in the United States. Surveys of black communities in which there is no evidence of malnutrition (although there may be dietary and nutritional differences) still show the average black IQ to be about the usual 15 points below the white average. Also, when groups of black children with IQs below the general black average have been examined for low nutritional status, no signs of malnutrition have been found.

The most recent and most thorough survey ever made of the nutritional status of U.S. blacks in relation to IQ concludes that there are significant differences between whites' and blacks' nutritional intakes, the blacks (and Hispanics) being the less well nourished. From the observed differences in the average nutrition of whites and blacks and the association of various indices of nutritional deficiency with IQ among individuals of the same race, the investigators attempted to estimate how much of the white-black IQ difference might be attributed to the nutritional differences. They estimated 1 or 2 IQ points overall, several points at most. It could possibly be more in some of the poorest segments of the black population. But apparently, unless there is severe and prolonged malnutrition, which is virtually nonexistent in the United States, dietary and nutritional variation, prenatally and postnatally, has little if any effect on later IQ.

Prenatal and Perinatal Disadvantages

The significantly higher rates of fetal loss, prematurity, low birth weight, and infant mortality in the black population may indicate disadvantages in prenatal health care and poor conditions attending birth. The causes of all these conditions, however, are not yet understood. It is puzzling, for example, that certain other minority groups—Jews and Asians—living in poverty have shown lower rates of fetal loss and infant mortality than are currently found in the white middle class.

Massive data from studies by the National Institutes of Health suggest that these reproductive factors, particularly birth weight, could account altogether for 2 to 4 points of the average black IQ deficit. These points would not necessarily be in addition to those contributed by poor nutrition, because the two variables are correlated and therefore overlap each other, so that their independent effects may not add up to more than 5 points. But these biologic factors would not begin to account for such phenomena as a rate of mental retardation (IQs below 70) six or seven times higher in the black than in the white population. However, it is interesting to note that the severest types of retardation—which are almost all caused by either a single mutant or a recessive gene (e.g., microcephaly), a chromosomal abnormality (e.g., Down's syndrome or "mongolism"), or brain damage due to disease or trauma—occur at similar rates in the black and white populations.

Styles of Child Rearing and Mother-Child Interaction

Another popular environmental hypothesis is that the cause of the black IQ deficit is to be found in the quality of mother-child interaction during the preschool years. The hypothesis is difficult to test, as it must rely on systematic observations comparing black and white children in their natural environments. Two developmental psychologists, Alfred and Clara Baldwin, have spent more than a decade in this kind of investigation, amassing several hundred recorded observations of mother-child interactions involving preschoolers in black and white families from lower and middle social classes. Many aspects of mother-child interactions were systematically observed in half-hour-long free-play settings and recorded in terms of thirty-five coded variables.

Only *one* statistically significant difference between blacks and whites showed up: black mothers were *more* likely than white mothers to adopt a didactic teaching role in their free-play interactions with their youngsters. The Baldwins noted that "white mothers were much more relaxed in general about the child's academic future. They felt considerably less pressure to teach him academic-type facts during the play session than did the black mothers" ("The Study of Mother-Child Interaction," *American Scientist* 61[1973]: 714–721).

The Baldwins question the language deprivation theory: "All these facts lead us to question deeply whether there is any social significance in the small difference in the syntactic complexity found in the mothers in the free-play session." They admit, "Frankly, when we began this investigation, we anticipated many more differences between the black lower class sample and the white upper middle class sample. . . . But as we observed these mother-child pairs, and then as we saw the results of the data analysis, we have become convinced that the most striking fact is the overall similarity of mother-child interaction in free play in all the samples."

It is hard to reconcile such observations with the view that the black IQ deficit is the result of the family environment, especially of middle- and upper-middle-class blacks. What environmental effects of the social interaction variety could produce the size of IQ differences we find? If such social interaction differences are so subtle as to go largely undetected in as thorough and careful a study as the Baldwins', one must wonder about the source of the IQ difference.

Some idea of the problem is conveyed by the observation that in all the large-scale studies that have been made, black children in the middle and upper-middle SES groups, on the average, score no higher, and usually score slightly lower, on IQ tests than do white children of the lowest SES. To take a quite typical finding, we can compare the average IQs of blacks and whites at two extreme SES levels in one of the more affluent California school districts. "High SES" in this study was defined as jobs requiring a college degree such as high-level administrator, supervisor, college teacher, high-level professional, engineer, and physician. Of the total black school population in the district, 7 percent were in this category, representing the topmost 7 percent of the black pupils in SES. One would have to call them environmentally "advantaged" by ordinary standards. "Low SES" was defined as manual and nonmanual workers in unskilled jobs ordinarily requiring less than a high school diploma. Of the entire white school population, 14.4 percent fall into this low SES category, representing the 14.4 percent socioeconomically *least* advantaged white pupils. But this low SES white group averages 3 IQ points *above* the high SES black group. (The high SES white group averages 15 IQ points above the high SES black group.) Clearly, in view of this typical finding, what we ordinarily think of as the child's environmental advantages associated with SES appears as completely inadequate in explaining the black IQ deficit.

Totaling Up Environmental Factors

One might imagine that each of the small decrements in IQ contributed by each of the disadvantaging environmental factors we have mentioned might total up to the full 15 IQ points of gap between whites and blacks. Attempts to combine properly all of the contributing IQ decrements that have actually been found to be associated with various environmental factors, however, fall far short of making up the full 15-point deficit. The IQ decrements found to be associated with each

environmental factor cannot be added up in a simple fashion, like totaling the cost on a grocery list, because the various environmental effects
are rarely independent. They are usually highly intercorrelated variables, and therefore overlap each other to a great extent. The effect on
IQ of any one variable also includes some of the effects of the other variables, and so the total, in this case, is much less than the sum of its
parts. If we say that a child's parents have had very little education, we
are also saying in part that generally they also have a smaller-than-
average income, a larger-than-average number of children, lower occupational status, poorer nutrition, and so on. And so it is with nearly
every feature of the environment, except for purely fortuitous circumstances.

There is a proper statistical technique, termed ''multiple regression
analysis,'' for totaling the combined effects of a number of intercorrelated variables. When it is applied to the present problem, the results
indicate that removing these correlated environmental effects reduces
the 15-point average white-black IQ difference by about 5 or 6 points,
leaving about two-thirds of the gap unaccounted for by assessed environmental effects. This gives rise to hypothesizing still other, more subtle environmental factors that either have not been or cannot be
measured—a history of slavery, social oppression, and racial discrimination, white racism, the ''black experience,'' and minority status con-
sciousness, to name the most commonly mentioned explanations.

But there is a still more serious technical problem that undermines
the interpretation of any result of adding up correlated environmental
effects by means of multiple regression analysis. This is because some
of the environmental effects are correlated with the parents' genotypes
for intelligence and are thereby indirectly correlated with their off-
springs' genotypes and IQs. The only way out of this bind is to eliminate the link between environment and genotype. With plants or animals, this could easily be done experimentally. With humans, the only
recourse available is to look at naturally occurring cross-racial adoptions, where infants of one race are adopted by parents of a different
race. Theoretically and ideally, cross-racial adoption is the one feasible
method available that could significantly reduce the uncertainty about
the causes of the black IQ deficit.

Cross-racial Adoptions

There is only one cross-racial adoption study worth mentioning, as
it is the only one based on American blacks and on reasonable-size

samples (S. Scarr and R. A. Weinberg, "IQ Test Performance of Black Children Adopted by White Families," *American Psychologist* 31 [1976]: 726–739).

The adoptive parents were mostly college-educated, professional and managerial level, upper-middle-class whites in Minnesota. All of the adoptees had been given up shortly after birth by their natural mothers, and most were adopted in infancy; some were placed in foster homes before adoption.

The adoptees could be classified into two groups: those whose natural mother is white and whose natural father is black (labeled "white/black"), and those whose natural parents are both black ("black/black"). Because the average black American has about 20 percent Caucasian genes, the interracial or white/black adoptees have at least 60 percent Caucasian genes, which makes them a very nontypical group for comparison with American blacks in general, who have at least twice as much African ancestry. Also, judging from the average educational level of the interracial parents, some of them were college students. Other studies have shown that black males involved in interracial mating are more likely to be above the black average in IQ. The black/black adoptees could be regarded as more typical, although a majority were selected from those states with the highest average black IQ: Minnesota, Wisconsin, and Massachusetts. (Armed forces test data indicate that in 1968 black males in Wisconsin averaged higher than blacks in any other state of the United States, with a mean IQ of about 95.)

IQs were not known for the natural parents, but the adoptive parents, their own children, and the adoptees were all given individual IQ tests, with the following results:

	Average IQ
Adoptive fathers	120.8
Adoptive mothers	118.2
Natural children of adoptive parents	116.7
White/black adoptees	109.0
Black/black adoptees	96.8

The IQ levels of the adoptive parents and their own children are typical for college-educated professional and executive level families.

The relative differences among all these averages appear to be consistent with a genetic hypothesis. However, the authors of the study put most of their emphasis on the fact that the adoptees' IQs average well above the general average of the black population. I think this emphasis on the absolute level of the IQ is unjustified, however, because of the probability of selective bias in those families who volunteered their adopted children for participation in the study. More than a third of the eligible adoptive families who were requested to participate refused or did not respond to repeated requests. Also, among the volunteers there were many more white/black than black/black adoptees. When volunteers are requested for a study involving mental tests, there is generally a tendency for the mean score to be biased upward. In addition to some self-selection for higher IQ in those who volunteered, it is also likely that there was selection by adoption agencies, which usually try to place the potentially brightest adoptees in well-educated upper-class families, especially if the adoptive parents have children of their own. But we really have no way of knowing just how much the IQs of the adoptees might be spuriously elevated by these selective factors. It is an unfortunate ambiguity inherent in any adoption study, in which, of course, participation cannot be coerced.

What about the difference of 12.2 IQ points between the white/black and black/black adoptees? It seems consistent with a genetic hypothesis. But the authors stress that such an interpretation is ambiguously weakened by the significantly different foster placement histories of the white/black and black/black groups prior to their legal adoption. The black/black children lived in foster homes for a longer time and in a greater number of foster homes. This explanation, however, seems quite *ad hoc*. It attributes a large effect on IQ—12.2 points—to differences in early environmental backgrounds of a type that has not been found to have any appreciable effect on IQ in other studies. It is doubtful that the quality of the foster care environments in which the black/black children were reared until they were legally adopted (at an average age of 2 years 8 months) and the qualities of their legal adoptive families were at all outside the range of environments that the authors, in their reports of another adoption study, refer to as "humane environments," variations among which, they claim, are functionally equivalent in their effects on IQ. They state that "the [IQ] differences among children at the end of the child rearing period have little to do with environmental differences among families that range from solid working class to upper middle class." The 12.2-point difference between the white/black and black/black adoptees is much greater than could be accounted for by any combination of the environmental variables that have been assessed for the magnitude of their effect on IQ in another adoption study (involving only whites) by Scarr and Weinberg.

Thus the only study of the type that theoretically could best reduce the uncertainty about the causation of the black IQ deficit is unfortunately rendered equivocal by these unavoidable methodological shortcomings.

The Genetic Hypothesis

Environmental factors, except those so vague, subtle, remote in time, or ill-defined as to be immune to objective assessment, are inadequate to explain all the observed phenomena connected with the white-black IQ difference. There has been no rigorous demonstration, or even the attempt, to show that all aspects of the black IQ deficit can be accounted for by environmental variables. Thus, after collaborating in the most painstakingly thorough and cautious review of the available evidence ever attempted in this field, two behavioral geneticists and an anthropologist drew the following conclusions:

> 1. Observed average differences in the scores of members of different U.S. racial ethnic groups on intellectual-ability tests probably reflect in part inadequacies and biases in the test themselves, in part differences in environmental conditions among the groups, and in part genetic differences among the groups. It should be emphasized that these three factors are not necessarily independent, and may interact.
>
> 2. A rather wide range of positions concerning the relative weight to be given to these three factors can reasonably be taken on the basis of current evidence, and a sensible person's position might well differ for different abilities, for different groups, and for different tests.
>
> 3. Regardless of the position taken on the relative importance of these three factors, it seems clear that the differences among individuals within racial-ethnic (and socioeconomic) groups greatly exceed in magnitude the average differences between such groups. [J. C. Loehlin, G. Lindzey, and J. N. Spuhler, *Race Differences in Intelligence*, W. H. Freeman, 1975.]

Hence, genetic factors, among others, are deemed part of the explanation. What is far less certain is just how much of the average white-black difference can be assigned to genetic and nongenetic causes.

The genetic hypothesis has the advantage of plausibility, but the disadvantage of there being no ethically feasible direct test that would reliably estimate the magnitude of the racial difference in the genes that affect the development of intelligence. I once proposed that the most parsimonious hypothesis—one that would comprehend virtually all of the established facts about the white-black IQ difference without the need to postulate any environmental factors besides those that are known to affect IQ and on which blacks in general are less advantaged—is that "something between one-half and three-fourths of the average IQ difference is attributable to genetic factors, and the remainder to environmental factors and their interaction with genetic differences."

A gross misconception about any genetic explanation, regardless of its hypothesized magnitude, is that there are "white genes" and "black genes" for intelligence. This is nonsense. A polygenic theory assumes that the very same genes that produce variation in intelligence among persons of the same race can produce variation between races or other population groups that are relatively segregated. The gene pools of such groups are hypothesized to possess different frequencies of the genes that enhance the trait in question. As pointed out earlier, such polygenic variation between human races in a host of observable characteristics is the rule rather than the exception. That the brain and its behavioral correlates should be the only exceptions would seem miraculous.

Yet there is nothing in the theory or methodology of quantitative and population genetics which, in connection with any present evidence, can provide a proper test of the genetic hypothesis regarding race differences in intelligence.

We would be faced by essentially the same problem if we were asked for a rigorous proof that genetic factors play a part in the difference in height (a polygenic character) between the average Pygmy and Watusi. I have tried this question on several professors of genetics, and all admitted they could not present any evidence or argument based thereon that would properly persuade a geneticist to believe that the Pygmy-Watusi difference involves genetic factors. Yet none of them doubted that the difference in height between Pygmies and Watusis is practically all genetic. In other words, they were appealing to plausibility. If someone had a strong vested interest in opposing that plausible conclusion, he could quite correctly argue that there is no direct evidence of a genetic difference between Pygmies and Watusis. (Moreover, it would be hardly feasible to obtain such evidence, without resorting to ethically objectionable techniques such as experimental cross-breeding and the random cross-fostering of offspring.) Hearing that, some people might then favor the conclusion that the difference is entirely environmentally caused. After all, Pygmies and Watusis have quite different habitats and diets—factors that possibly affect growth.

It is instructive to ask why so few people, including geneticists, would doubt that the Pygmy-Watusi height difference is largely genetic. What lends it plausibility? Two things: (1) the large size of the average difference—the tallest Pygmies are shorter than the average Watusi; and (2) the known very high heritability of height within each group—the correlation between genotypes and phenotypes for height is .95 or more. In other words, within each group, the variations in nutrition and other environmental conditions contribute so little to the variation in height (10 percent or less), and the differences between typical Pygmies and Watusis in these conditions do not appear as great as the differences between the extremes of these environmental conditions within either group, that we feel justified in doubting that these environmental conditions are entirely responsible for the difference in height. In the absence of any other environmental factors that differ between typical Pygmies and Watusis and that have sufficiently powerful effects on physical growth to produce such a difference in height, it seems reasonable to attribute the difference to the single most important factor known to control individual variation in height, namely the genes. This is a plausible explanation, and most people accept it.

Formally, the white-black IQ difference is perfectly analogous, although it is less extreme because the average IQ difference between whites and blacks is not nearly so great relative to IQ variability within the groups, and the heritability of IQ is not nearly so high—the correlation between genotypes and phenotypes for intelligence within each group being .75 to .80. Because the known environmental causes of IQ variation have relatively small effects within the typical American white and black populations, and because these populations, on the average, are not found to differ extremely enough in these environmental variables to account for even half of the 15 IQ points difference between the groups, it seems plausible that genetic factors contribute to the total difference. Only a relatively small average genetic difference would fill the explanatory gap, whereas it would take an unrealistically extreme environmental difference to do so, which is contradicted by our knowledge of environmental effects on IQ. Because genes importantly affect individual differences in IQ, they are a likely explanation for the part of the white-black IQ gap unaccounted for by environmental factors.

Why is this, just like our Pygmy-Watusi height analogy, an example of mere plausibility rather than of scientific "proof" of a genetic explanation, thereby rendering it only a genetic hypothesis?

The reason, in both cases, is that all other possible nongenetic causes have not been definitely ruled out. One can hypothesize other nongenetic factors to explain the gap—in height or in IQ. The hypothesized environmental factors may even be much less plausible than a genetic hypothesis, but all hypothesized factors, technically speaking, have equal status until they can be ruled out or the counter-hypothesis can be proved by direct evidence.

Competing hypotheses, of course, can certainly differ in our subjective estimates of their plausibility, and most people wouldn't bet a dime on some. But scientifically this is not the deciding criterion for any hypothesis, although it may direct the scientists' priorities for investigating what seem the most likely fruitful hypotheses.

No scientist, to my knowledge, has argued that a genetic hypothesis is not plausible or that it is even less plausible than any other hypothesis yet proposed. The present strictly nongenetic counter-hypotheses posit broad and subtle social factors that would have no effect on IQ within the white or Asian populations, but which severely depress black IQ. That such hypothesized factors apparently do not operate in the case of certain other minority groups with a history of discrimination and social disadvantage comparable to blacks', gives such hypotheses a very *ad hoc* status, and *ad hoc* hypotheses are poorly regarded in science.

This is not the case with the genetic hypothesis, as genes affect intelligence in all populations we know. If the present condition of our society or the history of blacks in America harbors the causes of the black IQ deficit, one should ask if there is any evidence that those sub-Saharan Africans who were the parent population of American blacks are now, or ever were, superior to American blacks in intelligence. I can find nothing in the extensive research literature on sub-Saharan Africans that would lead one to suppose that blacks in Africa or in any other part of the world are superior to American blacks in mental abilities.

What would constitute scientifically rigorous evidence for a genetic hypothesis? The most direct evidence would be to identify specific genes that contribute to IQ variance and to show a difference in the frequency of these genes in the white and black populations. This would be conceivably feasible only if a very small number of genes, say, two or three, could be found that would each have a large effect on IQ. Genetic linkage analysis could then possibly identify these few genes and permit a statistical estimate of their frequencies in any population.

If, as is more likely the case, however, genetic variation in IQ is highly polygenic, with numerous genes each contributing small and similar effects, there is no present genetic methodology that would permit a direct estimate of specific IQ-related gene frequencies in any population. The problem of racial differences in any highly polygenic trait is therefore scientifically uninteresting to geneticists in terms of anything they can at present do about it as geneticists. This of course says nothing about the scientific importance of the problem or its social interest.

There is another, less direct type of genetic evidence based on the progeny of cross-racial matings. Do the racially mixed offspring of white and black parents have higher IQs than the offspring of two black parents? In the United States today virtually all blacks have some Caucasian ancestry. It is possible to estimate the percentage of Caucasian admixture in black Americans by means of blood group analysis. This would seem to afford a method for testing the genetic hypothesis, by determining the correlation between IQ and percentage of Caucasian admixture. The outcomes of the few studies based on this approach are as totally inconclusive as can be imagined. The problems involve, first, the assumptions that must be made about the probable intelligence levels of white and black ancestors of present American blacks, and second, the extreme methodological problems posed by the data.

Unless the whites and blacks who mated interracially during the period of slavery were fairly representative of their respective populations in intelligence, the interpretation of any outcome of an admixture study is ambiguous. For example, if the cross-racial matings consisted largely of members of the intellectually upper half of the black population and the lower half of the white population, there would be less possibility of finding a positive correlation between percentage of Caucasian admixture and IQ. The same would be true if mulattoes had a greater probability of mating with the intellectually abler blacks, in which case the genes for higher intelligence in subsequent racially mixed generations would have come more from the African ancestry than from the white. Hence the great ambiguity inherent in this method.

But the more serious problems are inherent in the data themselves, which makes this an unpromising method to geneticists. There are three main difficulties. The first, but least intractable, is the fact that skin color and other physical characteristics, are correlated with degree of racial admixture and these physical attributes could be hypothesized to elicit social attitudes that affect mental development. This can be overcome theoretically by statistically removing the IQ-correlated effects of physical appearance from the correlation between the blood group index of Caucasian admixture and IQ. But this would also weaken the correlation between IQ and Caucasian admixture, if there is truly a genetic connection, because skin color and the other visible features are indices of amount of Caucasian admixture, just as are the blood groups.

The second difficulty is due to the fact that there is little variation in the percentage of Caucasian admixture among blacks drawn from the same locality or sufficiently similar background to ensure that degree of admixture is not spuriously correlated with environmental differences, as would be the case, for example, if we compared blacks in rural Georgia (with about 10 percent admixture) with blacks in the urban West (with about 20 percent admixture). Correlation essentially depends on sufficient variance in both correlated variables. Admixture studies are thus statistically handicapped because they depend on the correlation between IQ, on the one hand, and a variable—Caucasian admixture—with very restricted variance, on the other.

The third and probably most limiting difficulty is the fact that the entry of most of the Caucasian genes into the black gene pool took place so long ago that the linkages between the genes affecting intelligence and the blood group genes or other physical characteristics used to index degree of Caucasian admixture have by now largely broken up within the black population, so that there is very little correlation left between "intelligence genes" and any other genes. In studies of American blacks, for example, indices of Caucasian admixture based on certain blood groups correlate only slightly with the lightness of skin color or with other blood group indices, thus showing considerable disassociation between genetic indicators of admixture. Under such limiting conditions, it would take an enormous sample to be able to test any well-considered genetic or environmental hypothesis with a reasonable degree of statistical confidence. So this method has not seemed encouraging to most geneticists.

Perhaps methodological ingenuity will eventually come up with a genetic technique for obtaining evidence that would settle the present uncertainty. Until then, what we are left with is merely the considerable plausibility that genetic factors are involved in the IQ difference between certain racial populations. Although the preponderance of evidence is consistent with the hypothesis that genetic as well as environmental factors are the cause of the white-black IQ difference, it remains, by the strict rules of scientific evidence, too insufficiently tested to allow a definitive conclusion. This scientific uncertainty justifies an openly agnostic position. But many people are deeply gratified by the scientific uncertainty in this sphere—an attitude which works against the growth of knowledge. In the history of intellectual conquest, agnosticism concerning socially important natural phenomena has always been highly unstable. It invariably gives way either to dogmatic belief or to scientific knowledge.

7

Questions and Answers

As a consequence of my appearance on "The Phil Donahue Show" (a television interview and talk show) and several radio talk shows following the publication of my book *Bias in Mental Testing* (1980), I received a flood of letters from viewers and listeners—most of them friendly. A good many correspondents asked specific questions. My answers to most of these questions can be found in the preceding chapters. But in scanning my mail, I have found a number of questions that have not been answered in the preceding chapters. Some of these should be answered, especially those asked, with slight variations, by at least two or more correspondents. As the answers to these questions do not fit easily into any of the main topics considered in this book, I have decided to answer each one as directly as possible in this final chapter, consisting entirely of questions and answers about mental tests.

Q: When the National Education Association and a number of other teachers' organizations are so strongly opposed to IQ tests or other standardized scholastic tests, and if these groups reflect or influence teachers' attitudes toward such tests, how much confidence can we have in the test results when tests are administered and scored by teachers?

A: There is a common saying among test experts that a test is no better than the person using it. Studies have found that teachers who have favorable attitudes toward tests are more conscientious about closely observing the explicit requirements for administering and scoring standardized tests—such things as reading the test instructions aloud completely and clearly, accurately observing the prescribed time limits for each part of the test, maintaining a relaxed but businesslike atmosphere throughout the test session, and properly proctoring the whole proceeding to ensure that each pupil's performance is exclusively his or her own performance.

My own studies of teacher-administered tests have convinced me that the great majority of teachers are conscientious in giving tests. But a few, unfortunately, are not, and I could tell some real horror stories about such teachers' abuses of tests. I have found some teachers completely disregarding the standard instructions, which would make the pupils' scores noncomparable to the test norms. Still worse, some teachers violate the time limits—in both directions. In one school we found that the total time allowed by teachers for a standardized test with a prescribed 45-minute time limit ranged, for different teachers, from 15 minutes to several hours! One teacher allowed her class to take the test "cooperatively," the pupils consulting one another during the testing period. Then we have found teachers who alter the test questions to make them easier. One sixth-grade teacher, for example, read aloud the reading comprehension items of the Stanford Achievement Test, because, she complained, some of her pupils could not read the items! Another teacher, before scoring the tests, filled in any answers that the pupils left blank if she thought the answer was something the pupils ought to have known.

Even when the test has been administered faultlessly, the teacher may make gross scoring errors or misread the tables for converting the raw scores into standard scores or percentiles. I have seen IQs recorded that were as much as 40 points off as a result of such conversion errors. It is a shame that such undependable test scores are ever recorded anywhere. Pray that no decisions are ever based on them.

I could go on. But to sum it all up, an investigation in one school district showed significantly greater variability (about 25 percent greater variance) among class averages on IQ and especially on achievement tests when the tests were administered and scored by the classroom teachers than when they were administered and scored strictly according to the rules by a specially trained staff of testers working under the close supervision of a school psychologist. When teachers did the testing under supervision, after receiving preliminary instruction in testing procedures, they showed much less variability in the test scores obtained from their pupils; the results were then very comparable to those obtained by expert psychometrists.

Because of these dismaying experiences, which fortunately are not typical but are not too rare either, and because of the near impossibility of knowing just which teachers have or have not done the testing properly, I would put little stock in teacher-administered tests, especially if the scores are intended to be used for any individual purpose.

Teachers need to be better educated about the fact that standard achievement tests can provide valuable informative feedback to both the teacher and the pupils, and it is in their mutual interest to obtain as accurate scores as possible. It should not be a game of "beating the test" or "putting one over" on the school administration. Schools *should* use standardized achievement tests, but their administration and scoring should be handled more carefully.

Although achievement testing is an indispensable part of the educational process, I see little value in group-administered IQ tests, even under the best of testing conditions. A well-designed achievement test, administered after a unit of instruction, provides the teacher with the most essential information—the pupil's actual achievement. A teacher surely needs to know whether or not a pupil has learned what was taught. But it is hard to see why the teacher should need to know a pupil's IQ. If the pupil has a learning problem that the teacher and parents cannot remedy by ordinary means, the child then should be referred to a specialist for a psychological assessment of the problem; this may involve an individually administered IQ test.

Many psychologists would argue that all pupils should be given an IQ test, so that the teacher will know which pupils are or are not achieving "up to capacity." The room for abuses of this philosophy seems to me to outweigh its possible advantages. In the best of all worlds, I would be comfortable with it. But knowing what I do about teacher-administered group IQ tests and the prevalence of teachers' misconceptions about the interpretation of the IQ, I am inclined to believe that mass testing of IQ is a wasteful and dubious practice at best, and that schools are probably better off without group IQ tests. It is truly a pity, because some of these group tests are technically excellent from the standpoint of psychometrics. Properly administered and scored, they are highly reliable and valid for any of the legitimate uses of such tests.

Yet I think schools can do without group IQ tests, with the following three exceptions: (1) Group IQ tests can be extremely useful as statistical control variables in educational research, if reliably administered by a trained staff; (2) they are useful to a school psychologist, in exceptional cases, as an efficient preliminary screening device that may rule out the need for giving a child a more time-consuming individual IQ test; and (3) they are useful in screening for academic talent, which the schools should foster with appropriate programs. Culture-reduced tests can make an especially important contribution to the identification of academic talent among children from an educationally disadvantaged background, whose abilities are more apt to go unrecognized. Tests often discover children with superior aptitudes that were unsuspected by their parents and teachers.

Q: If group IQ tests are abandoned by the public schools, what would take their place?

A: Good standardized achievement tests given by teachers who are trained to use them properly. Achievement testing should be an integral part of the instruction, providing the teacher and pupil with information such as what knowledge and skills have or have not been mastered. In order to be an effective part of the feedback loop that can help guide the student toward achieving the instructional goals, tests should be given frequently, interspersing frequent teacher-made tests for small units of study with less frequent standardized tests for assessing achievement in broader units.

Except in the case of children with special reading disabilities, often called dyslexia, we have found that the one type of scholastic achievement test that gives the best indication of a pupil's general scholastic ability is reading comprehension. But one must be careful to distinguish between word reading or oral reading, on the one hand, and reading comprehension, on the other. Scores on reading comprehension are very highly correlated with IQ, even with purely nonverbal IQ. The important practical difference between a reading comprehension test and an IQ test is that teachers and parents have no trouble understanding what reading comprehension means, whereas for many there is a "mystique" surrounding the IQ; the misconceptions are frequently so deeply ingrained that it might even require a complete college course on mental testing to dispel them.

If a child's reading comprehension score is low for his age group, it could mean any of several things—low general ability, special reading disability, poor reading instruction, or an emotional block to reading. A high reading comprehension score, on the other hand, rules out low IQ.

In general, the schools should concentrate on improving achievement (which also implies objectively assessing achievement), rather than try to measure abilities, except for those pupils who are having unusual problems in school and warrant special attention by a psychologist.

Q: Where can I secure a psychological evaluation of my 8-year old child's ability?

A: I assume there is some legitimate reason for wanting an evaluation. I would begin by inquiring at the child's school; ask to see the school psychologist. If the school does not provide this service, ask your child's pediatrician to refer you to a psychologist, or try the local mental health clinic or a children's hospital, or talk to someone in the psychology department at the nearest college or university. As is true in medicine or law or any other professional service, the training, competence, experience, and wisdom of clinical psychologists vary enormously. Referrals from dependable professionals, established clinics, and the like are a safer bet than the yellow pages in the telephone directory.

Q: What is a "minimal competency" test? Should a passing score be required for a high school diploma?

A: The "minimal competency" tests that I have seen are tests of very basic scholastic skills in the three R's and in their applications to the kinds of practical, real-life demands that are made of every adult in our society. Questions involve such things as the following, for example: Given a specified amount of money, the student must be able to write that amount both in figures (e.g., $6.85) and in words. Given the hourly wage rate and the number of hours worked, they must compute the total wages. Told the rent on an apartment for one month, they must compute the yearly rent. They must be able to fill out a job application or a Social Security form, total up a weekly time card, follow the directions on the label of a medicine bottle, and so on.

Passing a minimal competency test is now required for high school graduation in several states, and many other states are now considering this. The use of these tests to determine who shall graduate has been strongly protested by some groups, because the tests are "failed" by much higher proportions of minority students, particularly blacks and Hispanics. This should come as no surprise, as scores on these minimal competency tests are highly correlated with scores on the usual IQ and scholastic achievement tests on which these ethnic group differences are already well known to school authorities.

Despite the fact that the minimal competency tests are well constructed from a psychometric standpoint, and have excellent "face validity," I can see no justification for their use as a criterion for awarding or withholding high school diplomas. Not only is it unnecessarily stigmatizing to those who fail, but it makes no sense psychometrically. "Minimal competence" is an arbitrary cutoff point on a continuum of ability and achievement. To divide graduating students into those who are "competent" and those who are "incompetent," and to award or withhold high school diplomas accordingly, serves no useful educational or social purpose that I can determine. What is competence for one purpose may be incompetence for another. The high school graduate who wants to go to MIT needs a higher level of scholastic competence than the graduate who wants to work in a filling station. Let every college and employer determine what is competence for their own requirements, and be free to use whatever assessment technique for selecting applicants that best suits their particular purpose. No single criterion of "competence" can possibly serve all these diverse purposes.

However, assessments of the basic scholastic skills and their practical applications that are represented in minimum competency tests should be made frequently throughout every student's scholastic career. No student should be deprived of knowing the kinds of practical scholastic skills that are commonly called for in adult life, or of knowing where he stands in those skills in relation to his peers. The main purpose of competency tests should be to periodically reveal a student's particular deficiencies in applying his scholastic skills. This should begin long before the final year of high school, so that deficiencies can be discovered and remedied as much as possible before graduation. But it seems unjust and unwise, as well as wasteful of taxpayers' money, to use competency tests only in the final year of school as a requirement for graduation or for awarding a diploma.

Q: Are the physically handicapped, such as those with cerebral palsy, or the deaf or blind, or those with speech handicaps, penalized on IQ tests because of their handicap, or can their intelligence be accurately measured?

A: Many of the usual tests are unsuitable for persons with severe sensory or motor disabilities. However, there are different tests that a clinical psychologist can select as appropriate for testing a person with a particular type of disability. For example, the Columbia Mental Maturity Scale and the Peabody Picture Vocabulary Test require no writing or manipulative skill. Various peformance tests and nonverbal paper-and-pencil tests are suitable for the deaf, aphasic, and speech-handicapped. The blind can be given all the verbal scales of the Wechsler and parts of the Stanford–Binet, and there is also a special adaptation of the Binet test for the blind. A competent clinician can make as accurate an assessment of a handicapped person's general mental ability as of anyone else's. But some clinicians are much more experienced than most in working with the physically handicapped, and they are usually known by the clinics, hospitals, or training centers that serve the handicapped.

Q: I have seen advertisements for books that claim to tell parents how they can raise their child's IQ. Which of these books would you recommend?

A: If you want to raise your child's *intelligence*, I recommend none of them. Their claims usually border on charlatanism. There is no real evidence to substantiate such promises. These books appear to have been written for the sole purpose of exploiting the gullibility of parents who are overanxious about their children. Such books and their authors should be held in contempt for selling a fraudulent bill of goods.

If you want to read these books just for amusement or interest, they can do you no harm. A few even give the reader some insight into how intelligence test items are composed. It is possible to gain familiarity with the key aspects of certain types of test items that one must pay attention to in order to get the right answer. With sufficient practice in using the most efficient strategies or ''rules'' for solving certain classes of problems, such as number series, figure analogies, or matrices, one can improve one's score on tests composed of such items. But there is no transfer of this gain to different types of items that are equally good measures of intelligence. Instruction and practice on matrices items, for example, won't improve a child's performance on Stanford–Binet or Wechsler items even a little. And vice versa. But a child who can get a high score on a matrices test without any prior coaching will also usually do well on the Stanford-Binet, Wechsler, and other highly *g*-loaded tests.

The effects of coaching in general, and the specific methods proposed in books on ''how to raise your child's IQ,'' can affect performance on *specific* tests. The scores on such tests, then, for the test-trained child, actually lose much of their *g* loading. That is, the artificially raised scores are no longer as accurately indicative of the child's level of general intelligence as they would be without the training. You may have "beaten the test," but you won't have raised the child's intelligence. It's like sucking on a piece of ice before the doctor takes your temperature. It will puzzle the doctor that the thermometer doesn't register a "temperature" when he sees all the others signs that you have a fever; and the piece of ice in your mouth won't fool anyone when the doctor takes your temperature rectally. It seems to me just as silly to want to train your child to "fake" his or her IQ.

In any case, a clinical psychologist always tries to elicit the child's best performance on an IQ test. If the test is being given to help answer a diagnostic question, which is the only legitimate use of an IQ anyway, what is to be gained by coaching the child on the test (or on a highly similar test) before the child is tested by the clinician?

This is a very different matter from brushing up on one's math, for example, before taking the SAT, which is intended in part as a measure of specific scholastic skills. The aim of an IQ test, however, isn't the measurement of any *particular* knowledge or skill, but of the broad *g* factor that underlies all cognitive tasks. I am not aware of any psychological prescription that can dependably raise a person's intelligence in the meaningful sense of *g*. If any of those who write books on how to raise your child's intelligence really had an effective prescription for doing this, you can be very sure they would be highly acclaimed. Not one of them is.

Q: What can I do for my child to raise his IQ?

A: If all you are interested in is raising your child's score on a particular test, then teach the child the answers to the test. But if you mean permanently raising the child's level of intelligence, so that his or her performance would be improved or made easier on *all* kinds of tasks to the extent that they involve mental processes of the kinds that characterize *g*, then that is quite another matter. Parents who ask this question, I find, are not thinking of a boost in intelligence that would be represented by 5 or 10 IQ points; they usually have in mind a much more conspicuous improvement.

I don't know of any psychological prescription that will lead to the fulfillment of this parental wish. No such formula has been discovered.

Assuming that the child receives regular medical checkups, has good nutrition, is not deprived of social interaction with loving and responsive adults and other children, and is allowed the freedom safely to explore every aspect of the environment to the fullest extent of his capability, then the child's mental ability will develop of its own accord in its own way.

What *can* be influenced by the parents and others, to some extent, are the interests and experiences into which mental growth is channeled, and the acquisition of habits that will permit the child to make the most of his natural ability. Inquisitiveness, curiosity, exploration, learning, practice to attain mastery, the self-discipline needed for sustained effort, and responsibility and dependability are all learnable habits to a large extent. Children at almost every level of IQ can acquire such habits, and, within broad limits, these will be at least as important to their well-being and "success" as the "IQ" (that is, the general ability that the IQ is intended to measure). Children acquire these personal assets mainly through the example and help of the adults who rear them. These are the things that determine what a person will make of his or her native gifts. This is what parents ought to be most concerned with, rather than "raising the IQ."

General mental ability or *g* is a scientifically important construct in psychology; it ties together a wide range of behavioral phenomena, and the eventual scientific understanding of *g* will explain one extremely important dimension of human variation. Although this *g* factor is of great scientific interest, it is not something one worries about personally or in connection with one's own children. It is somewhat like the other "*g*" in science—the so-called gravitational "constant" (which really isn't a constant). Even though a physicist knows that a complete scientific explanation of his weight must include the gravitational constant, he doesn't give this a thought when he steps on his bathroom scales to check his weight. Similarly, we don't think about our psychological *g* when we try to do something; but we are aware of our effort and persistence.

A high school student who wants to play basketball may realize that height has some (far from perfect) correlation with success in basketball; but there are other important factors as well. It is only if one entertains hopes of being a champion player that height becomes a crucial limiting factor. The student who wants to play doesn't think about trying to increase his height, but works at developing the specific skills that will improve his actual performance in basketball, and by so doing he will become a better player. The very few who become champions will have done much the same, perhaps more so, and in addition will have exceptional physical advantages (including being very tall) for which they (or their parents) should take no personal credit. The same sort of thing can be said of those who win a Nobel Prize or sing at the Metropolitan. As a popular song put it, "God decides who will write a symphony."

Q: Is it important that I should know my child's IQ?

A: Generally, no. It's not important that anyone know it, or even that it be measured. If a child lags consistently behind his age-mates in many capabilities, however, or has unusual difficulty in school, then he should be examined, at first by a pediatrician or the school psychologist. The results of the examination will be interpreted for the child's parents in terms that the examiner judges will be the most informative and helpful to them for understanding their child's development. This involves much more than merely reporting a test score, which may only convey misconceptions if not properly interpreted in a relevant context. Given a proper interpretive context, there should be nothing "secret" about the IQ or any other test scores or how they are arrived at. Only a poor practitioner would do anything that would promote a mystique about psychological testing. Nothing that the psychologist does or says should seem arcane to the client. If parents leave the conference with a feeling of mystery, either they have not asked enough questions or the psychologist has not done his job properly.

Q: How can I find out my own IQ? Is there any value in my knowing it?

A: The only value I can imagine is if you are anxiously concerned about your mental ability, for whatever reason. Then having an IQ test may help to allay your anxiety.

The only satisfactory way to find out your IQ is to take a well-standardized IQ test, such as the Wechsler Adult Intelligence Scale, which must be administered by a qualified person. It could cost you $50 or more to be tested by a psychologist. But just an IQ score may not be what you are really looking for. A good psychologist would try to find out what you really want to know about yourself and take it from there. A set of vocational aptitude tests and interest inventories, for example, may come closer to the kind of information you really want.

I've never bothered to find out my own IQ, because I don't know what I could do with it if I knew it. It has been much more useful to me to determine, in relation to my specific goals, what specific things I knew or could do and what things I didn't know or couldn't do, and then set about working to learn the necessary things. That done, you go on the same way to the next step, whatever it may be. Your acquisition of knowledge and skills gradually cumulates to some level of mastery in the things of importance for the realization of your ambitions. The notion of some neutral, norm-referenced level of intellectual capacity or potential never crosses one's mind in the whole process. This doesn't mean that I could do *anything,* but I can do what I try to do, with some effort, and I don't believe that knowing my IQ would ever have been of any use to me in the process of trying to achieve any of my goals. Even if I did happen to know my IQ, I certainly wouldn't let that knowledge limit what I would *try* to do.

There's no denying the statistical predictive validity of tests. But for *you,* personally, the best way to find out if you can achieve something is to *try* to achieve it. No person should approach a challenge as a statistic to be predicted by a test score in a regression equation. Statistical prediction is for the college or employer faced with the necessity for selection.

Q: Our two boys differ extremely in high school. The older boy is almost straight A, and always has been all through school. The younger boy is just making a C average, even though he works as hard or even harder at it. The older boy recently took an exam which won him a National Merit Scholarship to go to a top college next year. His brother won't have the grades to get into such a college. Their high school counselor told me I shouldn't try to push him or compare him with his brother, whose IQ, he said, is over 30 points higher. This seems terribly unfair. What can we do about it?

A: About one family in twenty has a pair of siblings who differ from each other by more than 30 IQ points. (The average difference between siblings is about 13 IQ points.) Of course it isn't fair! But fairness is a purely human concept; it is irrelevant to nature, which has nothing to do with our personal notions of fairness and unfairness. That is why we, as rational beings, must ourselves always try to be as fair as possible.

All perceptive parents notice differences between their children. Good parents try to emphasize the strong points of each child, whatever they may be, and give help where it is needed. The aim should be to help each child develop in his or her own way, each finding appropriate avenues for achievement, approval, reward, and self-esteem. Parents should not try to exact the same goals and the same standards for each child. Unquestionably the challenge of successful parenthood is greater when there are exceptionally large disparities between children in general ability, talents, or other natural gifts. Parental pride and a child's self-pride should stem from his own efforts and actual accomplishments, not from natural gifts. "Gift" implies just that. The recipient and his parents should feel lucky and humbly grateful, rather than be proud or boastful. Superiority in natural gifts is a blessing, not a moral virtue.

Q: My 6-year-old daughter obtained a Stanford–Binet IQ of 145, or so I was told by her first-grade teacher. Will her IQ still be that high by the time she goes to college?

A: Probably not. The odds are only about 1 to 10 that her IQ will be 145 or higher by age 17. This is, of course, a statistical prediction, which is all that is possible, short of clairvoyance. Statistical probability is never a *cause* of anything. From studies of IQ changes from early childhood to maturity, we know that, statistically, those who begin with low IQs will, on the average, show some gain, and those who begin with high IQs show some loss. Other children will take their places in the IQ distribution, so the total IQ distribution of all children will remain the same from year to year. There is some reshuffling of people's positions in the IQ distribution throughout the course of mental development, with "early bloomers" and "late bloomers" exchanging places to some extent.

The best statistical prediction of your child's IQ at age 17, made on the basis of our evidence on developmental trends in IQ, is that it will be 128 ± 13. Just what does "statistical prediction" mean? It means that if we draw a sample of, say, 100 children who have IQs of 145 from the total school population of 6-year-olds and then measure their IQs again when they are 17 years old, their average IQ will be 128. Two-thirds of these children will have IQs between 115 and 141, and only slightly fewer than 10 percent will still have IQs of 145 (or higher). Some children who at age 6 obtained IQs lower than 145 will have moved up by age 17 to replace those age-mates whose IQs have slipped. But we *can't* predict just who these replacements will be. (I fully explain the basis for calculating such statistical expectations in *Bias in Mental Testing*, on pages 277–288.)

Q: How can we know if our child is intellectually gifted?

A: So-called gifted children are not a distinct category of children, set apart from all the rest. Giftedness is part of the total continuum of mental abilities, including both general intelligence and special abilities or talents. Where one draws the line on this continuum to distinguish those one would characterize as "gifted" is fairly arbitrary. In identifying the intellectually gifted, most school systems use the criterion of obtaining an IQ of between 130 to 140, or higher, on an individual IQ test. Children suspected of being gifted are often referred to the school psychologist for an individual IQ test, to determine qualification for any special services, programs, or classes for the gifted that the school offers.

Aside from the use of psychological tests for identifying the gifted, parents and teachers may notice a number of behavioral characteristics that often distinguish gifted children from their age-mates. These have been so perfectly described by Dorothy A. Sisk, director of the U.S. Office of Education's Office of Gifted and Talented, that I cannot do better than to quote directly from her highly informative article on recognizing the gifted child ("What If Your Child Is Gifted?" *American Education,* October 1977):

1. *Early use of advanced vocabulary.* Most children at age two make sentences like: "There's a doggie." A two-year old who is gifted might say, "There's a brown doggie in the backyard and he's sniffing our flowers."

2. *Keen observation and curiosity.* A gifted child might pursue lines of questioning such as: What makes Scotch tape sticky on one side and smooth on the other? How can they make a machine that puts on the sticky part without getting the machine all gummed up? Why doesn't the sticky side stay stuck to the other side when you unroll the tape? A gifted child will also observe details. At a very young age the child might remember where all the toys go on the shelf and replace everything correctly.

3. *Retention of a variety of information.* Gifted children amaze parents and teachers by recalling details of past experiences. For example, one six-year-old returned from a trip to the space museum and reproduced an accurate drawing of a space rocket he had seen.

4. *Periods of intense concentration.* A one-year-old gifted child might sit for five minutes or more listening attentively to a story being read to an older brother or sister. Older gifted children can become totally engrossed in a book or project, becoming oblivious to the events happening around them.

5. *Ability to understand complex concepts, perceive relationships, and think abstractly.* Although an average four-year-old looks through a picture book of baby and mother animals with interest, a gifted four-year-old is more likely to observe concepts such as how much animal mothers and babies look alike except that the baby is smaller. Or, if a fifth-grade class were told to write a paper on what it's like to be poor, most of the children would write, "I would be hungry" or "I wouldn't have enough money." A gifted fifth grader would tend to view the problem more abstractly and might write something like: "Being poor would only be a problem if others were not poor. If everyone else also had very little money, then we would all have less to spend and things would be cheaper."

6. *A broad and changing spectrum of interests.* Gifted children often show an intense interest in a subject, perhaps dinosaurs one month, then

turn to a totally different subject like French literature or railroad engines the next.

× 7. *Strong critical thinking skills and self-criticism.* Gifted children evaluate themselves and others. They notice discrepancies between what people say and what they do. But they are usually most critical of themselves. For example, a gifted child who has just won a swimming race might complain, ''I should have beat my time by at least one second.''

× 8. *Characteristics of children gifted in other areas.* Children gifted in visual and performing arts or psychomotor skills will display many of the characteristics just cited as common to intellectually gifted children. In addition, such creatively or physically gifted children demonstrate their talents early. A visually gifted child might draw a man riding a motorcycle while classmates are still struggling to put nose, eyes, and mouth in the right places in drawing a face. Overall, children who have special creative abilities differ from intellectually gifted children in many ways. They are likely to have one or more of these characteristics: a reputation for having wild and silly ideas or ideas that are off the beaten track, a sense of playfulness and relaxation, a strong tendency to be nonconformist and to think independently, and considerable sensitivity to both emotions and problems.

Q: How can anyone really claim to measure a person's true worth with a test that takes only an hour or so to give?

A: I don't know of anyone who has ever made such a claim. A person's ''true worth'' means many things to many people. It is not a scientific or psychological concept, and there is surely no test that could measure it, whatever it may mean, given *any* amount of time.

We can best understand what any test measures in terms of the other behaviors of practical interest that are actually correlated with the test scores, and the degree of correlation. To be useful psychologically, a good test *shouldn't* measure a mishmash of a whole lot of different traits. The score on such a test would have little or no analytic or diagnostic value. It would be as if the physician tried to diagnose a patient's illness on the basis of a single composite ''score'' obtained by adding up the patient's blood pressure, temperature, pulse rate, blood count, and basal metabolic rate. Such a ''score'' would be uninterpretable. This is why it is silly to condemn a particular test because it does not measure all kinds of traits it was never devised to assess.

Ralph Nader's organization, for example, blasts the SAT because it does not measure the student's character. But the SAT was devised to measure academic aptitude in college. If certain traits of character were deemed important in college selection, separate inventories would have to be devised to assess them. So far no one has devised measurements of personality traits that will appreciably improve the prediction of college success over the prediction yielded by a combination of high school grades and SAT scores. Besides, one can well imagine the howl that would arise from some quarters if "tests" of personality or character were explicitly used as a basis for college selection! Foolishly blaming tests for not measuring all of the human virtues they were never intended to measure is merely a part of the whole anti-test syndrome that pervades the current social scene.

Q: (From the daughter of a world-famous Nobel laureate in literature.) My father is a world-recognized genius. Yet I am sure he would completely flunk any IQ test. What do you think of *that*?

A: Your statement says much more about your personal attitude toward IQ tests than about your father's IQ. I have read some of your father's works, and judging from the vocabulary, the complexity and subtlety of thought, and the general erudition displayed (to say nothing of the creative imagination), I would guess that his intelligence is very superior indeed. If he took an IQ test, he would probably score at least in the 99th percentile in general intelligence, and he is notably gifted in verbal ability.

Besides, one should never equate IQ with genius. Very few high-IQ persons ever become geniuses in the genuine sense of making contributions recognized by the intellectual, scientific, and artistic world as extraordinarily outstanding. Yet most of the world's geniuses come from the upper part of the IQ distribution, virtually without exception.

Superior intelligence is a necessary but far from sufficient condition for extraordinary intellectual achievement. The concept of "genius" has no authentic meaning except in terms of achievement. Shakespeare's genius is in his plays. Beethoven's genius is in his symphonies.

One often hears unfounded claims about the "low" IQs of persons with extraordinary accomplishments. A few outstanding persons make such claims themselves. But the claims are sheer nonsense. Whenever such persons have actually been tested, they are never found to have low IQs; they almost never have average IQs; by far the most of them score above the top 1 or 2 percent of the general population. A few did flunk certain subjects in school or were labeled as a problem by their teachers. But that is quite another matter. These persons are among those who account for the fact that the correlation between IQ and scholastic performance is far from perfect. I've noticed that the only persons I've ever heard disparage their own IQ scores are those who think they are so conspicuously gifted that there is no risk that people will believe them. Their claims that they "flunked an IQ test" are usually intended to provoke laughter and levity in the fashionable game of ridiculing tests.

Q: Do men and women differ in intelligence?

A: No, men and women do not differ in general intelligence, that is, the *g* factor. A few IQ tests, for example, the Stanford–Binet and Wechsler scales, have eliminated any items that show large sex differences and have balanced out the remaining items to create a zero sex difference in the overall score. Scores on such tests, of course, can't be the basis for determining if there is truly a sex difference in intelligence. However, studies based on tests that were not devised with any reference to sex, and studies based on factor analysis, which permits comparisons of males and females on the various separate ability factors that contribute to variation in all kinds of mental tests, fail to show a significant sex difference in the general ability factor that we identify with intelligence.

Males and females differ in certain other abilities, however. The most well-established difference is in spatial-visualization ability—the ability to mentally visualize complex objects, and to mentally manipulate relationships among objects in three-dimensional space. It is an important ability for geometry, organic chemistry, architecture, structural engineering, and the like. Spatial visualization is also a component of mathematical ability, in which mental spatial representation of quantitative relationships plays a part in problem-solving proficiency. In the best tests of spatial visualization ability, only about one-fourth of females surpass the average male.

The sex difference in spatial ability is evident in childhood, but increases markedly after puberty. There is some evidence that it is related to male hormones and also some evidence that other genetic factors play a part in the sex difference. I don't know of a single expert in this field who believes that cultural and environmental causes—such as the cultural difference in sex-role socialization—is anywhere near adequate to explain all the evidence related to the sex difference in spatial and mathematical ability.

Because of the connection between spatial ability and mathematical ability, there is a notable sex difference in the latter as well, and it cannot be explained by differences in amount of exposure to mathematics or differences in motivation to succeed in math. A great deal of excellent research is being done on this topic at present, and the next few years should see an increase in our knowledge and understanding of these phenomena.

Females surpass males in verbal ability, from the age at which children begin to talk (girls sooner than boys) all the way into adulthood. The sex difference in verbal ability is not as large as in spatial ability. But when a variety of tests are factor-analyzed, women do better on the verbal factor and men on the nonverbal, quantitative, spatial, and performance factors. On g, the general ability factor, the sexes are equal.

There is also an indication that males are slightly more variable in IQ than females, who cluster closer to the general average. Hence more males are found at the two extremes of the IQ distribution. There are more males than females above IQ 140 (in the ratio of about 1.2 to 1) and below IQ 70 (about 1.6 to 1). There is no generally established theory to explain the slightly greater variability of males, and some few authorities even dispute the evidence for the greater IQ variability of males.

Q: Are the persons who get high scores on IQ tests simply the ones who are most motivated and try hardest?

A: No. In fact, there is some evidence that those who get higher scores don't try as hard as those who get lower scores. Pupillary dilation, which is controlled by the autonomic nervous system, is a sensitive and reliable indicator of motivational arousal and mental effort. Measurements of pupillary dilation have been made while the subjects were being presented intelligence test items for solution. The subjects were selected beforehand from different regions of the IQ distribution, although they were all of average or above-average intelligence. It turned out that for any given test item, the less bright subjects showed greater pupillary dilation. They would show dilation even on the relatively easy items, whereas the brighter subjects showed a comparable amount of dilation only on the most difficult items. This finding contradicts the notion that the persons who obtain higher IQs do so because they are more highly motivated to perform well on the test. IQ differences are not merely a reflection of differences in motivation.

Q: Does the IQ decline with advancing years in middle age and after?

A: The average IQ itself, being a type of "standard score," remains constant across every age group in the population. That is, the average IQ is conventionally set or scaled at 100 within every age bracket, so that a person's IQ indicates his relative standing among persons of the same age in the general population.

The raw score (that is, the actual number of correct responses) on the IQ test, however, reaches its peak in the early to mid-twenties, remains on a fairly level plateau until the mid-forties, and thereafter shows a gradual decline, which becomes more severe after seventy.

The graph depicting the growth and decline of mental ability as a function of age, in the general population, closely parallels similar graphs of the growth and decline of vital capacity (the air capacity of the lungs) and brain weight.

The rate of decline in performance is not the same for all types of test items. Tests that involve crystallized ability, involving acquired knowledge and skills such as vocabulary, general information, and the like, hold up, and even increase, until very old age. Tests that call for fluid ability, which involves solving novel problems, learning something new, immediate memory, and the like, show the most rapid rate of decline. Also, speeded tests show more rapid decline with age than unspeeded power tests. (See Chapter 1.)

I am, of course, talking here about statistical averages. There is a very wide range of individual differences in the rate of mental decline with advancing age. In general, the higher the level of ability that is attained by the peak years (somewhere in the twenties), the slower is the rate of decline thereafter. Better-educated persons and those engaged in occupations that make some intellectual demands show less decline. The rate of mental decline is also related to health. Staving off arteriosclerosis is probably the best preventative against mental decline in old age.

It is an interesting fact that a sudden decline in mental power in old age is a statistically significant predictor of impending death. When a group of older persons were tested each successive year, those who showed the most marked decline from their score in the previous year were the ones most likely to die during the following year. The IQ thus reflects the person's general state of health, especially in old age.

Q: Is our national IQ declining?

A: No one can satisfactorily answer this question at present. It has not been directly researched. Some fifty years ago a number of prominent psychologists and geneticists expressed concern over the possibility that the average level of intelligence was declining in Great Britain and the United States. The basis for their concern was the finding (which still holds good) of a negative correlation (of about − .30) between schoolchildren's IQs and the number of siblings they have. In other words, the children with the lower IQs tend to come from larger families. Also, the relationship between socioeconomic status and IQ was noted in connection with the fact that lower-status parents, in general, have larger families.

As it was already known that there is a genetic component in IQ variation, it was argued that if the trend for larger families to produce children with lower IQs continued generation after generation, there would inevitably be a gradual impoverishment of the population's gene pool for intelligence. Although a few points loss of IQ at the mean would itself be scarcely noticeable, the effect on the extremes of the total distribution of IQ could be drastic—the percentage of intellectually gifted could be cut in half and the percentage of retarded doubled. (See Chapter 1.) It looked like a convincing argument, although there was no direct evidence for a decline in the population IQ. In fact, large-scale testing of schoolchildren in Britain and the United States between the 1920s and the 1940s revealed no downward trends. In some studies even the opposite was found—a slight rise in IQ. This was seen as a paradox at the time. Psychologists argued that the widespread improvement of education, the greater amount of schooling obtained by the average person, the increase in general literacy, and the rise in the overall level of culture and information available because of the common media provided by the advent of radio during this period were all reflected in the scores on IQ tests, and all these effects were just temporarily masking the gradual deterioration of the population's gene pool for intelligence. The insidious downward trend would reveal itself as soon as the rapidly improved environmental factors favorably affecting IQ scores leveled off.

A serious flaw was soon found in this whole argument, that is, the argument based essentially on the negative correlation between IQ and family size. The argument had taken into account only those members of the population who were married and had children. But what about those who never have children? Studies revealed that persons with low IQs have less tendency to marry or to have children than persons of average and above-average IQ. Lower-IQ persons who do marry, however, have a larger-than-average number of children. But if one looked at the total number of children born to *all* persons (i.e., both those who have children and those who do not) in the lower half of the IQ distribution of the population, they equal the number of children born to all persons in the upper half of the IQ distribution, more of whom marry but have fewer children per married couple. Thus, it appeared, the upper and lower halves of the IQ distribution have equal reproductive rates, when everyone in the population is taken into account. So overall there should be no negative selection for intelligence genes, and the gene pool for IQ should remain stable from one generation to the next. The IQ scores would fluctuate only because of possible environmental perturbations. Apparently there was really nothing to worry about.

A few "cranks" continued to worry, however, because the argument that the reproductive rates of the above- and below-averge segments of the population in IQ are in almost perfect balance was based largely on a single study of a very small and probably unrepresentative sample of the United States population, namely, the native-born white population of Kalamazoo, Michigan, before World War II. This group was largely Protestant, of above-average educational level, living in an urban environment. It is amazing how quick scientists were to accept the results of this small study (and one later study of comparable limitations) as being definitive enough to clamp the lid tightly on the whole question. No one has really looked at the matter since.

These small studies' chief value was not their conclusions, which surely do not warrant generalization to the national population, but their methodology, which emphasized that the crucial thing we must look at is the average number of children born to *all* persons (childbearing *and* childless) within each segment of the IQ distribution. This has never been done in any large representative sample of the population.

The closest approximation I can find to such a study is provided by the 1970 United States Census (*Current Population Reports: Population Characteristics,* Series P-20, No. 226, U.S. Bureau of the Census, November 1971). Because women's IQs correlate close to .70 with their final attained level of education, we can use educational level as a rough index of intelligence. The census provides a table that shows the average number of children (not including stillbirths) per woman ever born to all women in the U.S. in the childbearing age range 15 to 44 years (see Table 7). It is important to note that these data meet the crucial methodological requirement of including both married and unmarried women, and childless as well as childbearing women.

Table 7 shows that for both whites and blacks, the birth rate decreases as educational level increases. This trend is considerably more marked for blacks than for whites. Because there are intelligence differences (and probably differences in other desirable traits as well) between those who go furthest in school and those who leave school earliest, and because these differences involve genetic factors to some

TABLE 7

Average Number of Children per Woman Ever Born
to All Women 15–44 Years of Age in 1970 Census

| | YEARS OF SCHOOL COMPLETED BY WOMAN | | | | | | |
| | Elementary | | High School | | College | | |
RACE	Less than 8 years	8 years	1 to 3 years	4 years	1 to 3 years	4 years or more	TOTAL
White	2.596	2.222	1.393	1.794	1.279	1.315	1.634
Black	3.065	2.735	1.948	1.820	1.274	1.370	1.974

extent, the figures in Table 7 should have the following implication: If this same trend persists, each successive generation will have somewhat lower genetic potential for those qualities involved in scholastic performance and all its social correlates. Moreover, given the trend indicated by these census data, the black average should decline at a faster rate than the white, causing the two racial populations to grow still farther apart in their ability to compete educationally and occupationally in our technological society. Continuation of these trends, combined with the overall higher birth rate among blacks, whose average IQ is about 15 points below the white average, should result in a decline in the total population's average IQ and scholastic ability. Calculation of the exact amount and rate of decline would require knowing the average time between generations within each educational level for each race and the population frequencies within each category of Table 7. The precise implications of the trends suggested by these census data could be properly determined only by a full-fledged study aimed specifically at this question. The 1980 Census might provide the necessary data.

Q: Do different communities, localities, or geographical regions of the country show differences in IQ distributions? If so, does it make any practical difference?

A: The best evidence on this in the United States is provided by the armed forces mental test data, which show average differences between regions and between states. For example, considering only the white male population, the lowest-scoring state on the Armed Forces Qualification Test has a failure rate more than ten times higher than the highest-scoring state. In our IQ testing in different cities in California we find average differences of as much as 15 points, even considering only the white populations of these cities. There are, of course, corresponding differences in average levels of scholastic achievement.

These differences seem to come about as the result of selective migration of the population in terms of the types of employment opportunities and economic incentives, and their associated intellectual and educational demands, in different locales. Throughout the world there is a consistent average IQ difference between urban and rural populations.

The various social correlates of these average mental test score differences between localities have been intensively studied recently in Great Britain and France by Richard Lynn, a psychologist at the University of Ulster, Northern Ireland ("The Social Ecology of Intelligence in the British Isles," *British Journal of Social and Clinical Psychology* 18 [1979]: 1–12). Lynn obtained various statistics for each of the thirteen standard regions of the British Isles, including the mean IQ in each region. These quite large regions vary in mean IQ from 96.0 to 102.1. Despite the rather small average differences, Lynn found quite substantial correlations between the mean IQs of these thirteen regions and the following variables, each expressed as the rate per thousand in the population of the region (correlations with IQ shown in parentheses):

Fellows of the Royal Society (birthplace)	(+ .94)
Recipients of first-class honors degrees	(+ .60)
Per capita income	(+ .73)
Unemployment	(− .82)
Infant mortality	(− .78)

Similar results were found for ninety regions of France. Thus the slight mean IQ differences between regions are associated with differences in several socially significant variables. Lynn also looked at crime rates, which were positively correlated (+ .51) with mean population IQs only by virtue of the joint correlation of each variable with "urbanization"—the proportion of a region's population living in big cities. When the effect of this variable is statistically removed from the correlation between population IQ and crime, the correlation drops to zero. Big cities have a higher crime rate and a higher mean IQ. For individuals, however, most studies find a negative correlation between IQ and criminal behavior.

Q: Why do research psychologists seem to focus so much research effort on the IQs of blacks, and also perhaps Hispanics, but pay so little attention to the IQs of other groups—Japanese, Chinese, Italians, Irish, Germans, or other nationalities in this country?

A: True, the research literature on mental and scholastic tests involving blacks is vastly greater than that involving any other minority groups in the United States. (Hispanics of Mexican and Puerto Rican origin run a very distant second in this respect.)

The reason is twofold: (1) blacks are by far the largest minority population in the United States, and so the conditions of the black population are of very significant consequence to the whole society; and (2) the black population shows a disparity from the general average of the rest of the population in scholastic performance of such a magnitude as to have become a major national concern in the past three decades. The concern has focused on scholastic achievement because of its relationship to so many other socially and economically important conditions of the adult population.

Behavioral scientists and educators, with large-scale financial support from government agencies, have studied these matters with the tools of their disciplines. Because the IQ has long been known to be the single most potent predictor of scholastic performance, and it predicts equally well for blacks as for whites, a great deal of research was aimed at trying to understand the causes of the difference between the black and white IQ distributions.

Other population groups have not been studied on such a large scale mainly because they show no disparities in scholastic performance large enough to be of much social significance, and the disparities that are observed in some groups seem more obviously related to language *per se*. English is a second language for many Hispanics and first-generation immigrant Asians. For these bilingual groups, scholastic performance is positively related to the length of time they have been in the United States or have attended English-speaking schools. And so it has been with other non-English-speaking immigrant groups of the past. At present, Asian-Americans (Chinese and Japanese) scholastically perform on a par with the white population, and in those areas in which their numbers are most concentrated, as in California, their scholastic achievement even exceeds the general average. In relation to their total numbers in the population, they are in fact overrepresented in classes for the academically gifted, on college campuses, among scholarship winners, and in the learned professions. Ten times as many are elected to membership in the prestigious National Academy of Sciences as would be predicted from their number in the general population. (They are equaled only by Jews in this respect.)

Consequently there has been little concern by educators, or by the Asians themselves, over their scholastic aptitudes or preparation for assuming productive roles in our technological society.

A similar picture seems to be emerging in the Asian (Indian and Pakistani) population of Great Britain, despite their quite marked linguistic and cultural differences. The West Indian black population of Britain, in contrast, evinces much the same disparity in scholastic performance and all its socioeconomic correlates as we see in the black population of the United States. Blacks have not shown the same ascent on the educational ladder, relative to the majority, as have most other immigrant groups.

It is a false hope to believe that these facts will disappear automatically by refusing to recognize them. The search for possible solutions implies a search for causes. Hence research. What research has demonstrated most clearly so far is that the simple educational solutions that were predicated on what we now view in retrospect as the "naive environmentalism" of the 1950s and 1960s are not the answer.

Q: I've heard of using prize bulls for breeding cattle by artificial insemination. But what about the recent news item about some millionaire [Robert K. Graham] in California enlisting Nobel prizewinners as donors for the artificial insemination of young women volunteers who were selected for high IQs? Will this produce super-offspring?

A: This news item provoked many emotional reactions and a good deal of utterly fatuous commentary, some of it even from scientists. One would have thought the matter was all very daring and outlandish. But actually, artificial insemination by donors has been going on for a good many years, making it possible for a woman to bear children when her husband is infertile. About 20,000 babies are conceived by this method every year in the United States. The donors are usually medical students, often selected to resemble the parents in the most obvious physical characteristics. Medical students are on the whole a quite select group in terms of intelligence, scholastic aptitude, and drive. If one does not object to that degree of selection for the donors, why should there be objection to the more extreme selection implied by the Nobel prizes? Whatever other qualities and special talents may be found among Nobel laureates, two traits are virtually certain, and both undoubtedly involve genetic components: very superior intelligence and great intellectual energy and drive. These traits, combined with a remarkable capacity for hard work, are the common feature of the several Nobelists whom I've personally observed. In these respects, they would seem to be at least as desirable donors as medical students.

There is little reason to believe that the resulting offspring should be appreciably different from the natural offspring of Nobel prizewinners, whose wives would usually be of comparable intelligence to the women selected in Graham's "experiment." I am not aware of any studies of the children of Nobel prizewinners. What we can be quite sure of, however, is that, on the whole, they are not anywhere near as outstanding as their Nobelist parents. (There are, of course, marked exceptions. Five Nobelists in science have had children who also won a Nobel prize in science.) As was explained in Chapter 3, individuals cannot pass on their genotypes to their offspring. The offspring inherit only a random half of each parent's genes, and there is little likelihood that these would produce as unusual combinations of genetic factors as constitute the outstanding parent's genotype. (Cloning is theoretically the only method by which exactly the same genotypes could be reproduced.) The overwhelming majority of the world's future geniuses will continue to be the offspring of comparatively ordinary parents.

Yet on the basis of Terman's famous study of the offspring of high-IQ persons, it would seem a safe prediction that the average IQ of the children born to the bright young women who were artificially inseminated by Nobel laureates would most probably be in the top 1 or 2 percent of the total distribution of IQs in the general population. But the variability of IQs would be about as great as it is in the general population. In Terman's study, the 2,452 offspring of gifted parents (whose IQs averaged 138.5) had an average IQ of 132.7, but these children's IQs ranged all the way from mentally retarded (below 70) to over 190! The genetic lottery makes almost anything possible individually, even though the central tendency may be highly predictable if the number of persons is large. That, of course, is true whether the parent is a Nobel laureate or anyone else. The one possible disadvantage of artificial insemination by older donors (as Nobelists would tend to be) is the slightly increased risk of genetic mutations or chromosomal anomalies which may become more likely with advancing age. This disadvantage, however, may be more than offset by the positive advantage of having direct evidence of the donor's health and mental vigor in his later years. Heredity is also involved in longevity and freedom from senility.

Q: Isn't there a danger that scientific knowledge about such subjects as genetics, intelligence, and race might be misused by racists?

A: Should the discovery of fire have been avoided because arsonists can misuse it? Any kind of information can be misused by those who are determined to do so. The place to stop the misuse of knowledge is not at the point of inquiry, but at the point of misuse. Enforce laws against racial discrimination in all its forms. To avoid pursuing scientific inquiry for fear that racists will misuse it is to grant them the power of censorship of research.

An increase in knowledge and understanding increases people's freedom of choice. Beneficial outcomes are more likely to arise from scientific knowledge than from ignorance or dogma. One should not imagine that the educational and social correlates of mental test scores will disappear by not being studied or publicly recognized. As Harvard physiologist Bernard Davis has remarked, "The truths about the universals of human nature, and about the diversity of the human population, will be there whether or not scientists discover them; and this reality will affect the success of those social policies that depend on assumptions about these matters. Moreover, if we recognize justice as a constantly evolving social construct it is difficult to see how long any valid new knowledge can itself threaten justice. As we approach closer to truth . . . we should be able to build the institutions of justice on a more realistic foundation."

Genetic research on socially important human traits, especially intelligence, is scorned by some persons who fear that it could lead to the discovery of a genetic component in observed racial difference; or that such investigation, whatever its eventual outcome, lends scientific respectability to the question of racial differences in IQ or other behavioral characteristics. The question itself, they would declare, is to be scorned as insulting and racist. This fear reflects a gross failure to observe the important distinction between racism and the scientific study of racial variation, which logically must apply to *all* characteristics, mental as well as physical.

Racism is one of the major hindrances to the scientific study of racial variation in intelligence and other behavioral traits. Racism is the belief that human races can be distinctly ordered in a simple hierarchy in terms of some global evaluation of inferior-superior, and that individuals are justifiably treated differently—socially, educationally, legally, and politically—solely according to their racial origins or their socially defined racial group membership.

There is nothing in genetics or in the scientific study of racial variation that would lend support to these racist beliefs. In fact, already well-established findings in genetics and differential psychology clearly contradict the essential tenets of racism.

Racism should be fought wherever it actually exists, through education and enforced legal sanctions when necessary. The cause of racial justice is not furthered by condemning scientists who inquire into the nature and causes of racial variation in the same manner in which they might investigate any other natural phenomenon. Where certain racial differences are generally acknowledged to be of considerable social and educational importance, attempts to understand these phenomena warrant the best scientific effort we can bring to bear on them. One by-product of the study of racial differences that is rarely mentioned is that it will test whether psychology can actually behave as a science in dealing with a socially sensitive issue, or whether, in the final analysis, psychology can only rationalize popular prejudice and social ideology.

But to answer the question as it relates specifically to the main topic of this book: the sound use and interpretation of mental testing can help reinforce the democratic ideal of treating every person according to his or her *individual* characteristics, rather than according to race, sex, social class, religion, or national origin.

Suggestions for Further Reading

THE FOLLOWING BOOKS are recommended to readers who wish to delve further into the topics of the present book. They are selected so as to represent the main topics of this book while minimizing duplication of contents among the six selections. These books, in turn, provide an excellent guide to virtually the whole literature of this field.

My selection is based on four criteria: (1) the book is either wholly or largely nontechnical and can be easily read by the educated layman, (2) it deals with broad, socially significant issues rather than with highly specialized topics or a critical technical analysis of a limited field, (3) it is accurately informative and has received excellent reviews in scholarly journals by other distinguished scientists in the same field, and (4) the authors have achieved international recognition for their scientific and scholarly contributions to their respective fields.

JOHN R. BAKER. *Race.* New York and London: Oxford University Press, 1974. Written by the noted Oxford University zoologist, this is the most thoroughly informative work I have found on the taxonomic and biologic aspects of human racial variation; the last quarter of the book deals with the issue of racial differences in cognitive abilities, with greater emphasis on evolutionary and cultural interaction than is ordinarily found in discussions oriented toward quantitative genetics and psychometrics.

260

Lee J. Cronbach. *Essentials of Psychological Testing.* 3d ed. New York: Harper & Row, 1970. This has been the best book on the subject for over thirty years, and although it is a college textbook (probably the most widely used) for introductory courses on mental testing, it is highly readable. The author, a professor of psychology and education at Stanford University, has for many years been the world's leading figure in the field of psychological and educational testing.

H. J. Eysenck. *The Inequality of Man.* London: Temple Smith, 1973. The most famous contemporary British psychologist, a professor in the University of London, explores the social implications of individual and group differences in mental abilities, personality traits, mental illness, and crime. Besides being the most prolific writer in the history of psychology, the author is a major contributor of original research in all of the aspects of the field dealt with in his book.

R. J. Herrnstein. *IQ in the Meritocracy.* Boston: Little, Brown & Co., 1973. This information-packed little book by the noted Harvard psychology professor about the nature, inheritance, and social meaning of IQ raised a furor of popular protest when it first appeared, mainly because of its elaboration of what seemed to many the grim implications of the famous "syllogism" it put forth: (1) If differences in mental abilities are inherited, and (2) if success requires those abilities, and (3) if earnings and prestige depend on success, (4) then social standing (which reflects earnings and prestige) will be based to some extent on inherited differences among people. Herrnstein is one of the best writers in contemporary psychology; hence his book is a pleasure to read.

John C. Loehlin; Gardner Lindzey; and J. N. Spuhler. *Race Differences in Intelligence.* San Francisco: W. H. Freeman & Co. 1975. Two well-known behavioral geneticists, Loehlin and Lindzey (a past president of the American Psychological Association), and Spuhler, a genetic anthropologist, have provided an indispensable reference. This is the most thorough review and carefully balanced interpretation of the psychometric evidence on race differences in intelligence ever published. Most of the technical material in this very lucid work is confined to the appendices.

Philip E. Vernon. *Intelligence: Heredity and Environment.* San Francisco: W. H. Freeman & Co., 1979. Britain's leading educational psychologist and test expert has presented the most up-to-date and well-organized review and interpretation of the evidence relating to every aspect of the whole IQ controversy, written with the cool, clear, ascetic style and impeccable scholarship for which Vernon is noted. This is probably the best introduction to the whole literature on IQ.

Index